Dörte Andres / Martina Behr (eds.)
To Know How to Suggest …

Transkulturalität – Translation – Transfer, Band 16
Herausgegeben von
Dörte Andres / Martina Behr / Larisa Schippel / Cornelia Zwischenberger

Dörte Andres / Martina Behr (eds.)

To Know How to Suggest …

Approaches to Teaching Conference Interpreting

Verlag für wissenschaftliche Literatur

Umschlagabbildung: © Maren Dingfelder Stone

CIUTI

Die Publikation wurde von CIUTI gefördert.

2., unveränderte Auflage 2019
(1. Auflage 2015)

ISBN 978-3-7329-0114-2
ISSN 2196-2405

© Frank & Timme GmbH Verlag für wissenschaftliche Literatur
Berlin 2019. Alle Rechte vorbehalten.

Das Werk einschließlich aller Teile ist urheberrechtlich geschützt.
Jede Verwertung außerhalb der engen Grenzen des Urheberrechtsgesetzes ist ohne Zustimmung des Verlags unzulässig und strafbar.
Das gilt insbesondere für Vervielfältigungen, Übersetzungen,
Mikroverfilmungen und die Einspeicherung und Verarbeitung in
elektronischen Systemen.

Herstellung durch Frank & Timme GmbH,
Wittelsbacherstraße 27a, 10707 Berlin.
Printed in Germany.
Gedruckt auf säurefreiem, alterungsbeständigem Papier.

www.frank-timme.de

To know how to suggest is the art of teaching.
(Henri-Frédéric Amiel)

Contents

Foreword by Daniel Gile 9

Preface by the Editors 11

SYLVIA KALINA
Interpreter Training and Interpreting Studies –
    Which is the Chicken and which is the Egg? 17

CATHERINE CHABASSE
Aptitude 43

DÖRTE ANDRES / SOPHIA BODEN / CLAUDIA FUCHS
The Sense and Senselessness of Preparatory Exercises
    for Simultaneous Interpreting 59

CATHERINE CHABASSE / MAREN DINGFELDER STONE
Capacity Management in Interpretation: Efforts, Directionality,
    and Language Pair Considerations 75

DÖRTE ANDRES
Easy? Medium? Hard?
    The Importance of Text Selection in Interpreter Training 103

STEPHANIE KADER / SABINE SEUBERT
Anticipation, Segmentation ... Stalling?
    How to Teach Interpreting Strategies 125

MAREN DINGFELDER STONE
The Theory and Practice of Teaching Note-Taking 145

MARC ORLANDO
Implementing Digital Pen Technology
    in the Consecutive Interpreting Classroom 171

MARTINA BEHR
How to Back The Students – Quality, Assessment & Feedback.................. 201

JACQUY NEFF
Professionalisation: A Systematic Didactic Approach 219

MAREN DINGFELDER STONE
(Self-)Study in Interpreting: Plea for a Third Pillar 243

Foreword by Daniel Gile

Remarkable, highly talented personalities, who became interpreters because of historical circumstances but could probably have had brilliant careers in other fields as well, set high standards for conference interpreting around the middle of the twentieth century, when it became a prestigious professional career. Their personal influence was such that their ideas about training were adopted readily in the most prestigious schools where they taught and in association with certain ideals as set out by AIIC, the International Association of Conference Interpreters.

As time passed, the interpreting environment changed and became highly diversified. Today's conference interpreters face speeches, working conditions and expectations which sometimes differ considerably from those encountered by their illustrious predecessors. The background and aptitudes of many interpreting students are also quite different from those of the first- and second-generation conference interpreters. Finally, the didactic and institutional environments of interpreter training programs have changed considerably over time.

Ideas about training therefore had to be re-examined with a view to optimize programs and to comply with local academic and professional requirements. Moreover, scientific research about interpreting, and in particular about interpreting cognition, brought new insights which also had potential implications on the best teaching and learning practices. Finally, globalization and communication and information technology have been opening up new possibilities for knowledge and skills acquisition.

This could be one explanation of the reason why interpreter training has been and remains a central focal point in the interpreting literature, both professional and academic. A single, idealized model of the highly gifted 'born interpreter' no longer seems adequate. Neither does a simplistic, insensitive 'practice and sink or swim' philosophy of training. Not only because the stress-induced suffering in students who will not make it appears unnecessarily cruel, but also because it makes sense to assume that more systematic investigation into aptitudes, training methods and learning processes could lead to improvements and to better output, including successful training of candidates who might fail if their particular idiosyncrasies are not taken on board through appropriate tools and policies.

Canonical science (e.g. experiments, correlational studies etc.) may help in advancing towards better training, though due to variability and the numerous interacting variables, combined with technical difficulties in quantifying them meaningfully, it is not reasonable to expect it to yield many clear-cut answers with direct applications at this time. Theoretical reflection may also contribute: even without 'solid' evidence as required by canonical research, critical reflection and discussion among many scholars is likely to identify relevant issues and perhaps open up avenues for improvement. Experiential knowledge gained in the field, that is, classroom experience, is equally valuable. Maximum cross-fertilization could be achieved when the input of each is fed into a common pool of knowledge and ideas, to be discussed and evaluated.

This collective volume is a case in point: input from various sources and under various angles is provided as food for thought. This includes overviews of theories, discussions of related issues and examples of training practice and tools, including the most recent technological tools. Not on a prescriptive mode, but as a set of resources. I believe such resources could be useful to trainers who are only familiar with the training model which they experienced as students, perhaps with some reservations.

The publication in English of a collection of papers by authors from the German-speaking world (most of the authors in this volume are) is also welcome. Their research, reflection and training endeavours are less visible to the Interpreting Studies community at large than they deserve to be because they tend to publish more in German than in English. This book is a good opportunity for readers not familiar with them to get acquainted with their work and experience.

Daniel Gile

Preface by the Editors

In May 2011, at the General Assembly Meeting of the *Conférence Internationale des Universités de Traduction et d'Interprétation* (CIUTI) in Beijing, the members reinforced their goal of sharing expertise among the CIUTI member institutions. They agreed upon the creation of different work groups to develop and implement train-the-trainers schemes for interpreters and translators. Dörte Andres (University of Mainz/FTSK Germersheim) agreed to head a work group for conference interpreting. She developed an initial concept for a train-the-trainers workshop in cooperation with her colleagues Martina Behr, Catherine Chabasse and Sabine Seubert, all also from the University of Mainz/FTSK Germersheim, and distributed it to the other members of the CIUTI work group: Martina Behr (also for Saarland University, Germany), Bart Defranq (University College Ghent, Belgium), Catherine Chabasse (University of Mainz/FTSK Germersheim, Germany), Lena Menhem (ETIB Beirut, Lebanon), Marie Mériaud (ISIT Paris, France), Alessandra Riccardi (SSLMIT Trieste, Italy), Isabelle Seguela (ISIT Paris, France) and Olga Zharkova (MSU Moscow, Russia). These members met at a kick-off meeting in November 2011 at ISIT, Paris, which was organised by Marie Mériaud. The concept was discussed and revised in detail during the one-day meeting. Thanks to the valuable contributions of the colleagues involved, a template for a train-the-trainers workshop was created and later finalised by the Germersheim team in autumn 2011.

On the basis of this template, six interpreting trainers (Dörte Andres, Martina Behr, Catherine Chabasse, Stephanie Kader, Maren Dingfelder Stone and Sabine Seubert) developed a week long train-the-trainers seminar. It was held for the first time in August 2012 at the FTSK in Germersheim in the context of the *Germersheim International Summer School* (ISG), organised by Wini Kern. It was attended by ten Interpreting trainers from four countries. The success of this seminar led to a second workshop in September 2014.

The idea of publishing the contents of the seminar arose with the motivation to reach non-German-speaking educators. The teachers involved wrote one article per teaching unit. This publication comprises these articles, together with additional contributions from Sylvia Kalina (FH Köln), Marc Orlando (Monash University) and Jacquy Neff (FTSK Germersheim).

The importance of didactic training in conference interpreting has become the subject of increased discussion due to the differentiation of interpreter training, such as in the novel concepts for imparting fundamental court interpreting as well as specialist interpreting skills. The number of interpreter-training offerings in non-European countries has risen as well. New institutions are being created that could benefit from a didactic approach to the development of interpreting competence. This also means that an increased exchange of information between training centres must occur in order to make the didactics of (conference) interpreting an integral part of training. This fulfils a demand already articulated by the conference interpreter and renowned expert on the didactics of interpreting Daniel Gile in 1982:

Les cours d'interprétation dispensés dans les écoles spécialisées, universitaires, et autres établissements sont nombreux, mais le détail des démarches, techniques et méthodes utilisées reste largement inconnu, faute d'un échange d'information suffisant. [...] Dans cette optique, les échanges d'information entre enseignants, notamment par le biais d'articles [...], sont susceptibles d'apporter une contribution importante en permettant à tous de profiter des initiatives de chacun. (GILE 1982: 350f)[1]

Didactically oriented publications have existed since the early days of conference interpreting, when practicing interpreters such as Jean Herbert, Jean Francois Rozan and Henri van Hoof expressed initial reflections on this profession and its training. The theoretical elaboration of the phenomenon of interpreting in the context of interpreting studies has also provided us with insights into the processes that occur during interpreting. This allows us to divide the overall interpreting process into individual components during training, which can then be practiced in a focused manner. An essential requirement based on insights from the psychology of cognition and learning is

---

1   There are numerous interpreting courses offered by specialised schools and university departments as well as other institutions, but details about the procedures, techniques and methods used remain largely obscure due to an inadequate exchange of information. [...] Given this situation, the exchange of information between teachers, particularly in the form of articles [...], is likely to make a significant contribution and to allow everyone to benefit from the efforts of each individual. (Translation: Yann Kiraly)

that the student be at the centre of the learning process. The CIUTI, which, at its general assembly meeting in Shanghai in May 2014, declared that "Teaching quality means putting the student in the centre", shares this goal.

This volume does not aim to present in-depth scientific theories. Individual theoretical perspectives are discussed where they provide the basis for a specific application in interpreter training and if exercise types can be derived from them, which are then explained in detail. Some of the resulting concepts introduced here already have a longer tradition within training institutions. Others are based on new developments that will influence both interpreting training and practice.

The contributions in this volume are meant to serve as suggestions for experienced interpreter training practitioners who may not have received theory-based training in this domain during their studies. It may provide them with a new perspective on various topics. Their current teaching activities can be complemented by and confirmed through new explanations. This volume also includes discussions on the relative usefulness of various exercise types as well as suggestions for making teaching in the days of short master's degree programmes even more efficient and student-oriented.

At the same time, this book is also geared towards teachers just starting out in conference interpreter training, either at an existing institution or in the context of the creation of new ones in countries that may lack a long tradition of interpreter training. As editors and authors we are well aware that this volume has an inevitable Eurocentric perspective. The views and ideas presented here can certainly not adequately account for all countries, language combinations and culturally specific forms of teaching. We hope, however, that it can still provide encouragement to consider new approaches with a view toward adapting them to individual requirements.

In the first contribution in this volume, **Sylvia Kalina** describes the long development from the beginnings of (conference) interpreting and on-the-job training to a didactically well-founded form of interpreter training. The author also discusses new insights gained in the increasingly interdisciplinary field of interpreting studies and illustrates their importance. Kalina ends her discussion with thoughts on the future of training and practice in these times of new technologies, evolving study habits and the changing relevance of bodies of knowledge.

The institutionalisation of conference interpreting and therefore the abandonment of the idea of a natural aptitude for interpreting increasingly pose the question of which abilities students must have in order to complete their interpreting studies successfully. In her contribution, **Catherine Chabasse** explains the necessary competencies and skills for performing simultaneous as well as consecutive interpreting. She shows which examination methods can be used in the context of aptitude tests and therefore provides a scientific basis for an improved prediction of a student's future performance.

There is a consensus in the interpreting studies literature that it is important to introduce students to the process of interpreting in a step-by-step manner and initially to familiarise them with sub-competencies. Preliminary exercises are the ideal teaching technique for this purpose. As these exercises are the subject of controversial discussions in the relevant literature, **Dörte Andres, Sophia Boden** and **Claudia Fuchs** discuss the didactic relevance of preliminary exercises for the development of skills relevant to interpreting, which have been developed by researchers and teachers in order to provide an easier entry into the field of simultaneous interpreting.

Attention is of great importance in conference interpreting. **Catherine Chabasse** and **Maren Dingfelder Stone** explain Daniel Gile's Effort Models and apply them to the topics of directionality and language pair specificity. They provide practical didactic suggestions for various learning stages and language pairs. The primary goals are to increase the students' sensitivity to capacity allocation shifts and therefore to facilitate their acquisition of the necessary problem-solving skills.

Comprehension is a basic prerequisite for successful interpreting and is dependent on the level of difficulty of the source text. Interpreting didactics has so far not paid much attention to the difficulty level of texts and effective text selection. **Dörte Andres** therefore discusses text-internal and presentation-based difficulty parameters and examines the didactic relevance of exploring interpreting texts and their difficulties (under consideration of the master's thesis completed by Henriette Kilger at the FTSK on text comprehension and text difficulties in interpreter training).

Student-oriented learning in interpreting means that students must be able to reflect critically on the skills they have acquired. This requires the conscious use of interpreting strategies. **Stephanie Kader** and **Sabine Seubert** collect various interpreting strategies in their contribution and illustrate their complex interaction in the interpreting process. The description of the strategies shows the importance and function of these strategies in simultaneous and consecutive interpreting. The specific examples of teaching the strategies in courses take the different learning levels of the students into account.

Systematic note-taking was one of the first topics in conference interpreting to be dealt with didactically. Over time a number of significantly different opinions emerged on whether a note-taking system should be taught and, if so, how this should be done. **Maren Dingfelder Stone** evaluates the various approaches in her contribution and highlights the most important and generally accepted recommendations in note taking training. She explains how the systematic and structured as well as language-independent teaching of systematic note-taking can be made an integral part of conference interpreter training.

Digital interpreting facilities, which emulate real-life interpreting situations, for example with the digital audio and video recording of interpretations, are increasingly being integrated into interpreter-training courses. The digital pen is also one of these interpreter-training tools. **Marc Orlando** discusses its application in the development of note-taking systems. He uses specific examples to show that the digital pen technology provides students and teachers with insights into the process of note taking. This illustrates the relationship between note taking, comprehension, analysis and the memorisation of a source speech.

High-quality interpreter training ensures adherence to high quality standards in interpreting practice. This training involves very regular and frequent evaluation of the students. **Martina Behr** describes the relevant quality criteria for interpreting practice and presents evaluation sheets for use in training. She also provides a detailed discussion of the contribution of good feedback to helping students learn in a motivated and goal-oriented way, while also providing specific hints on how to phrase such feedback in a fair and performance-enhancing manner.

The demand for employability, a topic of constantly increasing importance, is also geared towards interpreter training institutions. In his contribution, **Jacquy Neff** shows that teaching market-relevant skills is often neglected, even though professional associations do emphasise this topic. He shows what knowledge students must possess in order to compete on the current conference interpreting market by describing his course on professionalisation.

Teaching units in conference interpreter training aim to guide students in an efficient and goal-oriented manner. The acquisition of interpreting competence is largely achieved through intensive self-study. Digital media and information technologies offer new possibilities in this domain. In the final contribution, **Maren Dingfelder Stone** presents the *Moodle Online Platform, Self-Study in Interpreting* (MOPSI) platform that she has developed. She explains how this mode of self-study allows the students to correct their individual weaknesses with appropriate exercises.

We would like to thank everyone who has contributed to the creation of this volume. We would like to mention the CIUTI, which provided the funding for this publication. We would also like to thank the authors for their contributions as well as the translators for their efforts. Special thanks go to Flora Boegel for the careful formatting and the thorough review of the articles and to Charlotte Kieslich for supporting her.

Karlsruhe, December 2014
The editors, Dörte Andres and Martina Behr

Translated from German by Yann Kiraly

Interpreter Training and Interpreting Studies – Which is the Chicken and which is the Egg?

Sylvia Kalina
sylvia.kalina@fh-koeln.de
Cologne University of Applied Science, Germany
Sylvia.kalina@iued.uni-heidelberg.de
Heidelberg University, Germany

1. Early Interpreting and Interpreter Schools: On-the-job Training

The history of conference interpreting is full of impressive, self-trained personalities who interpreted in the consecutive mode and whose extensive knowledge and language skills provided an excellent basis for their interpreting activities. One might therefore assume that training in conference interpreting only began with the advent of the simultaneous mode. But a look at the history of this profession reveals that interpreters had been receiving some kind of training long before.

There is evidence that there must have been some training of professional interpreters in the ancient world. As early as the 9th century, boys were sent to missionary and other schools for the purpose of learning other languages, which they used later as interpreters (Schneider 2012). Their training included the mastery of foreign languages, but also specific interpreting skills (Wiotte-Franz 2001), whatever they may have consisted of at the time. From the 12th century on, highly qualified *dragomans* (the Egyptian and then Turkish term for interpreters) assisted in the negotiation of contacts between authorities and consulates (in Arabic, Turkish and Persian) in Egypt (Schneider 2012), and groups of boys were instructed in these languages so that they could become dragomans.

During the Roman Empire, interpreters were regularly used for high-level negotiations after military conflicts (Hermann 1956). These very first 'conference interpreters' with a command of scholarly languages enjoyed high academic status, whereas other interpreters were widely regarded as irresponsible rogues and potential traitors (GLÄSSER 1956). Clerical institutions explicitly obliged their interpreters to keep the information they obtained confidential and heed the principles of fidelity and correctness (SCHNEIDER 2012). At that time, consecutive interpreting (CI) was mostly expected to render the sense of an utterance in a compressed version, although at times there was a need for word-for-word renderings (SCHNEIDER 2012). Since then, the great debate about literal/free renderings, compression and completeness has never ceased.

Efforts to train interpreters at scholarly institutions can be traced back to the 13th century, when the Chancellor of the University of Paris was requested to establish a so-called Oriental College where students were taught languages, law, sciences, mathematics, theology and medicine (THIEME 1956). Christopher Columbus requested training for the native Indian-Americans he brought back from his voyages (cf. MOSER-MERCER 2005a, KURZ 2012), hoping that once they had learned Spanish, they would be able to act as interpreters. In the 17th century Ottoman Empire, apprentice dragomans were trained for seven years in Istanbul (AIIC 2005), and another Oriental Academy was set up in Austria (JOUKOVA 2002), while the Turkish Translation Chamber started their own training of Muslim dragomans in 1833, suspecting that Greek interpreters might falsify the intended meaning with their translations (ADAMS 2014). Interpreting for high-level contacts was practised long before the profession of the conference interpreter developed, and in some places it was taught as a skill long before university courses started offering specific training to aspiring conference interpreters.

The first exponents of consecutive interpreting to appear at an international level had become professionals because of their bi- or multilingual and -cultural upbringing and experience. They had devised CI techniques of their own, and many of them relied on their phenomenal memories. It was only during and after the Paris Peace Conference (1919) and the establishment of the League of Nations that there turned out not to be enough of these natural and multilingual talents. To cover the growing need for conference interpreters, some sort of formal training had to be provided.

In the late 1920s, the International Labour Organisation (ILO) in Geneva introduced ad hoc sessions for consecutive training (BAIGORRI-JALÓN 2004). Initial trials with early equipment for simultaneous interpreting (SI) were organised in 1928, both by ILO in Geneva and the Comintern Congress in Moscow (MOSER-MERCER 2005a), and when, after the end of World War II, SI was used systematically at the Nuremberg trials, it became evident that even if consecutive had been practised largely without any formal and specific training, working in the simultaneous mode required a certain degree of prior instruction. For the Nuremberg trials, this training took place under the aegis of Colonel Leon Dostert, himself an interpreter for U.S. President Eisenhower, on an ad hoc basis (GAIBA 1998). However, before any interpreters could be trained for simultaneous work during the trials, they had to undergo a selection procedure. It became apparent that testing for the ability to work in the simultaneous mode would have to be more demanding than testing for consecutive.

In addition to language proficiency, resilience to stress, and the ability to concentrate, mental agility to find equivalents under pressure, physical stamina to keep up high-level performance over time, as well as good voice quality, and clear enunciation were required. (MOSER-MERCER 2005a: 207)

Most of the subsequent training can best be described as 'learning by doing', or, as Baigorri-Jalón (2004) put it, "on-the-job" training. Training methods were as yet unknown, and "trial and error were the order of the day" (MOSER-MERCER 2005b: 62).

One of the questions that was debated at that early stage of SI and is still a matter of controversy today was whether the interpreters chosen should work into their A- or their B- language; a number of them actually worked into their B-language (cf. MOSER-MERCER 2005a, see SEUBERT & KADER in this volume).

Texts used for practising SI were often taken from newspapers, as there was no awareness of the criteria determining whether a text was appropriate for interpreting in the simultaneous mode. Later, speeches were read or improvised by one person with gradually increasing speed and complexity, the interpreters translated into a telephone-like device and another person listened and reviewed the interpreter's output (BAIGORRI-JALÓN 2004). Mock conferences and trials were held and interpreted; other components were the writing of summary reports of meetings, studying thematic subjects, and translation, especially at sight. The two crucial criteria for evaluation during courses and at examinations were accuracy and clarity of the message (BAIGORRI-JALÓN 2004).

Léon Dostert turned to the Geneva School of Translation and Interpretation (ETI), where conference interpreting was already being taught, though only in the consecutive mode. He recruited some of his interpreters from the students and teachers he met there. Only two to three weeks were available to prepare the future SI interpreters for the Nuremberg trials, and when simultaneous was introduced at the United Nations (again by Dostert) and the Council of Europe a few years later, two to three months had to suffice.

2. Practice and Theory: Training and Reflection

Despite the reluctance of many professional CI interpreters to go simultaneous, for fear of being unable to maintain the quality of their work (cf. BAIGORRI-JALÓN 2004: 50), some of the 'grand old' consecutive interpreters agreed to work in the booth, where some of them even managed without any further training. This may explain why the Paris school has always held the view that once a student fully masters consecutive, simultaneous will be no hurdle for him/her and will be learned quite naturally.

Soon it became obvious that interpreters working at high-level meetings needed training even for CI, and as a result universities, mainly in Europe, developed courses for conference interpreting. There was no doubt that universities were the only institutions where such highly specialised training could be provided. The School of Translation and Interpretation (now ETI) in Geneva was founded in 1941; SI was introduced there officially only in 1949 and did not become an integral part of the curriculum before 1953, after students had introduced it unofficially with their own technical equipment in 1947 (MOSER-MERCER 2005a). In the years thereafter, other schools followed in Heidelberg, Vienna, Mainz (Germersheim), Saarbruecken, Graz, Paris and other places. The courses offered were mostly postgraduate or were combined translation and interpreting courses. Fully-fledged conference interpreter degrees with SI were introduced in the 1950s and 1960s. Here, as before, simultaneous was accepted only after a tough battle with the defenders of CI (BAIGORRI-JALÓN 2004) who were the great interpreters and teachers of the time.

Even before SI was widely taught in university courses, the first contributions to what was to become the discipline of interpreting studies (IS) came from teachers of the famous Geneva school, all of them experienced high-level conference interpreters. Apart from passing on their own experience to their students, some of them soon started to reflect upon their teaching methods. Until then, interpreting had been practised without anyone caring much about how and why it worked; but as soon as full university courses were set up, the first handbooks with recommendations for future conference interpreters were published. One pioneering figure was Jean Herbert, who penned a famous handbook (HERBERT 1952), in which he sets out what an aspiring conference interpreter needs, why and how interpreting is different from translation, and which kind of challenges must be confronted. It also contains a few judgements on appropriate interpreter behaviour in cases of uncertainty, e.g. whether and when to correct a speaker's error, how to handle ambiguities, and note-taking in CI. It is interesting to note that most of his recommendations have remained valid to this day and are quoted frequently by contemporary interpreting teachers. Rozan taught CI and put together the principles and methods of note-taking (1956). Though few in number, they continue to form the basis for note-taking today. Research has meanwhile shown what mental processes are at work during note-taking and target-text production in the consecutive mode (ALBL-MIKASA 2007; ANDRES 2002), and its results have proved Rozan's method to be correct. Gérard Ilg described not only what he had observed while working as a consecutive interpreter himself but also sketched out a framework for the teaching of it, with references to, and critical comments on, the articles published by teachers at other schools. He thus laid the groundwork for a scholarly discussion of training methods (ILG 1959, 1980/1988).

These conference interpreting teachers all described regularities they had observed in their own and their colleagues' interpreting practice; they concluded that those regularities provided a model for quality interpreting and should therefore be taught. They explained the ways in which professional interpreters solved typical interpreting problems and compared their methods with those chosen by students. From their findings, they derived hypotheses regarding interpreting processes.

With translation studies gradually developing into the overall discipline of translation and interpreting (T&I), Otto Kade (1968) attempted to derive a theory of interpreting from translation theory based, at that time, on an early information-theoretical approach which held that equivalence in the communicative content of texts drafted in different codes is the core of translation. According to this view, the operations performed include substitution of code signs, grammatical transformation, lexical-semantic modulation, interpretation and paraphrase (as a result of a recoding operation). Though anchored in the theoretical thinking of the period and based on a conception of languages as codes, this approach provides some early references to strategic processing and therefore paved the way for subsequent research on interpreting. Hella Kirchhoff (1976) took up Kade's ideas and defined interpreting as a complex and multiple problem-solving task to be tackled with sequences of strategic operations. It is a multi-phase process, where segments of the target text are produced in phase shift as against the production of the source text. Crucial factors are situation-determining conditions (such as source text delivery rate), the principle of economy (i.e. formal reduction in interpreter output) and automatisation of routine operations. These automatisms and operations have to be trained.

As the interpreting school in Paris (ESIT) started to develop its postgraduate course under the aegis of an outstanding interpreter and committed teacher, Danica Seleskovitch, some (pre-)theoretical concepts of university training for conference interpreters were developed. As Seleskovitch herself had mainly amassed her interpreting experience in the consecutive mode, she focused on that mode and developed a first theoretical model of how, in her opinion, it worked. This resulted in her well-known theory of deverbalisation, or *théorie du sens*. For Seleskovitch (1975), comprehension is the crucial process, and analysis of what a speaker has said should enable the interpreter to find out what his/her intention is. Seleskovitch (1968) regarded this as interpreting proper based on deverbalisation, whereas proceeding word-for-word was transcoding and not really interpreting. In the teaching of interpreting proper (in the consecutive mode) she deemed it unnecessary to provide systematic note-taking training, as comprehension of the *sens* in the deverbalised mode is the only requirement. Her focus on CI led her to suggest that SI, though proceeding more on a word-for-word level, is not different from CI, except for the temporal factor, and that it should only be taught after students had fully mastered consecutive.

An even more important contribution made by Seleskovitch was her insistence on IS as a discipline in its own right that needed cooperation from other disciplines beyond the confines of translation studies. She invited her most ambitious students to engage in theoretical work and established the famous Paris *cycle de doctorat* which was to become the cradle of conference interpreting studies. Meanwhile, most university courses havetheoretical modules as part of their conference interpreting curricula.

Seleskovitch's *théorie du sens* has been criticised for many reasons, among them for being purely speculative and pre-scientific with no empirical evidence furnished to prove the statements made (cf. GILE 1990, KALINA 1998,

DAM 1998, PÖCHHACKER 2000). Dam, one of the critical voices, studied the choices made by student and professional interpreters for lexical items and found that when the choice was between form-based and meaning-based equivalents (transcoding vs. deverbalisation), professional interpreters also tended to produce a high number of form-based solutions, even when the mode was consecutive. Her conclusion was that if professionals behaved that way, they probably had good reasons for doing so, one of them being that technical source texts are frequently presented fast, with many figures and enumerations. This meant that students should be acquainted with types of processing where lexical similarity figures more often than lexical dissimilarity.

Notwithstanding this criticism, the deverbalisation approach is very useful as a teaching model, as students need to be told over and again to forget about the wording of a source text and instead express the meaning they have understood in their own words in the target language. Seleskovitch's approach to note-taking contrasted starkly with the systematic teaching of note-taking in Germany established by Matyssek (1989), and there ensued a heated debate on the appropriateness of note-taking instruction, including when it should be taught and whether notes should be SL, TL or symbolic/iconic (cf. MEISTER 1970; ANDRES 2002, AHRENS 2005; ALBL-MIKASA 2008; see DINGFELDER STONE (07) in this volume). The note-taking issue is a good example of how the practical experience of a few may lead to generalised teaching approaches that need to be reflected on in methodological terms if they are to become the basis for sound academic training.

Somewhat later, Marianne Lederer (1981), another teacher of the Paris school who cooperated with Seleskovitch but focused on SI, published one of the first empirical studies based on authentic interpreting data. She did not have the technological tools available today (see ORLANDO in this volume) but nevertheless transcribed and analysed comparatively large volumes of data. The result was a description of the different ways interpreters choose to solve problems raised by enumerations of figures and names, complicated syntax etc., and she found that for some of these problems transcoding, which – according to Seleskovitch – could not be regarded as interpreting proper, was in fact what interpreters did.

3. Extra- and Interdisciplinarity: Approaches to Explaining Interpreting

The phenomena at work during simultaneous interpreting subsequently aroused the interest of other disciplines, and a number of extra-disciplinary studies cast light on how interpreting, above all SI, actually functioned. Selective attention was investigated by Lawson (1967), input segmentation to facilitate SI by Goldman-Eisler (1972), while Treisman (1965) was interested in measuring *décalage* (time-lag, ear-voice span); this latter was also measured by Oléron & Nanpon (1965) with authentic interpreting products.

Professional interpreter and teacher interest and criticism was triggered by a linguistic study by Barik on error typologies (1971), which compares written texts, i.e. transcripts of texts read to test subjects and transcripts of the interpreted versions. Although the method used by Barik was not genuinely representative of interpreting products, its result, a categorisation of types of errors, was an instrument that could be used by teachers to enhance students' insight into the many things that could go wrong. The study prompted the interpreting community to make explicit the factors they found important but which were missing in Barik's purely product-oriented approach. These included paraverbal and nonverbal communication, the preferences and expectations of speakers and listeners, situational and processing conditions, and the fact that an omission is not always the same as an error but may, in some cases, even prove to be the optimum solution. Error research then became an important field in IS (cf. GILE 1985, 1990; KALINA 1998 (process and product) and others).

David Gerver, a psychologist, pointed out the relation between errors and a high input rate and the latter's influence on ear-voice span; after his test subjects (who were professional interpreters) had interpreted a text, he also questioned them about their comprehension of the text and their mnemonic capacity; the results confirmed that interpreting is a highly demanding cognitive task (GERVER 1969, 1976). Somewhat later, a very important contribution by a linguist to interpreting studies was made by Hildegund Bühler. Her survey (1986) aimed at identifying quality characteristics, and for this purpose she questioned interpreters themselves, not their users. The criticism of this method from interpreting professionals led to a number of user surveys with rather heterogeneous results, but again the attention of interpreting teachers to user preferences had been raised, and the categories defined by Bühler are used in conference interpreting classes everywhere.

Information processing and psycholinguistics were subjects that continued to show an interest in SI processes. As the interpreting community itself was more and more attracted by research on such questions, cases of interdisciplinary cooperation became more numerous. Moser's early flow chart model (1978) of the interpreting process is based on Massaro's (1978) psychological approach, and both Shlesinger (1989, 1990) and Kalina (1998) have cooperated with discourse studies scholars to establish categories of phenomena that need to be explained if one is interested in analysing interpreter comprehension as well as interpreting products.

Interpreting studies as an established subdiscipline of T&I has made use of models of translation (example: Pöchhacker (1994) who tested the functionalist Skopos theory for its ability to explain phenomena encountered in conference interpreting) and has meanwhile been seeking cooperation with other disciplines, such as psychology and neurophysiology, and with intercultural communication studies. Interdisciplinary research projects are the order of the day, and volumes such as Gran & Dodds (1989), Kurz (1996), Danks et al. (1997) and Englund Dimitrova & Hyltenstam (2000) demonstrate the wealth and depth of interdisciplinary research. Accordingly, the question to be addressed now is what effect all these research efforts have had on conference interpreting training.

4. Interpreting Studies: A Foundation for Training

Teachers who take their job seriously will undoubtedly be curious about how interpreting processes work, what differences can be identified between translating, CI and SI and what errors appear most frequently in which mode. They will not necessarily consult theoretical publications dealing with the most recent research results but look for advice on how to proceed in training. Although there is no such thing as a coursebook from which students can learn all the skills needed to become a good conference interpreter, a number of training manuals aimed at teachers have indeed been published. Some of them are collections of practical classroom experience and are useful especially for the less experienced trainer who, after having gained professional interpreting experience, sets about to share that experience with the younger generation; they include Matyssek (1989), Szabó (2003), Kautz (2000), Gillies (2001), Jones (1998). Others are the result of theoretical or empirical research and discuss different teaching methods or break down the overall competence to be acquired into subskills first taught separately and then integrated (cf. ANDRES 2002).

The first volume with a full theory-based account of teaching conference interpreting came from Seleskovitch and Lederer and expounded the approach of the Paris school. It is based on deverbalisation theory as an explanation for comprehension and production processes and regards CI as the mode to be mastered first, after which SI is mainly a question of training practice (SELESKOVITCH & LEDERER 1989). It also emphasises the view held by Seleskovitch that CI can be learned without any systematic note-taking expertise. In the same year, Matyssek published his manual on note-taking, and as a result the dispute mentioned above over what is right (systematic or ad hoc notes, symbols or abbreviations, source or target language notes) became even fiercer.

In 1995 Daniel Gile, one of the scholars who had always argued both for interdisciplinarity and for IS as an independent discipline, proposed a volume on interpreter and translator training that was to become a milestone on the road towards well-founded interpreting training. His Effort Models for CI and SI, originally published in 1985, have since served as a most valuable and illustrative model for students and teachers alike, as it has proved able to explain the reasons for difficulties, errors and weaknesses occurring during the interpreting process.

The differences between expert and novice interpreters in terms of knowledge, automated processes, and stages of skill acquisition were at the heart of Moser-Mercer's (2000a) study. With a small-scale empirical study of student groups at different stages of progress, she carried out task analyses and interviews to elicit their learning experience. As in Gerver's previous studies, the difficulties encountered by students were measured in the shadowing and simultaneous modes. This method enabled her to break down skills into subskills to be trained and learned by students and thus improve class planning and student progress towards expertise. Expertise and its acquisition are also major topics in Moser-Mercer's research (cf. also 2000b, 2005a, 2005b, 2008), and her suggestions for training are derived from models of learning theory and psychology. The expert/novice approach has also been taken up by Sunnari (2003), while learning styles are analysed by Kurz et al. (2000), who identify differences between translators and interpreters and similarities between student and professional interpreters.

Another teaching approach is that of Kalina whose work is based on the model of strategic processing first published in Kohn & Kalina (1996) and subsequently refined (KALINA 1996, 1998). It contradicts the view of the Paris school that consecutive must be fully mastered before simultaneous is taught and suggests that interpreting-specific strategies have to be developed and automated. It proposes a distinct set of preparatory exercises that help students acquire some of the skills they need for doing simultaneous and provides for a gradual increase in difficulty with emphasis on the type of feedback teachers offer their students (cf. KALINA 2000; ANDRES 2014). Feedback is also discussed by Kutz (1990, 2010) who argues that the identification of individual interpreting errors in class is largely irrelevant as long as there is no inquiry into the causes of these errors. For him, the aim of all training must be to enable students to take specific, cognitively monitored decisions on how to act, and that global objectives have to be split up into partial objectives. An empirical study on interpreter training aimed at devising a methodologically based curriculum was carried out by Sawyer (2004) who also defined levels of expertise and steps towards acquiring skills within the scope of an approach based on educational theory. The result is an instrument for curriculum assessment with clear-cut goals and suggestions for improving interpreting training.

Teachers who have engaged in, or at least read extensively about, the findings produced by interpreting studies will find it easier to design their courses in such a way that students can learn the necessary skills stepwise, from simple to more complex operations. For example, knowledge about comprehension processes will create conditions for helping students going through such processes, i.e. improve their comprehension skill (cf. HÖNIG 1992, GILE 1995, KUTZ 2000a, 2000b). Assessment of text difficulty is more successful if teachers know about the factors that make a text difficult to interpret, some of which apply specifically to CI or SI respectively (see ANDRES in this volume).

Determining the quality of interpreter output is a topic that has occupied researchers, teachers and practitioners in all phases of IS. Starting with Bühler's study, numerous surveys of users and interpreters have been conducted to obtain reliable data (e.g. ZWISCHENBERGER 2013 and PÖCHHACKER 2012), and specific components of interpreting quality have been analysed (COLLADOS AÍS et al. 2011). Indispensable prerequisites for quality interpreting have been emphasized by Kopczyniski (1994) and Moser-Mercer (1996). All these contributions have had a strong impact on how the quality question is dealt with in class; they have enabled informed teachers to better explain aspects addressed by IS and have helped to bring teaching more in line with the demands of professional practice.

One of the perennial talking points in interpreter training is the question of student evaluation. IS offers a number of different ways of proceeding, referring both to actual assessment and to ways of giving feedback to student interpreters. In exam sessions, assessors tend to assume the perspective of a user, but as they usually understand the source text, they cannot claim to go through all the comprehension processes a user requires. Kalina (1995) has suggested categories and factors to be weighted in accordance with the characteristics of source text presentation. Kutz (2005) has gone into the different perspectives that have to be considered when assessing student interpreting performance, such as the problem-solution approach and general behavior during a presentation, while Behr (2013) has presented a study on how emotions may influence teacher evaluation of interpreting products (cf. also the articles by ANDRES and by BEHR in this volume). Kutz (2000a, 2000b) points to the need to make students aware not only of the techniques of interpreting but also of efficient preparation. An empirical study with results on the preparation of technical conferences has been published by Gile (2002).

Interpreting studies has also laid the foundation for a wealth of preparatory exercises for CI and SI. Some of these are rather controversial, such as shadowing, which has been used not only in empirical studies for comparison with listening, CI and SI (GERVER 1976), but as a method of testing for aptitude (LAMBERT 1992a, MILZOW & WIESENHÜTTER 1997). The pros and cons of shadowing exercises are discussed in Kurz (1992), Kalina (1994) and Christoffels & De Groot (2004). Anticipatory text mapping was devised by Hönig (1997) and cloze as a preparatory exercise is discussed in Lambert (1992b) and Kalina (1998) (see ANDRES et al. in this volume).

Research into testing for interpreting aptitude is an excellent example of interdisciplinary cooperation. It has engendered test designs that notwithstanding their continuing uncertainties and weaknesses enable testers to give a reasonably justified assessment of the potential that candidates may have or lack (see CHABASSE in this volume).

How attractive are theory and IS to conference interpreting students? In the past, students largely preferred to engage in practical work, i.e. language and knowledge acquisition and, above all, interpreting exercises, especially in the SI mode. Meanwhile, however, IS has so many interesting answers to their questions that they feel an engagement with theory is no longer a laborious chore but a rewarding exercise. Ways in which they can embark on theoretical work have been suggested by Gile (2001), Pöchhacker (2001) and others. After all, the students of today will be the interpreting teachers of tomorrow, and that challenge can only be mastered by way of a thorough training in IS.

5. Conference Interpreter Training: Trends and Adjustments

In the decades since the introduction of SI as an increasingly important component of conference interpreting training, a great many proposals for specific training methods and entire training designs have been made. We must now ask ourselves whether the methods developed in decades past are still relevant and appropriate today. The present generation of students has grown up with entirely different ways of processing information and has at its disposal completely different communication channels from those available to their trainers when they were students. The relatively unsurprising answer is that training must be adapted to these circumstances and innovative training methods must be developed.

In comparison with the older generation, students today searching for an answer to a problem have to deal with excessive amounts of information; they find it extremely difficult to distinguish between what is helpful or important and to decide what is worth remembering in the long term. Their storage processes are related to electronic storage media rather than to mnemonic structures. Knowledge of history, the arts and current political and cultural events and trends is not something the young generation finds very intriguing. Interpreting students have to be made to understand the importance of such knowledge for the field of conference interpreting. Their memory capacity can be trained with specific analysing and summarising exercises, with which they can practise generalising, hyperonym-finding, the use of economical wording etc. and learn to rely on their memories.

Another factor is that the younger generation's comprehension processes work differently, a phenomenon observable not only in interpreters but also in conference participants and people in general. Though the criticism voiced by Spitzer (2012) that excessive use of the computer reduces children's ability to think in complex structures may be somewhat exaggerated, it is certainly true that they have their own, maybe less intricate ways of understanding relations between things and are often unable to relate facts from the present to those of the past. These changes (plus other factors) have also led to the rise of what is termed 'simplified language', a recent phenomenon in many languages that is gaining ground in oral and print media. At first glance, these texts resemble machine translations from a different language, yet simplified language has its own rules and standards. Initially developed for people with speech/comprehension deficits or functional illiterates and migrants with insufficient knowledge of the host language, it is being used by more and more people who find its limited scope of expression sufficient for their needs (cf. STRASSMANN 2014). If this trend establishes itself on the conference podium, this may make life for interpreters somewhat easier, but at the same time it is likely to endanger their very profession, as simplified language is easier to understand for those without any genuine proficiency in the language concerned. It is an open question whether the use of simplified language by interpreters will facilitate listeners' comprehension, and one may well doubt whether detailed and fine-tuned comments will be possible at all when everybody uses simplified language.

Also, rhetorical skills, though still admired where they are used effectively, have lost their importance, the reason being that electronic media do not rely on them. It is therefore all the more necessary to train public speaking skills and effective communication, be it for interpreting or for survival as such. Admittedly, new technologies place high demands on young people that have little to do with verbal and communicative skills, but as long as speakers at conferences are able to make use of the rhetorical resources that are part and parcel of public speaking in the traditional sense, interpreters must be able to follow suit and do the same. Linguistic ambition, too, appears to be a thing of the past; official registers no longer play a role in the everyday lives of young people, nor does style matter very much. Interpreting trainees who wish to base their career on language and communication, however, must develop a feeling and an ambition for register and stylistic differences. For them this is something quite new, so a lot of effort has to be put into this. But the interpreting community can help to actively cherish the treasures that languages hold.

International communication today largely uses English as its lingua franca. The English language has obtained a dominant role not only in everyday life but even more so in international conferences and organisations, and this trend, if it continues, will affect thought and linguistic expression in other languages and therewith entire cultures. Possible solutions to the question of whether to leave a term in English or find an equivalent in the target language may be manifold and challenging.

But there are also major opportunities to capitalise on in training a new generation of conference interpreters. Technology has provided teachers with a wealth of authentic speeches and conferences to be downloaded on easy-to-handle media, and interpreting products can be easily stored so that researchers have much greater possibilities of analysing them than could have been imagined just a few decades ago. Young people have fewer problems coping with technically mediated source texts and find it easier to interpret speeches from video conferences and even via the telephone. For them, digital libraries are not a novelty, and they know how to embark on advanced search operations. Conference technology, which used to be expensive equipment for classes at universities, can now be used easily with software assistance that students can program for themselves. They no longer need a full conference hall at university if they want to practise on their own. Instead, they can organise an electronic workshop environment where everybody who takes part in a practising session can do so from their own office desks.

One of the great opportunities for teaching today lies in the social media which, when used intelligently and professionally, can be a great help to students. In addition to the advantages that the computerised age has brought, students can exchange experiences, documents for preparation, glossaries and also comments on each other's interpreting output, thoughts about teaching etc. At the same time, they are confronted with the principles of confidentiality and will find out when not to make use of any social media communication, e.g. when working in the booth.

Today's students have developed their own learning styles, and this, too, requires adjustment of courses and new approaches by teachers. A number of e-learning module formats and blended learning environments have been devised to combine periods of face-to-face teaching with teacher-supported virtual training and distance-learning modules. Supervised practice can be combined with self-study activities and learning journals (cf. GROSS-DINTER 2007, CLASS & MOSER-MERCER 2013, SCHOMAKER & KAGON 2011). As independent self-training is attractive to the generation of students now at university, learning portfolios and diaries give them a degree of structure and control in monitoring their progress. In class, new technologies such as the digital pen help increase the identification of processes that go wrong or can be improved not only in SI, but also in CI (see ORLANDO in this volume). The strengths of today's trainees are the ease with which they master technical challenges, the speed at which they process huge amounts of information and the way in which they communicate with people all over the world through social media, and these strengths must be put to good use.

6. Theory and Practice: the Future of the Profession

Interpreting studies was once the 'poor relation' of translation studies proper, particularly after the functionalist turn and the focus on the translation of specialised texts. In the past few decades, however, IS has caught up and now stands revealed as a multi-faceted subdiscipline in its own right (cf. SALEVSKY 1992, SHLESINGER 1998, PÖCHHACKER 2000). With its emphasis in recent years on types of interpreting other than conference interpreting, the functionalist approach has gained ground in IS, too. What implications does this development have for interpreter training? Do interpreters of all types regard themselves as belonging to one profession? And, as the focus of this article is on conference interpreting, do conference interpreters regard those who work in the nonconference sector as peers? Unanswered research questions still abound in all fields of interpreting, and shared research efforts may open up ways of addressing such questions that will benefit theory and practice alike. Interpreter training, which, as we have seen, has to adapt to new circumstances anyway, will be enriched by joint research activities.

It is also important to closely observe market trends. For some decades, the consecutive mode was no longer practised ininternational meetings. Where the equipment was available, full simultaneous was provided, and in other cases, tour guide equipment was used, to the distress of the interpreters concerned. Meanwhile, there are signs that CI is recovering; one of the reasons for this trend is definitely the high costs of simultaneous technology. So far, most interpreting schools are still providing thorough consecutive training for their students, although some of the teachers there do not practise it any longer and have lost contact to consecutive technique. Recruitment tests held by international organisations, national ministries and other bodies continue to largely rely on the quality of a candidate's consecutive performance – not least because testers find it difficult to listen to an original and an interpreted version at the same time. If the trend towards more consecutive assignments on the market continues, this will be a chance for the young generation of interpreters, who are usually at the height of their consecutive skills because they have practised it in exercises day in, day out. It will also require teachers to take CI more seriously and improve their own mastery of it. In a digital age, one may also wonder why CI is still done with nothing but a note-pad and pencil as the only tools that interpreters have at their disposal. And indeed, the scenario may soon change. Different types of combinations of CI and SI have been studied (cf. PÖCHHACKER 2007), but so far they have not shown enough potential to represent a novel mode of interpreting in their own right.

Results of aptitude tests suggest that for a number of reasons fewer and fewer candidates are found eligible for taking up a Master's course in conference interpreting; testing results by international employers show a similar trend. Is it really true that the younger generation does not possess the talent, skills and knowledge that are needed for conference interpreting? Or do we need to revise our notions about the skills future conference interpreters must have and adjust our teaching methodologies to account for new ways of processing language and information and new approaches to studying whatever subject one has chosen? The young generation may find it more difficult to cope with criticism from their teachers, and they may also be less resistant to stress and fatigue. But if they are properly initiated and motivated, they will acquire all that is necessary for them to pass their tests and assert themselves on the market. After all, preferences may have changed not only among would-be conference interpreters but also among their potential clientèle, who may be also less demanding in terms of linguistic polish and whose world knowledge may not be all that different from that of their interpreters but who will certainly expect them to be fully acquainted with the very latest technological communication gadgets.

Although IS has done a lot to establish a firm basis for training conference interpreters in practice and theory, the question is whether its insights have been accepted and implemented in practice. The training of conference interpreters has adapted to new media available for use as source texts, to technologically advanced teaching/interpreting equipment, and to new formats for speeches and presentations. 'Training for trainers' courses are now available at some places where conference interpreting is taught, though at some schools the practice of hiring free-lance professionals without any prior didactic experience or training for trainers still lives on. This recalls the days that one hoped had gone forever, when some teachers who simply regarded giving interpreting classes as another easy source of income took the speeches they had interpreted on a given day and read them to their students in the evening. This led to much frustration as they never thought twice about the state of progress of their students, nor did they have any strategy for training progression. They had not reflected on the craft and the skills they were teaching, and in contrast to their students, who had undergone theoretical as well as practical training, they ignored what IS has found out about interpreting. Trainers like these gather their teaching experience as they go, a time-wasting business pursued at the expense of the unfortunate trainees concerned. This way, opportunities are missed and unnecessary experiments are done with the students. It is therefore imperative that theoretical interpreting studies be and remain part and parcel of any conference interpreting curriculum, so that future practitioners are able to reflect upon what they actually do when interpreting, and future teachers are aware of the findings and insights generated by IS. To conclude, IS should be more closely integrated at all levels and in all fields of conference interpreter training, and practitioners, employers and users should be made more aware of the fact that interpreting and, for that matter, conference interpreting, is a highly expert professional activity with conditions and processes of its own.

References

ADAMS, Christine (2014): *Looking for interpreter zero: (5) Dragomans.* http://aiic.net/blog/post/6653/looking-for-interpreter-zero-5-dragomans/2014/02/04/lang/1 (16.04.2014).

AHRENS, Barbara (2005): "Rozan and Matyssek: Are they really that different? A comparative synopsis of two classic note-taking schools", *Forum* 3(2), 1-15.

AIIC (2005): *From-dragomans-to-interpreters-a-brief-overview-of-the-profession-in-turkey.* http://aiic.net/page/1525/from-dragomans-to-interpreters-a-brief-overview-of-the-profession-in-turkey/lang/1 (17.04.2014).

ALBL-MIKASA, Michaela (2007): *Notationsprache und Notizentext. Ein kognitiv-linguistisches Modell für das Konsekutivdolmetschen.* Tübingen: Gunter Narr.

ALBL-MIKASA, Michaela (2008): "(Non-)Sense in note-taking for consecutive interpreting", *Interpreting* 10:2, 197-231.

ANDRES, Dörte (2002): *Konsekutivdolmetschen und Notation.* FASK Publikationen des Fachbereichs Angewandte Sprach- und Kulturwissenschaft der Johannes-Gutenberg-Universität Mainz in Germersheim, Reihe A. Frankfurt a. M.: Peter Lang.

ANDRES, Dörte. (2014): "Lust verkürzt den Weg: Shakespeare und die Ausbildung im Dolmetschen". In: FORSTNER, Martin; GARBOVSKY, Nikolay & LEE-JAHNKE, Hannelore (eds.): *CIUTI-Forum 2013. Facing the World's New Challenges. The Role of T&I in Providing Integrated and Efficient and Sustainable Solutions.* Frankfurt a. M.: Peter Lang, 181-192.

BAIGORRI-JALÓN, Jesus (2004): "Interpreters at the United Nations: A History. Translated from Spanish by Anne Barr". In: BAIGORRI-JALÓN, Jesus: *La interpretación de conferencias: el nacimiento de una profesión. De París a Nuremberg.* Granada: Edition Comares, Ediciones de la Universidad de Salamanca, 36-84.

BARIK, Henry C. (1971): "A Description of Various Types of Omissions, Additions, Errors of Translation Encountered in Simultaneous Interpretation", *Meta* 16(4), 199-210.

BEHR, Martina (2013): *Evaluation und Stimmung. Ein neuer Blick auf Qualität im (Simultan-)Dolmetschen.* Berlin: Frank & Timme.

BÜHLER, Hildegund (1986): "Linguistic (Semantic) and Extra-linguistic (Pragmatic) Criteria for the Evaluation of Conference Interpretation and Interpreters", *Multilingua* 5(4), 231-235.

CHRISTOFFELS, Ingrid & DE GROOT, Annette (2004): "Components of SI: Comparing Interpreting with shadowing and paraphrasing", *Bilingualism: Language and Cognition* 7(3), 227-240.

CLASS, Barbara & MOSER-MERCER, Barbara (2013): "Training conference interpreter trainers with technology – a virtual reality". In: GARCÍA BECERRA, Olalla; PRADAS MACÍAS, E. Macarena & BARRANCO-DROEGE, Rafael (eds.): *Quality in interpreting: widening the scope.* Granada: Editorial Comares. Volume 1, 293-313.

COLLADOS AÍS, Ángela; IGLESIAS FERNÁNDEZ, Emilia; PRADAS MACÍAS, E. Macarena & STÉVAUX, Elisabeth (eds.) (2011): *Qualitätsparameter beim Simultandolmetschen, Interdisziplinäre Perspektiven*. Tübingen: Gunter Narr.

DAM, Helle Vronning (1998): "Lexical similarity vs. Lexical Dissimilarity in Consecutive Interpreting", *The Translator* 4(1), 49-68.

DANKS, Joseph; SHREVE, Gregory M.; FOUNTAIN, Stephen B. & MCBEATH, Michael K. (eds.) (1997): *Cognitive Processes in Translation and Interpreting. Applied Psychology Vol. 3*. Thousand Oaks, London/New Delhi: Sage Publications.

ENGLUND DIMITROVA, Birgitta & HYLTENSTAM, Kenneth (eds.) (2000): *Language Processing and Simultaneous Interpreting. Interdisciplinary Perspectives*. Amsterdam/Philadelphia: John Benjamins.

GAIBA, Francesca (1998): *The Origins of Simultaneous Interpretation. The Nuremberg Trial*. Ottawa: The University of Ottawa Press.

GERVER, David (1969): "The effects of source language presentation rate on the performance of simultaneous conference interpreters". In: FOULKE, Emerson (ed.): *Proceedings of the 2nd Louisville Conference on Rate and/or Frequency Controlled Speech*. University of Louisville, 162-184; and in: PÖCHHACKER, Franz & SHLESINGER, Miriam (eds.) (2002): *The Interpreting Studies Reader*. London and New York: Routledge, 52-66.

GERVER, David (1976): "Empirical studies of simultaneous interpretation: a review and a model". In: BRISLIN, Richard W. (ed.): *Translation: applications and research*. New York: Gardner Press, 165-207.

GILE, Daniel (1985): "Le modèle d'efforts et l'équilibre d'interprétation en interprétation simultanée", *Meta* 30(1), 44-48.

GILE, Daniel (1990): "Scientific Research vs. Personal Theories in the Investigation of Interpretation". In: GRAN, Laura &TAYLOR, Christopher (eds.): *Aspects of Applied and Experimental Research in Conference Interpretation*. Udine: Campanotto, 28-41.

GILE, Daniel (1995): *Basic Concepts and Models for Interpreter and Translator Training*. Amsterdam/Philadelphia: John Benjamins.

GILE, Daniel (1997): "Conference Interpreting as a Cognitive Management Problem". In: DANKS, Joseph; SHREVE, Gregory M.; FOUNTAIN, Stephen B. & MCBEATH, Michael K. (eds.): *Cognitive Processes in Translation and Interpreting. Applied Psychology Vol. 3*. Thousand Oaks, London/New Delhi: Sage Publications, 196-214.

GILE, Daniel (2001): "Useful Research for Students in T&I Institutions", *Hermes* 26, 97-117.

GILE, Daniel (2002): "The Interpreter's Preparation for Technical Conferences: Methodological Questions in Investigating the Topic", *Conference Interpretation and Translation* 4(2), 7-27.

GILLIES, Andrew (2001): *Conference Interpreting: A Student's Companion*. Krakow: Tertium.

GLÄSSER, Edgar (1956): "Dolmetschen im Mittelalter. Ein Beitrag zur Entwicklung des Völkergedankens". In: THIEME, Karl & HERMANN, Alfred & GLÄSSER, Edgar (ed.): *Beiträge zur Geschichte des Dolmetschens*. Band 1. München: Isar, 61-79.

GOLDMAN-EISLER, Frieda (1972): "Segmentation of input in simultaneous translation", *Journal of Psycholinguistic Research* 1, 127-140.
GRAN, Laura & DODDS, John (eds.) (1989): *The Theoretical and Practical Aspects of Teaching Conference Interpretation. Proceedings of the Trieste Symposium, 1986.* Udine: Campanotto.
GROSS-DINTER, Ursula (2007): "Portfolio für das bilaterale Konsekutivdolmetschen. Ein Instrument der Verbesserung von Unterrichts- und Lernqualität". In: SCHMITT, Peter A. & JÜNGST, Heike E. (eds.) *Translationsqualität. Leipziger Studien zur angewandten Linguistik und Translatologie.* Frankfurt a. M.: Peter Lang, 222-236.
HERBERT, Jean (1952): *Manuel de l'interprète/The interpreter's handbook/Handbuch für den Dolmetscher.* Genf: Georg & Cie.
HERMANN, Alfred (1956): "Dolmetschen im Altertum. Ein Beitrag zur antiken Kulturgeschichte". In: THIEME, Karl; HERMANN, Alfred & GLÄSSER, Edgar (eds.): *Beiträge zur Geschichte des Dolmetschens.* Band 1. München: Isar, 25-59.
HÖNIG, Hans G. (1992): "Verstehensoperationen beim Konsekutivdolmetschen – gehirnphysiologische Grundlagen, psycholinguistische Modellbildungen und didaktische Konsequenzen", *TexTconTexT* 7(3/4), 145-167.
HÖNIG, Hans G. (1997): "Using text mappings in teaching consecutive interpreting". In: HAUENSCHILD, Christa & HEIZMANN, Susanne (eds.): *Machine Translation and Translation Theory.* Berlin/New York: De Gruyter, 19-34.
ILG, Gérard (1959): "L'enseignement de l'interprétation". Off-print of three articles published in *L'Interprète.* Genf: Georg & Cie.
ILG, Gérard (1980/1988): "L'interprétation consécutive. Les fondements", *Parallèles* 3, 109-136. [Revised version: ILG, Gérard (1988): "La prise de notes en interprétation consécutive. Une orientation générale", *Parallèles* 9, 9-13.]
JONES, Roderick (1998): *Conference Interpreting Explained.* Manchester: St. Jerome.
JOUKOVA, Alexandra (2002): *Dolmetscher- und Sprachausbildung an der Orientalischen bzw. Diplomatischen Akademie in Wien* (Diplomarbeit). Zentrum für Translationswissenschaft, Universität Wien.
KADE, Otto (1968): "Kommunikationswissenschaftliche Probleme der Translation", *Beihefte zur Zeitschrift Fremdsprachen* II. – VEB Leipzig, 3-19.
KALINA, Sylvia (1994): "Some views on the theory of interpreter training and some practical suggestions". In: SNELL-HORNBY, Mary; PÖCHHACKER, Franz & KAINDL, Klaus (eds.): *Translation Studies – An Interdiscipline. Selected papers from the Translation Studies Congress, Vienna, 9-12 September 1992.* Amsterdam/Philadelphia: John Benjamins, 219-226.
KALINA, Sylvia (1995): "Dolmetschen und Diskursanalyse – Anforderungen an Dolmetschleistungen". In: BEYER, Manfred; DILLER, Hans-Jürgen; KORNELIUS, Joachim; OTTO, Erwin & STRATMANN, Gerd (ed.): *anglistik und englischunterricht. Realities of Translating.* Heidelberg: C. Winter, 233-245.
KALINA, Sylvia (1996): "Zum Erwerb strategischer Verhaltensweisen beim Dolmetschen". In: LAUER, Angelika; GERZYMISCH-ARBOGAST, Heidrun; HALLER, Johann &

STEINER, Erich (ed.): *Übersetzungswissenschaft im Umbruch. Festschrift für Wolfram Wilss zum 70. Geburtstag.* Tübingen: Gunter Narr, 271-279.

KALINA, Sylvia (1998): "Strategische Prozesse beim Dolmetschen. Theoretische Grundlagen, empirische Untersuchungen, didaktische Konsequenzen", *Language in Performance* 18. Tübingen: Gunter Narr.

KALINA, Sylvia (2000): "Interpreting competences as a basis and a goal for teaching", *The Interpreters' Newsletter* 10, 3-32.

KAUTZ, Ulrich (2000): *Handbuch Didaktik des Übersetzens und Dolmetschens.* München: Iudicium/Goethe-Institut.

KIRCHHOFF, Hella (1976): "Das Simultandolmetschen: Interdependenz der Variablen im Dolmetschprozeß, Dolmetschmodelle und Dolmetschstrategien". In: DRESCHER, Horst W. & SCHEFFZEK, Signe (ed.): *Theorie und Praxis des Übersetzens und Dolmetschens.* Band 6, Reihe A der Publikationen des Fachbereichs Angewandte Sprachwissenschaft der Universität Mainz in Germersheim. Frankfurt a. M.: Peter Lang, 59-71.

KOHN, Kurt & KALINA, Sylvia (1996): "The strategic dimension of interpreting", *Meta* 41(1), 118-138.

KOPCZYŃSKI, Andrzej (1994): "Quality in Conference Interpreting: Some Pragmatic Problems". In: SNELL-HORNBY, Mary; PÖCHHACKER, Franz & KAINDL, Klaus (eds.): *Translation Studies – An Interdiscipline.* Amsterdam/Philadelphia: John Benjamins, 189-198; and in: LAMBERT, Sylvie & MOSER-MERCER, Barbara (eds.): *Bridging the Gap: Empirical RESEARCH on Simultaneous Interpretation.* (Benjamins Translation Library 3.) Amsterdam/Philadelphia: John Benjamins, 87-99.

KURZ, Ingrid (1992): "'Shadowing' exercises in interpreter training". In: DOLLERUP, Cay & LODDEGAARD, Anne (eds.): *Teaching Translation and Interpreting – Training, Talent and Experience. Papers from the First Language International Conference, Elsinore, Denmark, 31 May – 2 June 1991.* (Copenhagen Studies in Translation). Amsterdam/Philadelphia: John Benjamins, 245-250.

KURZ, Ingrid (1996): *Simultandolmetschen als Gegenstand der interdisziplinären Forschung.* Wien: Wiener Universitätsverlag.

KURZ, Ingrid; CHIBA, Doris; MEDINSKAYA, Vera & PASTORE, Martin (2000): "Translators and Interpreters: Different Learning Styles?", *Across Languages and Cultures* 1(1), 71-83.

KURZ, Ingrid (2012): *Acceptance speech. Danica Seleskovitch Prize 2012. Discours prononcé par Ingrid KURZ, lauréate du Prix Danica Seleskovitch 2012, à l'occasion de la remise du Prix le 20 mars 2012 à Paris (ESIT).* http://www.prix-danica-seleskovitch.org/Discours_Kurz_10mars12.pdf (17.04.2014).

KUTZ, Wladimir (1990): "Zur Überwindung aktueller Entsprechungslücken – Zu einer dolmetschspezifischen Fähigkeit". In: SALEVSKY, Heidemarie (ed.): *Übersetzungswissenschaft und Sprachmittlerausbildung. Akten der 1. Internationalen Konferenz.* Berlin: Humboldt-Universität, 405-408.

KUTZ, Wladimir (2000a): "Warum zum Teufel sagt er das? Verstehensleistung und Gedächtnistechniken beim Konsekutivdolmetschen". Teil 1, *MDÜ* 46(4-5), 27-31.

KUTZ, Wladimir (2000b): "Warum zum Teufel sagt er das? Verstehensleistung und Gedächtnistechniken beim Konsekutivdolmetschen". Teil 2, *MDÜ* 46(6), 11-14.

KUTZ, Wladimir (2005): "Zur Bewertung der Dolmetschqualität in der Ausbildung von Konferenzdolmetschern", *Lebende Sprachen* 50(1), 14-34.

KUTZ, Wladimir (2010): *Dolmetschkompetenz. Was muss der Dolmetscher wissen und können?* Translation 1. Berlin/Bochum: Europäischer Universitätsverlag.

LAMBERT, Sylvie (1992a): "Shadowing", *Meta* 37/2, 263-273.

LAMBERT, Sylvie (1992b): "The Cloze Technique as a Pedagogical Tool for the Training of Translators and Interpreters", *Target* 4(2), 223-236.

LAWSON, Everdina A. (1967): "Attention and simultaneous translation", *Language and Speech* 10, 29-35.

LEDERER, Marianne (1981): *La traduction simultanée – Expérience et Théorie. Lettres modernes.* Paris: Minard.

MASSARO, Dominic W. (1978): "An Information Processing Model of Understanding Speech". In: GERVER, David & SINAIKO, Henry W. (eds.): *Language Interpretation and Communication.* New York: Plenum Press, 299-314.

MATYSSEK, Heinz (1989): *Handbuch der Notizentechnik für Dolmetscher. Ein Weg zur sprachunabhängigen Notation. Teil 1 und Teil 2.* Heidelberg: Julius Groos.

MEISTER, Elisabeth (1970): "A propos du livre de D. Seleskovitch. L'interprète dans les conférences internationales", *L'Interprète* 25(1), 7-8.

MILZOW, Maria & WIESENHÜTTER, Angela (1997): "Shadowing", *Folia Translatologica* 5. Prague: Charles University. Institute of Translation Studies, 21-28.

MOSER, Barbara (1978): "Simultaneous Interpretation: A Hypothetical Model and its Practical Application". In: GERVER, David & SINAIKO, Henry W. (eds.): *Language Interpretation and Communication.* New York: Plenum Press, 353-368.

MOSER-MERCER, Barbara (1996): "Quality in Interpreting: Some Methodological Issues", *The Interpreters' Newsletter* 7, 43-55.

MOSER-MERCER, Barbara (2000a). "The rocky road to expertise in interpreting: Eliciting knowledge from learners". In: KADRIC, Mira; KAINDL, Klaus & PÖCHHACKER, Franz (ed.): *Transationswissenschaft. Festschrift für Mary Snell-Hornby zum 60. Geburtstag.* Tübingen: Stauffenberg, 339-352.

MOSER-MERCER, Barbara (2000b): "Simultaneous interpreting: Cognitive potential and limitations", *Interpreting* 5(2), 83-94.

MOSER-MERCER, Barbara (2005a): "The Teaching of Simultaneous Interpretation: The first 60 years (1929-1989)", *Forum* 3(1), 205-225.

MOSER-MERCER, Barbara (2005b): "Challenges to interpreter training". In: MAYER, Felix (ed.): *20 Jahre Transforum: Koordinierung von Praxis und Lehre des Dolmetschens und Übersetzens.* Hildesheim: G. Olms. S. 61 – 72.

MOSER-MERCER, Barbara (2008): "Skill Acquisition in Interpreting. A Human Performance Perspective", *The Interpreter and Translator Trainer* 2(1), 1-28.

OLERON, Pierre & NANPON, Hubert (1965): "Recherches sur la traduction simultanée", *Journal de Psychologie Normale et Pathologique* 62(2), 73-94.

PÖCHHACKER, Franz (1994): *Simultandolmetschen als komplexes Handeln*. Tübingen: Gunter Narr.

PÖCHHACKER, Franz (2000): *Dolmetschen. Konzeptuelle Grundlagen und deskriptive Untersuchungen. Studien zur Translation.* Tübingen: Stauffenburg.

PÖCHHACKER, Franz (2001): "Working within a theoretical framework". In: GILE, Daniel; VAN DAM, Helle; DUBSLAFF, Friedel; MARTINSEN, Bodil & SCHJOLDAGER, Anne (eds.): *Getting Started in Interpreting Research*. Amsterdam/Philadelphia: John Benjamins, 199-219.

PÖCHHACKER, Franz (2007): "'Going Simul?' Technology-assisted Consecutive Interpreting", *Forum* 5(2), 101-124.

PÖCHHACKER, Franz (2012): "Interpreting Quality: Global professional standards?" In: REN, Wen (ed.). *Interpreting in the Age of Globalization: Proceedings of the 8th National Conference and International Forum on Interpreting*. Beijing: Foreign Language Teaching and Research Press, 305-318. http://lourdesderioja.com/tag/franz-pochhacker/ (13.05.2014).

ROZAN, Jean-François (1956): *La prise de notes en interprétation consécutive*. Genf: Georg.

SALEVSKY, Heidemarie (1992): "Dolmetschen – Objekt der Übersetzungs- oder Dolmetschwissenschaft?" In: SALEVSKY, Heidemarie (ed.): *Wissenschaftliche Grundlagen der Sprachmittlung. Berliner Beiträge zur Übersetzungswissenschaft.* Frankfurt a. M.: Peter Lang, 85-117.

SAWYER, David B. (2004): *Fundamental Aspects of Interpreter Education*. Amsterdam/Philadelphia: John Benjamins.

SCHNEIDER, Reinhard (2012): *Vom Dolmetschen im Mittelalter. Sprachliche Vermittlung in weltlichen und kirchlichen Zusammenhängen* (Beihefte zum Archiv für Kulturgeschichte 72), Köln: Böhlau.

SCHOMAKER, Anja & KAGON, Barbara (2011): "Blended Learning im Konferenzdolmetschstudium", *MDÜ* 57(1), 54-57.

SELESKOVITCH, Danica (1968/1988): *L'interprète dans les conférences internationales. Problèmes de langage et de communication.* Lettres modernes. [German translation in *TexTconTexT* 1988, Beiheft 2]. Paris: Minard.

SELESKOVITCH, Danica (1975): *Langage, langues et mémoire. Etude de la prise de notes en interprétation consécutive.* Lettres modernes, Cahiers Champollion. Paris: Minard.

SELESKOVITCH, Danica & LEDERER, Marianne (1989): *Pédagogie raisonnée de l'interprétation*. Collection 'Traductologie' 4. Paris: Didier Erudition.

SHLESINGER, Miriam (1989): *Simultaneous Interpretation as a Factor in Effecting Shifts in the Position of Texts on the Oral-Literate Continuum.* Unpublished M.A. Thesis, Faculty of Humanities, Tel Aviv University, Dept. of Poetics and Comparative Literature.

SHLESINGER, Miriam (1990): "Factors affecting the applicability of the oral-literate continuum to interpretation research", *Hebrew Linguistics* 28-30, 49-56.

SHLESINGER, Miriam (1998): "Interpreting as a Cognitive Process. What do we Know About How It is Done?" In: FÉLIX FERNANDEZ, Leandro & ORTEGA ARJONILLA, Emilio (eds.): *Actas de la II Jornadas Internacionales de Traduccion e Interpretacion*. Gruppo de Investigacion de Linguistica Aplicada y Traduccion de la Universidad de Malaga, 749-766.

SPITZER, Manfred (2012): *Digitale Demenz. Wie wir uns und unsere Kinder um den Verstand bringen*. München: Droemer.

STRASSMANN, Burkhard (2014): "Deutsch light", *DIE ZEIT* 6, 35 (30.01.2014).

SUNNARI, Marianna (2003): "Expert and novice performance in simultaneous interpreting: implications for quality assessment". In: COLLADOS AíS, Ángela; FERNÁNDEZ SÁNCHEZ, Manuela & GILE, Daniel (eds): *La evaluación de la calidad en interpretación: investigación*. Granada: Comares, 235-247.

SZABÓ, Csilla (ed.) (2003): *Interpreting: From Preparation to Performance. Recipes for Practitioners and teachers*. Budapest: British Council Hungary.

THIEME, Karl (1956): "Die Bedeutung des Dolmetschens für die 'Weltgeschichte Europas'". In: THIEME, Karl; HERMANN, Alfred & GLÄSSER, Edgar (ed.): *Beiträge zur Geschichte des Dolmetschens*. Band 1. München: Isar, 9-24.

TREISMAN, Anne M. (1965): "The effects of redundancy and familiarity on translating and repeating back a foreign and a native language", *British Journal of Psychology* 65, 369-379.

WIOTTE-FRANZ, Claudia (2001): *Hermeneus und Interpres. Zum Dolmetscherwesen in der Antike*. Saarbrücken: Saarbrückener Studien zur Archäologie und Alten Geschichte 16.

ZWISCHENBERGER, Cornelia (2013): *Qualität und Rollenbilder beim simultanen Dolmetschen*. Berlin: Frank & Timme.

Aptitude

CATHERINE CHABASSE
chabasse@uni-mainz.de
Johannes Gutenberg University Mainz/Germersheim, Germany

1. Introduction

Before interpreter training was offered at European universities and other institutions of higher education, interpreters entered the profession based on their bilingual upbringing or their previous career path, without ever actively preparing for or planning to enter this line of work. They were often colourful characters and excelled at their work. This led many to assume that a natural, innate talent for interpreting exists (RUSSO 2011). The introduction of programs of study for conference interpreting in the 1940s and 1950s encouraged a more sober perception of interpreting as a teachable and acquirable competency[1]. Experience has shown, however, that students must meet certain prerequisites in order to successfully complete a degree in conference interpreting.

What are these prerequisites? How and when should they be assessed? In order to answer these questions objectively and not based on a 'gut feeling', a scientifically rigorous approach is necessary[2] (GERVER et al. 1980; MOSER-MERCER 1985, 1994; MACKINTOSH 1999; CHABASSE 2009). Many conferences have dealt with the topic of aptitude, the most recent one having taken place in Antwerp in 2008[3]. Following a brief definition of the term 'aptitude' and the introduction of a model of aptitude for interpreting, this chapter will cover various assessment methods and will focus on a few promising tests in more detail.

---

1   Seleskovitch and Lederer used the term 'teachability' in the context of interpreting studies.
2   A detailed description of the current state of research on the topic can be found in the article by Russo, who gave the keynote speech at the conference in Antwerp.
3   The talks held during the conference in Antwerp were published in *Interpreting* 2011(13). No. 1.

2. What is Aptitude?

The *Advanced Learner's Dictionary of Current English* (ALD) defines 'aptitude' as "the natural ability to acquire knowledge or skill". An aptitude test has to assess an ability to learn and not an existing competency. The question of talent or giftedness as an individual ability to perform in a certain way is investigated in the fields of psychology as well as pedagogical research. In the area of intelligence research, Thurstone defined so-called primary factors of intelligence, which are seen as the basis for different types of talent. The following factors are relevant to interpreting (THURSTONE 1938):

Verbal Comprehension (V): The ability to grasp meaning and relationships through language; dealing with verbal concepts.
Word Fluency (W): The ability to produce words based on association rather than content
Memory (M): Mechanical memory performance or short-term memory.
Reasoning (R): The ability to perform logical reasoning, pattern recognition (induction) and deduction.
Perceptual Speed (P): The ability to quickly distinguish relevant from irrelevant information.
Speed of Closure: The ability to create holistic entities and order.
Flexibility of Closure: Agility; the ability to restructure, recentre and reshape.

Educational researchers have created a large number of models of talent based on Thurstone's theory of multi-faceted intelligence, which represent different talent factors and their interaction (RENZULLI 1978, WIECZERKOWSKI & WAGNER 1985, PERLETH et al. 1993, MÖNKS 1999, GAGNÉ 2000). In his *Differentiated Model of Giftedness and Talent* (DMGT) Gagné models the interaction between natural abilities (for example intelligence, creativity or the ability to communicate), intrapersonal catalysts (for example health, motivation and concentration) as well as environmental catalysts (for example a person's social background, their family and their life situation). Gagné also introduces chance into his model, which influences natural abilities as well as intrapersonal and environmental factors.

Pedagogical models of talent such as these refer to children. Since the question of interpreting aptitude arises in the context of university-level education, however, acquired cognitive knowledge has to be taken into account as well.

Therefore, the term aptitude is defined as the interaction of talent and cognitive competences (knowledge). Talent consists of cognitive abilities (ability, that is the targeted and strategic use of knowledge) as well as cognitive competences (knowledge) and non-cognitive personality traits such as resistance to stress, concentration and motivation. These competences can be represented as follows.

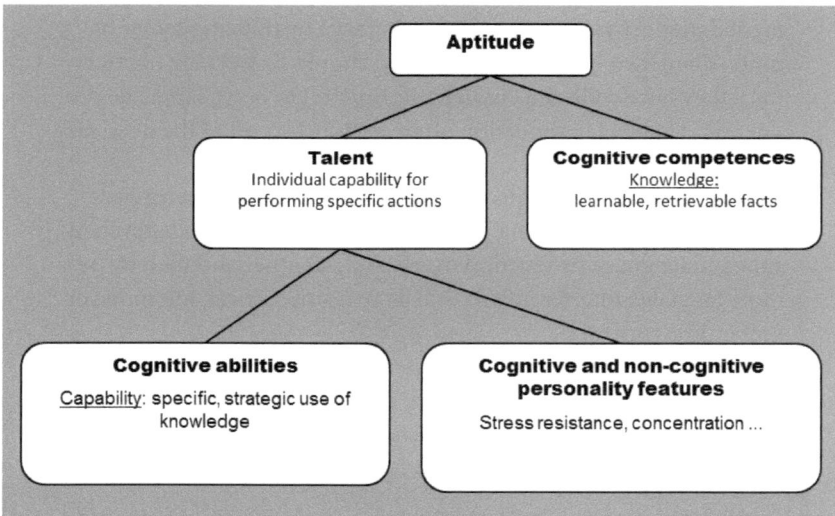

Fig. 1: Definition of aptitude

3. Aptitude Model for Interpreting

Interpreting is too complex an activity (PÖCHHACKER 1994) to be studied holistically. It should therefore be divided into processes in order to examine which competences and skills form the basis of these components. In his Effort Model (see CHABASSE & DINGFELDER STONE in this volume) Gile divides simultaneous interpreting (SI) into listening and analysis, production, short-term memory und coordination (GILE 1995: 159ff). In consecutive interpreting (CI) note-taking is added in the first phase as well as remembering und note-reading in the second.

The processes of comprehension and language production differ between mediated and unmediated communication (KOHN & KALINA 1996: 123) as they have to occur almost simultaneously and also given that they compete with one another. SI and CI differ in the demands they pose:

3.1 Simultaneous Interpreting

- In order to understand the source text, interpreters have to form a mental model based on the source language by utilizing semantic units. They then have to commit these chunks to working memory until they have collected enough information to begin language production. Language production often starts before all of the necessary information is present.
- In order to ensure high quality language production, interpreters must unload their working memory as fast as possible. Comprehension and language production overlap one another and thereby promote language interference as well as syntactic, lexical, idiomatic or semantic errors.
- In order to prevent these errors, interpreters have to constantly monitor their language production. This then consumes resources and attention, which are then no longer available when trying to interpret difficult passages (GERNSBACHER & FAUST 1991, GILE 1995).

3.2 Consecutive Interpreting

Phase 1: Listening and note-taking. This phase is paced by the speaker. The processes of comprehension occurring in this phase are equivalent to the ones occurring in simultaneous interpreting. The interpreters do not face the same amount of time pressure as they experience during SI because they can adapt their notes to the speed or the content and do not have to pay attention to grammatical correctness. However, they are simultaneously working in two modes (oral & written[4]). Insufficient mastery of note-taking technique can mean that this mode switching will consume a lot of time and attention. This negatively impacts listening and analysing and can lead to errors and omissions in language production.

---

4 Comprehension and production take place in the oral mode while note-taking takes place in the written mode.

Phase 2: Speech production phase. This phase is paced by the interpreter. In contrast to SI, the interpreters have already heard the entire message by the time the language production phase begins. They can therefore utilize text elements that were mentioned later in the text during reproduction. If they have focused too much on their notes and if they have not sufficiently analysed the macro-structure of the text, this information ends up missing. The memory performance required differs from SI as it refers to the text as a whole and therefore represents a more macro-analytic approach. The temporal separation of source and target language reduces the risk interferences between them compared to SI.

In order to successfully perform these parallel processes, interpreters must make use of strategies that facilitate comprehension (inference, anticipation, segmentation etc.), language production or coherence (compression, expansion) (see KADER & SEUBERT in this volume). These strategies require abilities that are not solely language-related. They are shown in the column on the left in the model depicted in figure 2.

The necessary cognitive competences are: native language and foreign language skills as well as intercultural competence and general knowledge. The cognitive capacities consist of: command of words, language-based thinking, logical thinking, memory (ultra short-term and working memory) and speed (word fluency, verbal comprehension, reasoning, memory and perceptual speed).

The column on the right in figure 2 shows the non-cognitive characteristics: a) motivation – consisting of the determination and stamina necessary to complete the programme of study, b) self-management, i.e. the concentration, stress resistance and language transfer that are essential components of success (CHABASSE 2009) and finally c) non-cognitive personality traits: flexibility, communication, self-esteem and the ability to work in teams, i.e. the so-called soft skills. Below these two columns there are two arrows pointing upwards: coincidences and experiences as well as the environment. They represent unforeseen circumstances or events that can have either a positive or a negative influence on an individual's performance. The third arrow representing the development process and training points downward and refers to the work that is necessary in order to reach the goal of systematically developed expertise. Expertise cannot develop without practice, no matter how much aptitude a person may have.

4. Aptitude Testing

4.1 Aptitude model for interpreting

The goal of an aptitude test is to identify the applicants that will most likely be able to successfully complete their studies within the time allotted. The result is therefore a prediction. Like with all predictions, however, there are many variables involved (compare the three lower arrows in the model, figure 2). In order to come to a conclusion as objectively as possible, specific criteria must be agreed upon that must then be applied uniformly for all language combinations and by all teaching staff members.

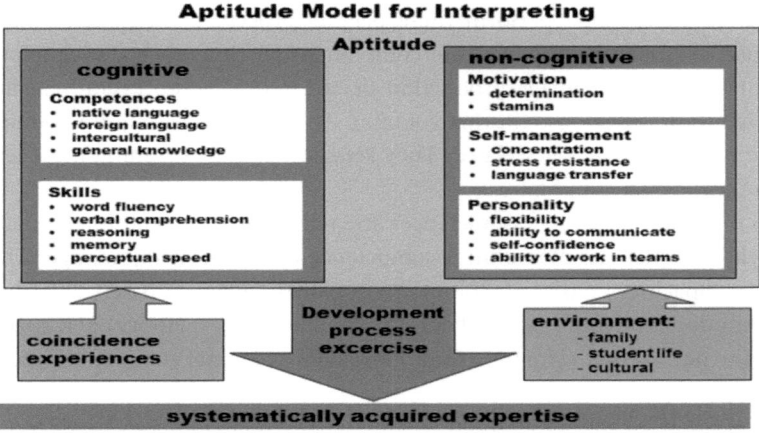

Fig. 2: Aptitude Model for Interpreting

A decision should only be reached jointly and should take all aspects and assessment components into account in order to provide a complete picture for each applicant: cognitive and non-cognitive abilities as well as language proficiency in all languages of the applicant's language combination (see Fig. 2).

Since some applicants have backgrounds outside of translation studies, tests directly involving interpreting (for example consecutive with notes or short simultaneous exercises) should be avoided. Tasks related to interpreting (for example: summarising texts, cognitive shadowing, paraphrasing[5]) should, however, be included.

---

5   Shadowing refers to the repetition of a recited text. It is used by some instructors to introduce

The following table (Fig. 3) provides an overview of possible assessment methods[6]. Every skill is assigned one or more methods. Some methods allow the assessment of multiple skills simply by evaluating different aspects of their outcomes. The tests marked with an * are explained later.

---

students to simultaneous interpreting. This method is controversial, however, as it can potentially lead students to see simultaneous interpreting as 'parroting'. Cognitive shadowing includes a phase of cognitive processing before speaking. The assessment methods of cognitive shadowing and paraphrasing are described in detail on the following pages.

6   This table was compiled from the overview of major skill categories and most popular associated tests (TIMAROVÁ & UNGOED-THOMAS 2008: 39), the *Überblick der Übungen bei Eignungsprüfungen* (CHABASSE 2009: 131) and other sources which can provide more detailed information on the testing methods. If no reference is provided, the testing method has not been studied scientifically.

Category of Skill	Skill	Method	Reference
	Native language	Short consecutive	Timarová & Ungoed-Thomas
		Short speech made by candidate	
		Interview	
		Summary	
		Translation	
		Cloze*	Lambert; Longley; Moser; Gerver et al.; Chabasse
		Aural discrimination: Recognizing grammatical, phonological and lexical errors in a text.	Arjona-Tseng; Longley; Gerver et al.
		Paraphrasing*	Longley, Moser, Russo & Pippa
		SynCloze*	Pöchhacker
	Foreign language	Short consecutive	Timarová & Ungoed-Thomas
		Short speech made by candidate	
		Summary	
		Translation	
	Intercultural competence	Critical incidents	Chabasse
		Intercultural Development Inventory (IDI)	Hammer & Bennett
		CQ Self assessment	Ang et al.
	General knowledge	Interview	Timarová & Ungoed-Thomas
		Written test	
		Short speech made by candidate	
Cognitive skills[7]	Word fluency	SynCloze*	Pöchhacker
		Paraphrasing*	Longley; Moser, Russo & Pippa
		Synonyms	Chabasse
		Cue-based impromptu speech *	
	Verbal comprehension	Summary	Timarová & Ungoed-Thomas
		Short consecutive	
		Translation	
	Reasoning	Paraphrase: Simplyfing a text	Chabasse
	Memory	Memory test	Lambert; Longley;

....

7   In order to test cognitive competences, a study used the WILDE intelligence test (CHABASSE 2009). The individual competences are assessed using multiple sub-tests and provide a general overview of the strengths and weaknesses of the subjects. The test is very time-consuming, however, and can therefore not be used in the context of an aptitude assessment.

			Moser; Arjona-Tseng; Gerver et al.
	Perceptual speed	Cognitive Shadowing*	Chabasse; Chabasse & Kader
Non-cognitive elements	Motivation	Interview	Timarová & Ungoed-Thomas
	Self-management Concentration	Cognitive Shadowing*	Chabasse; Chabasse & Kader
	Self-management Stress resistance (Simultaneity)	Dual-task exercise (listening and counting simultaneously, subsequently summarising what was said)	Moser
		Paraphrasing*	Longley; Moser, Russo & Pippa, Russo
		Shadowing	Lambert; Longley; Moser; Gerver et al.
		Processing of numbers	Moser
		Cognitive shadowing*	Chabasse; Chabasse & Kader
		Personalized cloze*	Chabasse; Chabasse & Kader
	Self-management Language transfer	Sight translation	Lambert; Moser
		Cognitive shadowing*	Chabasse; Chabasse & Kader
Non-cognitive personality traits	Flexibility	Short speech made by candidate	Timarová & Ungoed-Thomas
		Cue-based impromptu speech*	
		Short presentation without presentation	
	Ability to communicate	Short speech made by candidate	Timarová & Ungoed-Thomas
		Short consecutive	
		Summary	
		Interview	
		Short presentation without preparation	
	Self confidence	Interview	Timarová & Ungoed-Thomas
	Ability to work in teams	Interview	Timarová & Ungoed-Thomas
		Completing a team exercise	

Fig. 3: Skills and Tests

4.2 Suggestions for aptitude tests

4.2.1 Cloze

Every fifth or tenth word is removed from a text. The other sentences remain unchanged in order to allow a knowledge context to develop. The applicants have to reconstruct the missing words by activating their language proficiency, capturing the inner structure of the text, anticipating information and coming to a conclusion (closure) (CHABASSE submitted). Cloze tests therefore assess vocabulary as well as listening or reading comprehension. They also test the ability to anticipate (OLLER & CONRAD 1971), short-term and long-term memory as well as creativity (ANAYA & LOPEZ 1990).

4.2.2 Paraphrasing (Test in a Booth)

The students listen to an approximately five-minute long text in their native language and simultaneously paraphrase it in the same language. There is no language switching involved. The assessment is performed using a table of criteria. The focus lies on the use of synonyms and the maintenance of coherence (RUSSO & PIPPA 2004). Paraphrasing tests mental flexibility as well as expressive ability (RUSSO 2014).

4.2.3 SynCloze (Test in a booth)

The students listen to a text in their native language or one of their foreign languages that is read at a speed of about 100 words per minute. Every second sentence is missing a word, usually near the end. The students have to complete the missing parts of the expressions as fast as possible using as many synonyms as possible. The SynCloz test is a combination of semantic cloze and lexical paraphrase. The test assesses expressive ability as well as anticipation ability. It also tests memory performance because it is an oral test: working memory (process and recording) and long-term memory (lexis and content comprehension) (PÖCHHACKER 2011).

4.2.4 Cue-based impromptu speech

Arbitrary terms (concrete and abstract) are written on cards (for example: diapers – traffic jam – conference – international – sewage system – soccer etc.). The students are handed one card after another in rapid succession and have to spontaneously and orally produce a reasonably coherent text while integrating the terms shown on the cards as fast as possible.

4.2.5 Cognitive Shadowing (Test in a booth)

This test was initially developed by Kurz (1996) as an introductory exercise to SI and was then further developed as an aptitude test by me (CHABASSE 2009). The students hear a series of questions quickly one after the other, which they answer with yes or no and repeat while they listen to the next question (the yes-or-no answer serves to ensure that they have understood the content of the question and are not repeating it mechanically). This is a test to determine whether they are able to speak and listen simultaneously and if they can restore their concentration if it is broken. During the first phase of the test, the questions are answered with yes or no and in the same language (the native or foreign language). The second part consists of questions starting with 'why' and the answers are open-ended. The third part contains the same task with the question and the answer in two different languages.

Examples
First part: "Are diamonds a girl's best friend?" – "Yes, diamonds are a girl's best friend" or: "Is the Netherlands a mountainous country?" "No, the Netherlands isn't a mountainous country".
Second part: "Why are airports far from cities?" – "Because planes make a lot of noise".
Third part: The question is posed in the B-language and answered in the A-language and the other way around.

This test allows the evaluation of language proficiency, fluency and the ability to concentrate.

4.2.6 Personalized cloze (Test in the booth)

This test was developed by Timarová and presented at the conference in Antwerp. The students hear a text recounting a stranger's biography. They have to repeat the text in the same language while replacing the biographical information with their own. This test examines analytical and expressive ability.

In a study performed in 2009/2010 three of these aptitude tests geared towards simultaneous interpreting were investigated: cognitive shadowing, syncloze and personalized cloze (CHABASSE & KADER 2014). These tests were performed with 24 students at the beginning of their studies and their test results were correlated with the scores they achieved on their exams one year later. All three tests achieved significant results between .39 and .52. A new study of paraphrasing by M. Russo shows that primarily the criterion 'finding synonyms' correlates with the students' final grades and the time taken to complete their studies (RUSSO 2014).

5. Conclusion

German universities have had to concern themselves with aptitude testing since the Bologna reform and the introduction of the MA in conference interpreting. The process has been modified and streamlined a great deal over the last few years due to the high number of applicants. Written tests were not utilized as interpreting is an exclusively oral activity. In addition, the aptitude for simultaneous interpreting was evaluated using cognitive shadowing. This test has the major advantage that scoring occurs during the test and the complete results are therefore available immediately afterwards. This allows the examination committee to come to a decision promptly. Finally, one of the decisive factors in choosing an aptitude test is pragmatic feasibility. Nonetheless, researchers must keep evaluating the reliability of aptitude tests over the long term by regularly comparing the test results with the students' exam scores (CHABASSE & KADER 2014).

Translated from German by Yann Kiraly

References

Advanced Learner's Dictionary of Current English (ALD) (1969³).
ANG, Soon; VAN DYNE, Linn; KOH, Christine; NG, K. Yee; TEMPLER, Klaus J.; TAY, Cheryl & CHANDRASEKAR, N. Anand (2007*):* "Cultural Intelligence: Its Measurement and Effects on Cultural Judgment and Decision Making, Cultural Adaptation and Task Performance", *Management and Organization Review* 3(3), 327–458. http://onlinelibrary.wiley.com/doi/10.1111/more.2007.3.issue-3/issuetoc (18.11.2014).
ARJONA-TSENG, Etilvia (1994): "A Psychometric Approach to the Selection of Translation and Interpreting Students in Taiwan". In: LAMBERT, Sylvie & MOSER- MERCER, Barbara (eds.): *Bridging the Gap. Empirical Research in Simultaneous Interpretation.* Amsterdam/Philadelphia: John Benjamins, 69-86.
CHABASSE, Catherine (2009): *Gibt es eine Begabung für das Simultandolmetschen? Erstellung eines Dolmetscheignungstests.* Berlin: Saxa.
CHABASSE, Catherine (submitted). "Cloze". In: PÖCHHACKER, Franz (ed.): *Routledge Encyclopedia of Interpreting Studies.* London: Routledge.
CHABASSE, Catherine & KADER, Stephanie (2014): "Putting interpreting admissions exams to the test: The MA KD Germersheim Project", *Interpreting* 16(1), 19-33.
GAGNÉ, Françoys (2000): "Understanding the Complex of Talent Development Through DMGT- Based Analysis". In: HELLER, Kurt; MÖNKS, Franz J.; STERNBERG, Robert J. & SUBOTNIK, Rena F. (eds.): *International Handbook of Giftedness and Talent.* Amsterdam: Pergamon, 67-79.
GERNSBACHER, Morton Ann & FAUST, Mark (1991): "The Role of Suppression in Sentence Comprehension". In: SIMPSON, Greg B. (ed.): *Understanding Word and Sentence.* Amsterdam: North-Holland, 97-128.
GERVER, David; LONGLEY, Patricia; LONG, John & LAMBERT, Sylvie (1984): "Selecting Trainee Conference Interpreters", *Journal of Occupational Psychology* 57, 17-31.
GILE, Daniel (1995): *Basic Concepts and Models for Interpreter and Translator Training.* Amsterdam/Philadelphia: John Benjamins.
BENNETT, Milton J. & HAMMER, Mitchell R. (2002): *The Intercultural Development Inventory: Administrator's manual.* Portland: The IDI Corporation.
HELLER, Kurt (1996): "Aktuelle Trends, Paradigmen und Strategien der Hochbegabungsforschung unter besonderer Berücksichtigung der musikalischen Begabung". In: BASTIAN, Hans Günther (ed.): *Interdisziplinäre Aspekte und praktische Probleme der Begabungsforschung und Begabtenförderung.* Mainz: Schott, 15-31.
KOHN, Kurt & KALINA, Sylvia (1996): "The Strategic Dimension of Interpreting", *Meta* 41(1), 118-138.
LAMBERT, Sylvie (1989): "The Use of Aptitude Testing in the Selection of Students for Conference Interpretation Training". In: GRAN, Laura & DODDS, John (eds.): *The Theoretical and Practical Aspects of Teaching Interpretation.* Udine: Campanotto, 105-108.

LAMBERT, Sylvie (1991): "Aptitude Testing for Simultaneous Interpretation at the University of Ottawa", *Meta* 36(4), 586-594.
LAMBERT, Sylvie (1992): "Aptitude Testing for Simultaneous Interpretation at the University of Ottawa", *The Interpreters' Newsletter* 4, 25-32.
LAMBERT, Sylvie (1992): "Shadowing", *Meta* 37/2, 263-273.
Longley, Patricia (1989): "The Use of Aptitude Testing in the Selection of Students for Conference Interpretation Training". In: GRAN, Laura & DODDS, John (eds.): *The Theoretical and Practical Aspects of Teaching Interpretation*. Udine: Campanotto, 105-108.
MACKINTOSH, Jennifer (1999): "Interpreters are Made not Born". In: KURZ, Ingrid & BOWEN, Margareta (eds.): *History of Interpreting*. Special issue of *Interpreting* 4(1), 67–80.
MÖNKS, Franz. (1999): "Begabte Schüler erkennen und fördern". In: PERLETH, Christoph & ZIEGLER, Albert (eds.): *Pädagogisches Psychologie: Grundlagen und Anwendungsfelder*. Bern: Huber, 65-73.
MOSER-MERCER, Barbara (1984): "Testing Interpreting Aptitude". In: WILSS, Wolfram & THOME, Gisela (eds.): *Die Theorie des Übersetzens und ihr Aufschlußwert für die Übersetzungs- und Dolmetschdidaktik*. Tübingen: Gunter Narr, 318-325.
MOSER-MERCER, Barbara (1985): "Screening potential interpreters", *Meta* 30(1), 97-100.
MOSER-MERCER, Barbara (1994): "Aptitude Testing for Conference Interpreting: Why, when and how". In: LAMBERT, Sylvie & MOSER-MERCER, Barbara (eds.): *Bridging the Gap. Empirical Research in Simultaneous Interpreting*. Amsterdam/Philadelphia: John Benjamins, 57-68.
MOSER-MERCER, Barbara (1997): "Methodological issues in interpreting research: An introduction to the Ascona workshops", *Interpreting* 2(1/2), 1-11.
MOSER-MERCER, Barbara (2000): "Searching to define expertise in interpreting". In: ENGLUND DIMITROVA, Brigitta & HYLTENSTAM, Kenneth (eds.): *Language Processing and Simultaneous Interpreting: Interdisciplinary Perspectives*. Amsterdam/Philadelphia: John Benjamins, 1-11.
PERLETH, Christoph; SIERWALD, Wolfgang & HELLER, Kurt (1993): "Selected Results of the Munich Longitudinal Study of Giftedness: The Multidimensional/Typological Giftedness Model", *Roeper Review* 15, 149-155.
PÖCHHACKER, Franz (1994): *Simultandolmetschen als komplexes Handeln*. Tübingen: Gunter Narr.
PÖCHHACKER, Franz (2011): "Assessing Aptitude for Interpreting: The SynCloze Test", *Interpreting* 13(1). Amsterdam/Philadelphia: John Benjamins, 106-120.
RENZULLI, Joseph S. (1978): "What Makes Giftedness: Reexamining a Definition", *Phi Delta Kappan* 60, 180-184.
RUSSO, Mariachiara (1989): "Text Processing Strategies: a Hypothesis to assess Students' Aptitudes for Simultaneous Interpreting", *The Interpreters' Newsletter* 2, 57-64.
RUSSO, Mariachiara. & PIPPA, Salvador (2004): "Aptitude to Interpreting: Preliminary Results of a Testing Methodology Based on Paraphrase", *Meta* 49(2), 409-432.

Russo, Mariachiara (2011): "Aptitude Testing Over the Years", *Interpreting* 13(1). Amsterdam/Philadelphia: John Benjamins, 5-30.

Russo, Mariachiara (2014): "Testing Aptitude for Interpreting. The Predictive Value of Oral Paraphrasing, with Synonyms and Coherence as Assessment Parameters", *Interpreting* 16(1), 1-18.

Thurstone, Louis Leon (1938): *Primary Mental Abilities*. Chicago: University of Chicago Press.

Timarová, Šarka & Ungoed-Thomas, Harry (2008): "Admission Testing for Interpreting Courses", *The Interpreter and Translator Trainer* 2(1), 29-46.

Wieczerkowski, Wilhelm. & Wagner, Harald (1985): "Diagnostik von Hochbegabung". In: Jäger, Reinhold; Horn, Ralf & Ingenkamp, Karlheinz. (eds.): *Tests und Trends 4. Jahrbuch der Pädagogischen Diagnostik*. Weinheim/Basel: Belz, 109-134.

The Sense and Senselessness of Preparatory Exercises for Simultaneous Interpreting

Dörte Andres & Sophia Boden & Claudia Fuchs
andres@uni-mainz.de
Johannes Gutenberg University Mainz/Germersheim, Germany

1. Introduction

Simultaneous interpreting is an intricate cognitive process requiring specialized strategies and competences. Due to the complex nature of the overall process, it can be useful to identify and isolate individual operations, to practice them separately and to automate them as far as possible. Researchers and teachers have therefore developed various preparatory exercises in order to facilitate the initiation into simultaneous interpreting. In the following section these exercises will be introduced briefly, their advantages and disadvantages will be highlighted and their didactic relevance will be evaluated.

2. Dual-Task Training

Dual-task training is generally seen as a suitable form of preparatory practice for simultaneous interpreting. It is made up of two consecutive exercises and "[...] besteht in der parallelen Bewältigung verschiedener Operationen"[1] (Małgorzewicz 2003: 61). The goal of the exercise is to convince students that they are able to focus on two cognitive tasks at the same time (cf. Déjean Le Féal 1997: 617). The exercise is usually performed in the interpreting booth. The students listen to a text through headphones and have to understand the content of what is being said and to commit it to short-term memory. Seleskovitch and Lederer recommend starting out with a text the context of which is familiar to the students but the specific content of which is not

---

[1] "consists of the performance of multiple operations in parallel"

(cf. SELESKOVITCH & LEDERER 1989: 168). The students have to simultaneously focus on another task.

The nature of this task can differ based on the difficulty of the exercise. They may be asked to list days of the week or months while focusing on the acoustically presented text, for example. In order to increase the level of difficulty, the task can also be to list the days of the week or the months in reverse. Counting backwards or forwards out loud is a very popular variation of this exercise (cf. KURZ 1996: 103). The difficulty can also be increased incrementally in this situation by having the students count in steps of one, then two and then three. Three-digit numbers should be used, as they require more concentration than one- or two-digit numbers. In addition, attention should be paid to the students maintaining a uniform tempo in their counting (cf. SELESKOVITCH & LEDERER 1989: 168). This aspect is important because a constant speed requires additional focus and therefore represents a greater challenge for the students.

Once the first part of the exercise, which takes place in the booth, has been completed, the students are asked to repeat the text they listened to out loud as accurately as possible to their fellow students. This provides a way to evaluate whether the students were able to focus on the main task of listening, while performing multiple activities, all competing for their attention (cf. MAŁGORZEWICZ 2003: 61). This exercise is usually performed without *code switching*, i.e. the use of two different languages. The students hear a text in their native language and perform the second, simultaneous task in their native language as well.

When the first level of difficulty of *dual-task training* has been completed successfully, a text in a foreign language – ideally the students' B-language – is used. The additional task as well as the repeating of the text out loud, however, are performed in their native language. A further increase in difficulty can be achieved by using complicated texts for this exercise, such as texts with a higher degree of specialized content.

Dual-task training is often recommended in the literature (cf. MOSER-MERCER 1984, LAMBERT 1989, SELESKOVITCH & LEDERER 1989) as a suitable form of preparatory practice in order to enhance the students' ability to divide their attention between two different processes. This division of attention plays an important role in simultaneous interpreting because different processes such as listening, comprehending, storing, producing text and monitoring occur in parallel. These processes take up mental capacity, i.e. require attention to be distributed across the different operations (cf. KALINA 2000: 177).

Kurz, on the other hand, does not see the purpose of this exercise as being comprehensible in any way (cf. KURZ 1996: 103). Language comprehension and language production are related to each other regarding their content during simultaneous interpreting while *dual-task training* involves two processes that have no connection to each other. Kurz, as well as Déjean Le Féal (1997: 617), do not deem it sensible for and do not recommend it to prospective interpreters:

The goal is not to train the students of interpreting in some form of dual-task performance. Instead, the aim should be to achieve a proceduralisation of the individual operations necessary for their future interpreting work. (KURZ 1996: 103, own translation)

3. Shadowing

The most well-known and at the same time also the most controversial preparatory exercise is *shadowing:* "Shadowing is a paced, auditory task which involves the immediate vocalization of stimuli presented acoustically, for example the word-for-word repetition, *in the same language,* parrot-style, of a message presented through headphones" (LAMBERT 1992b: 17, emphasis in original)[2]. The aim of the exercise is to prepare the students for simultaneous listening and speaking. It is recommended to initially perform this exercise in the students' native language, as this is significantly easier than in their foreign language (cf. SCHWEDA NICHOLSON 1990: 35). *Phonemic shadowing* and *phrase shadowing* are distinguished in the literature. *Phonemic shadowing* involves the repetition of the words or individual syllables immediately. The distance to the original is therefore minimal. *Phrase shadowing* requires a unit of meaning to be completed before it is repeated (cf. NORMAN 1976, as quoted by LAMBERT 1989: 738). Schweda Nicholson developed *adjusted lag shadowing* as a third form based on these first two. The student is required to stay a certain number of words (for example five to seven) behind the original (cf. SCHWEDA NICHOLSON 1990: 34). The students do not have to grasp the meaning of what they are

....

2 The emphasis is taken from the original if no other indication is given.

hearing. They do however learn to keep a certain distance from the speaker. This taxes the short-term memory more than pure *phonemic shadowing*, which is why Schweda Nicholson sees *adjusted lag shadowing* as intermediate in difficulty between *phonemic* and *phrase shadowing* (cf. SCHWEDA NICHOLSON 1990: 34). It should be noted, however, that no constant *décalage*[3] is adhered to in interpreting as it depends strongly on the content, speaker and the direction of interpreting.

In contrast with the more mechanical shadowing exercises (especially the *phonemic* variant), cognitive *shadowing* requires the comprehension of the content and meaning of the original. Kurz develops three types of exercises for monolingual cognitive *shadowing*. Students start out with pure *phrase shadowing*. Next, simple yes/no questions must be repeated and answered. In the last exercise type, the students come up with individual answers to why-questions (cf. KURZ 1992: 249). Chabasse expands on these exercises by leaving out *phrase shadowing* and performing the other tasks with code switching. These tasks are used at the School of Translation, Linguistics and Cultural Studies (FTSK) of the Johannes Gutenberg University in Germersheim to test the aptitude of applicants for the master's degree in conference interpreting (cf. CHABASSE 2009: 153). First, the students listen to statements. They evaluate the correctness of these statements, answer them with yes or no and repeat them while the next sentence is already being read (example: "Die Pyrenäen trennen Frankreich von Spanien". – "Ja, die Pyrenäen trennen Frankreich von Spanien".[4] (CHABASSE 2009: 155). This task must first be completed in the native language and then in the B-language. The exercise extends beyond simple shadowing because "der Bedeutungsinhalt des zu wiederholenden Satzes muss analysiert und kognitiv verarbeitet werden, sodass eine Entscheidung bezüglich des Wahrheitsgehalts gefällt werden kann"[5] (CHABASSE 2009: 154).

The second task resembles the first, except that questions are read instead of statements. These in turn must be answered with yes or no and repeated as a statement (Example: "Ist eine Armbanduhr größer als ein Wecker?" – "Nein, eine Armbanduhr ist nicht größer als ein Wecker"[6] (CHABASSE 2009: 155)). This

---

3 *Décalage* refers to the distance from the original.
4 "The Pyrenees separate France and Spain". – "Yes, the Pyrenees separate France and Spain".
5 "the meaning of the sentence that is to be repeated must be analysed and processed on a cognitive level in order to allow a decision regarding the truth value of the statement"
6 "Is a wrist watch larger than an alarm clock?" – "No, a wrist watch is not larger than an alarm clock".

task is also performed in the A-language as well as the B-language. In the third and fourth sections, why-questions must be answered first in the A- or the B-language (part 3), then with a code switch between the question and the answer (part 4). This type of task is not shadowing in the classical sense because the students must formulate their own responses.

All of these types of exercises involve individual sentences and questions being read aloud that do not share a specific context. This allows the student to recover from getting behind when, while answering one question, he or she does not hear the following one. The student can simply skip over that one and catch up by moving on to the next question. This method is well-suited for aptitude tests for prospective students of interpreting because abilities relevant to interpreting such as simultaneous listening and speaking can be tested without requiring the applicants to have any interpreting experience (cf. CHABASSE 2009: 154). It can, however, also be used in teaching, as examples later in this text show.

Kalina suggests another variant of *shadowing*, which she calls "transformation" (1992: 255). In this exercise, the students either have to correct syntactic and morphological errors in a text or they have to modify the text, for example by turning passive sentences into active ones or by transferring the text into a different register. The students must then answer questions in order to ensure that they have understood its meaning. This exercise helps train their expression skills and the monitoring of language production (cf. KALINA 1992: 256f). This variant can also be called cognitive *shadowing* because, in order to recognize errors or change the style of the text, the student must have analysed and comprehended it.

As discussed above, *shadowing* is controversial among interpreting experts. Its advocates hold the view that the exercise is a good way to initially practice the ability to listen and speak in parallel, which is essential for simultaneous interpreting. This simultaneous activity can initially be vexing for students because either their own voice distracts them or language production is impaired by the need to listen at the same time. Lambert compares *shadowing* to learning to drive a car. Driving students also start out learning the basics of controlling the vehicle before being allowed to drive in normal traffic (cf. LAMBERT 1992b: 16). Schweda Nicholson also recommends the use of *phonemic, phrase* and *adjusted lag shadowing* for aptitude tests as an introductory exercise as well as an exercise for more advanced students. According to her interpretation, *phonemic shadowing* helps students improve their pronunciation and articulation in the foreign language in addition to simultaneous listening and speaking. Phrase shadowing is already somewhat similar to simultaneous interpreting in that in both activities, a unit of meaning has to be completed before language production starts. She describes *adjusted lag shadowing* as an intermediate step, which serves to train the students' memory because a certain distance to the original has to be consciously adhered to (cf. SCHWEDA NICHOLSON 1990: 33f).

According to Lambert, the length of the *décalage* during shadowing promotes analytical abilities (cf. LAMBERT 1992b: 18). She refers to Chistovich et al., according to whom test subjects who kept a short distance from the original and produced especially accurate repetitions of the text could not recall its contents later. The test subjects who were able to recall the contents after performing shadowing had a longer *décalage* (cf. LAMBERT 1992b: 18, citing CHISTOVICH et al. 1960). This study supports the conclusion that *phrase shadowing*, that is *shadowing* with a larger distance to the original, is more similar to simultaneous interpreting than *phonemic shadowing*. This is why Lambert recommends starting out with *phonemic shadowing* in order to practice simultaneous listening and speaking and to then continue with *phrase shadowing*. In addition, the difficulty of the exercise can be raised by increasing the speed at which the text is read (cf. LAMBERT 1989: 738).

Gerver arrives at a different conclusion from Lambert regarding analytical capabilities and text comprehension. In his experiment he interviewed test subjects about their text comprehension following listening and *shadowing* exercises as well as after simultaneous interpreting. The best results were achieved through listening. Gerver concludes that "[…] comprehension was impaired by simultaneous listening and speaking" (GERVER 1976: 184). Simultaneous interpreting led to significantly better results than *shadowing*: "[…] simultaneity of listening and speaking affected comprehension more when simple repetition of the message was involved than when the task involved the more complex decoding and encoding of simultaneous interpretation" (GERVER 1976: 184). This experiment shows that *shadowing* involves significantly less analysis than simultaneous interpreting. Lambert sees this as an advantage of *shadowing*, however, as it makes the process easier for beginners.

The advocates of *shadowing* therefore see its greatest benefit in allowing students to learn how to listen and speak at the same time in an exercise that is less demanding than simultaneous interpreting. It should be noted, however, that it has not been scientifically demonstrated that *shadowing* has a positive effect on the ability to listen and speak simultaneously.

Seleskovitch and Lederer have a critical view of *shadowing*. They argue that *shadowing* encourages people to only pay attention to words and not to their meaning. In addition, they doubt that simultaneous listening and speaking actually presents a major problem during simultaneous interpreting (cf. SELESKOVITCH & LEDERER 1989: 168; see CHABASSE & DINGFELDER STONE in this volume).

For these very reasons, Thiéry calls *shadowing* "[…] a pointless and potentially harmful exercise" (THIÉRY 1989: 4), and Van Dam also considers the exercise "[…] a totally counter-productive introduction to conference interpreting" (VAN DAM 1990: 5) as it promotes clinging to every word. She does however see this exercise as valuable for advanced learners – like Déjean Le Féal, but for different reasons – in order to improve the flow of speaking or to work on pronunciation (cf. VAN DAM 1990: 5f). Déjean Le Féal, on the other hand, recommends *shadowing* for improving the B-language, "[…] precisely because it draws attention to every single word of an utterance, especially structure words which normally do not even register when heard" (DÉJEAN LE FÉAL 1997: 621). Both authors stress that *shadowing*, in this case, is no longer a preparatory exercise for simultaneous interpreting at all. Déjean Le Féal also considers *shadowing* unsuitable for preparatory practice because it focuses on words instead of on context. She even advocates leaving out preparatory exercises for simultaneous interpreting entirely and expanding on the techniques of consecutive interpreting instead, which she thinks should be taught before simultaneous interpreting (DÉJEAN LE FÉAL 1997: 617f).

Kurz follows a different approach. She relies on results from research in neuropsychology which suggest that *shadowing* and interpreting place different demands on the brain because the former is pure repetition, which tends to activate the left half of the brain, while the latter requires active analysis and therefore depends more on the right half of the brain (cf. KURZ 1992: 248). She also concerns herself with the question of whether simultaneous listening and speaking is hard to learn and what influence practice has on this activity. For this purpose, she performed a study with students of interpreting who had already had a semester of instruction in simultaneous interpreting and then retested the same test subjects after four more months of class. For this experiment, she used the three types of exercises that Chabasse refined for her aptitude test model (cf. KURZ 1996: 107ff). With this experiment, she proves that practice has a major influence on simultaneous listening and speaking and that the ability can be acquired in a relatively brief period of time (cf. KURZ 1996: 124). In addition, she was able to show in the same study that, after four months, the greatest improvements were found for the why-questions. This exercise is most similar to simultaneous interpreting because the students do not only have to grasp the meaning of the text and comprehend it, but they also have to formulate their own answers. *Shadowing*, on the other hand, does not require a deeper understanding of the text, from which one could conclude that this exercise can confer the abilities necessary for simultaneous interpreting.

Overall, proponents and opponents both base their judgments primarily on personal experience from the classroom as well as on their own theories. There are few scientifically sound studies on the topic. It would definitely be sensible to take heed of these few studies when developing class designs:

In developing preparatory exercises for would-be interpreters, instructors are well advised to corroborate their intuitions – which may often prove to be right – with scientific evidence. Although it is true that our students will each learn in their own way, with our help or despite us, they can be expected to learn better if we apply what new knowledge is available to us. (KURZ 1992: 250)

4. Cloze

"The term 'cloze' comes from the psychological concept of closure, which is the perception of apparent wholeness of visual or auditory inputs that are actually incomplete" (LAMBERT 1992b: 26). The term closure reflects the goal of the cloze exercise, which is to add missing ends of sentences or to insert missing sentence elements. "Traditionally, clozing consists in the random or regular suppression of an element […] from the phonic chain the student is supposed to interpret" (VIAGGIO 1992: 40).

In a cloze exercise, students are supposed to understand the meaning of the incomplete sentence and to then complete it. In order to accomplish this, they must not only be able to grasp the structure of the text but also to anticipate information and to draw logical conclusions (cf. CHABASSE 2009: 157). Texts missing every tenth word are well suited for use in cloze exercises. Leaving a few sentences intact at the beginning of the text is recommended in order to allow the students to develop a basic understanding of the text by providing the necessary context (cf. LAMBERT 1992b: 27). Cloze exercises are usually done in the interpreting booth in order to create a situation that is typical for interpreting.

When the students listen to the text for the first time, they either write down the missing text elements or incorporate them into the gaps orally. It makes more sense to perform the exercise orally for interpreting purposes. Kautz recommends playing back a text from a recording and pausing it in regular intervals as a variation on the original cloze exercise. The students must then continue or complete the paused text. In order to anticipate the ending of the sentence, they must rely on context, on the information they have received so far from the text as well as on their own knowledge of the world (cf. KAUTZ 2000: 371). Anna Małgorzewicz also considers this exercise important in order to teach the students to develop textual logic (cf. MAŁGORZEWICZ 2003: 159).

Lambert recommends combining cloze exercises with a *shadowing* exercise. The students perform shadowing for a text being presented to them acoustically while adding in the missing text elements orally (cf. LAMBERT 1992b: 27). Depending on the desired degree of difficulty, cloze exercises can be performed in the students' A- or B-languages.

In order to change the difficulty of the cloze exercises and to introduce more variety into a course, modified versions of this preparatory exercise can be used, for example *SynCloze* or *PersonalizedCloze*. *SynCloze* keeps the basic design of the conventional cloze exercise but increases the difficulty. The students not only have to insert the missing words while listening to the gap text, they also have to give synonyms for the missing part of the sentence (cf. CHABASSE 2012). The ability to find a large number of synonyms for a term as quickly as possible is very important in simultaneous interpreting. *SynCloze* exercises focus on improving this ability and should therefore play a major role in the training of prospective interpreters.

In contrast with conventional cloze exercises, *PersonalizedCloze* requires the use of a text containing biographical information about a person, for example their name, age, date of birth and residence. An example could be the following text: "My name is Sean Miller. I am American. I'm from Memphis. I went to school in Memphis. I'm single. I have one brother and one sister. I was born in 1968. I'm 29 years old. I went to university when I was 16" (TIMAROVÁ 2009: 8). The students are supposed to *shadow* this text while replacing the personal information in it with their own personal details: "My name is Pavel Novák. I am Czech. I am from Pardubice. I went to school in Pardubice. I'm single. I have two sisters. I was born in 1979. I am 23 years old. I went to university when I was 19" (TIMAROVÁ 2009: 8).

This exercise allows students to practise listening in a focused and detail-oriented manner as well as reacting to what they hear – two abilities that are essential to simultaneous interpreting.

Interpreting researchers agree that cloze exercises present a sensible form of practice for prospective interpreters because they promote abilities relevant to interpreting, such as anticipation, finding synonyms and flexibility. In addition, cloze exercises allow the language skills of future interpreters to be assessed (cf. CHABASSE 2009: 158, LAMBERT 1992a: 27f).

According to Viaggio cloze exercises help train the important ability of paying attention to the meaning of what is being said and not to individual words. "Substituting concepts for missing figures and names is an extremely useful exercise that helps develop the students' ability to constantly analyse the speaker's *vouloir dire,* i.e. the *sense* he is trying to make" (VIAGGIO 1992: 41, emphasis in original).

5. Fairy Tales

Another exercise that is frequently used when teaching prospective interpreters is the interpreting of fairy tales. This is the exercise that is most similar to actual simultaneous interpreting because it requires simultaneity and code switching. A fairy tale that is known in both the culture of the source and the target language should be chosen for this exercise. This form of practice is especially suitable as a preparatory exercise because the students already know the content as well as certain phrases from the fairy tale. In addition, fairy tales can easily be visualized, which makes it easier for the students to follow the story. Due to their prior knowledge, they do not need to focus their entire attention on the process of listening and hearing and have more free mental capacity available for language production and monitoring. They will therefore find transferring this type of text from one language to another easier than would be the case for other types of texts.

The interpreting of fairy tales helps students recognize that they can express themselves in a completely natural way in their native language as long as they adhere to language conventions (cf. SELESKOVITCH & LEDERER 1989: 169). "Ils font spontanément autant appel à leurs connaissances thématiques et terminologiques qu'à leur perception auditive de l'énoncé, et leur interprétation est d'emblée excellente"[7] (SELESKOVITCH & LEDERER 1989: 170). This exercise only makes sense, however, if the interpreting takes place from the B- to the A-language because the required vocabulary and register are only available and accessible in the A-language. Interpreting into the foreign language would be counterproductive because the words of fairy tales are only known to the students from their childhood in their native language and not in the foreign language.

Fairy tales are therefore very well suited as introductory texts for simultaneous interpreters. Due to prior knowledge, the known content and the appropriate style of the text the prospective interpreters learn that they are capable of listening and speaking simultaneously, of understanding texts, and of transferring them into a target language, all while paying attention to their tone of voice. Success of this kind helps motivate the students and strengthens their self-confidence and self-awareness – an important factor in training interpreters.

6. Summary

There is a consensus in the literature that students should be introduced to the process of interpreting step by step and should be familiarized with sub-competencies first. Preparatory exercises are a suitable tool for this purpose. These are, however, the subject of controversial discussions in the relevant literature and there is considerable disagreement concerning their usefulness. Overall, the discussion is dominated by subjective, intuitive judgment and personal theories and that 'objective data' is only rarely used to support the various arguments.

There are especially large differences concerning *shadowing*, for which some researchers offer high praise while others reject it categorically. The discussion focuses on two important questions that proponents and opponents answer differently:

---

[7] "They automatically draw on their knowledge of the topic and terminology as well as their auditory perception of the utterance, and their interpretation is excellent from the start".

1. Is simultaneous listening and speaking really a major challenge for beginners in simultaneous interpreting?

2. Are *shadowing* and simultaneous interpreting two activities with comparable traits, therefore making *shadowing* a sensible choice for a preparatory exercise?

There is, in general, a consensus that simultaneity is an important part of simultaneous interpreting. The proponents of *shadowing*, however, believe that it can teach this necessary simultaneity while its opponents argue – based on the empirical study by Kurz – that it is an ability which can be easily acquired through other exercises and is not as important as is often assumed.

There seems to be a recent trend against *shadowing* due to the issue of the comparability of simultaneous interpreting and *shadowing*, and therefore the question of the usefulness of *shadowing*. The main argument in this development is that the exercise poses the risk of training people to think in terms of words instead of concentrating on comprehending meaning. *Phonemic shadowing* in particular has very little support left as an introductory exercise and is only seen as an exercise for improving pronunciation and language skills in the B-language. Cognitive *shadowing* however is still seen as a sensible alternative because it assigns much greater importance to analysis.

Dual-task training is also controversial. Its proponents argue that this exercise helps improve the students' ability to split their attention. Opponents state that *dual-task training* involves performing two completely independent activities at the same time while the various sub-processes of simultaneous interpreting are related to each other through their content.

Cloze exercises are universally seen as useful introductory exercises that are also very valuable when performed in the foreign language because they improve abilities such as analysis and anticipation as well as the rapid calling up of words and synonyms, all of which are relevant to simultaneous interpreting. The simultaneous interpreting of fairy tales is also seen as a useful preparatory exercise. It allows students to gather positive initial experiences because they usually intuitively pick the correct register and some of their mental capacity is freed up to deal with language production thanks to the familiarity of the texts.

Experiences of success as provided by sensible preparatory exercises strengthen the students' self-confidence, reduce their risk aversion and improve their faith in their own abilities and skills, thereby promoting their motivation and performance.

Translated from German by Yann Kiraly

References

CHABASSE, Catherine (2009): *Gibt es eine Begabung für das Simultandolmetschen?* Berlin: Saxa.

DÉJEAN LE FÉAL, Karla (1997): "Simultaneous Interpretation with 'Training Wheels'", *Meta* 42(4), 616-621.

GERVER, David (1976): "Empirical Studies of Simultaneous Interpretation: A Review and a Model". In: BRISLIN, Richard W. (ed.): *Translation: Application and Research*. New York: Gardner Press, 165-207.

KALINA, Sylvia (1992): "Discourse Processing and Interpreting Strategies. An Approach to the Teaching of Interpreting". In: DOLLERUP, Cay & LODDEGAARD, Anne (eds.): *Teaching Translation and Interpreting: Training, Talent and Experience*. Amsterdam/Philadelphia: John Benjamins, 251-257.

KALINA, Sylvia (2000): "Zu den Grundlagen einer Didaktik des Dolmetschens". In: KALINA, Sylvia; BUHL, Silke & GERZYMISCH-ARBOGAST, Heidrun (eds.): *Dolmetschen: Theorie, Praxis, Didaktik*. St. Ingbert: Röhrig, 161-189.

KAUTZ, Ulrich (2000): *Handbuch Didaktik des Übersetzens und Dolmetschens*. München: Iudicium.

KURZ, Ingrid (1992): "Shadowing Exercises in Interpreter Training". In: DOLLERUP, Cay & LODDEGAARD, Anne (eds.): *Teaching Translation and Interpreting: Training, Talent and Experience*. Amsterdam/Philadelphia: John Benjamins, 245-250.

KURZ, Ingrid (1996): *Simultandolmetschen als Gegenstand der interdisziplinären Forschung*. Wien: WUV.

LAMBERT, Sylvie (1989): "La Formation d'Interprètes: La Méthode Cognitive", *Meta* 34(4), 726-744.

LAMBERT, Sylvie (1992a): "Aptitude Testing for Simultaneous Interpretation at the University of Ottawa", *The Interpreters' Newsletter* 4, 25-32.

LAMBERT, Sylvie (1992b): "Shadowing", *The Interpreters' Newsletter* 4, 15-22.

MAŁGORZEWICZ, Anna (2003): *Prozessorientierte Dolmetschdidaktik*. Wrocław: Oficyna Wydawnicza ATUT.

MOSER-MERCER, Barbara (1984): "Testing Interpreting Aptitude". In: WILSS, Wolfram & THOME, Gisela (eds.): *Die Theorie des Übersetzens und ihr Aufschlußwert für die Übersetzungs- und Dolmetschdidaktik/Translation Theory and its Implementation in the Teaching of Translating and Interpreting. Akten des Internationalen Kolloquiums der Association Internationale de Linguistique Apliquée (AILA) Saarbrücken, 25. – 30. Juli 1983*. Tübingen: Gunter Narr, 318-325.

SCHWEDA NICHOLSON, Nancy (1990): "The Role of Shadowing in Interpreter Training", *The Interpreters' Newsletter* 3, 33-37.

SELESKOVITCH, Danica & LEDERER, Marianne (1989): *Pédagogie Raisonnée de l'Interprétation*. Brüssel-Luxemburg: Didier Erudition.

THIÉRY, Christopher (1989): "Letter to the Editors", *The Interpreters' Newsletter* 2, 3-5.

VAN DAM, Ine (1990): "Letter to the Editors", *The Interpreters' Newsletter* 3, 5-6.

VIAGGIO, Sergio (1992): "Cognitive Clozing to Teach Them to Think", *The Interpreters' Newsletter* 4, 40-44.

Speeches:

TIMAROVA, Šárka: Aptitude for conference interpreting: One test or two? Language: English. Lessius University Antwerp, Belgium. 28.05.2009.
CHABASSE, Catherine: Les tests d'aptitude à l'interprétation: pronosticou divination? Language: French. FB 06 Johannes Gutenberg-Universität Mainz, Germany. 27.04.2012.

Capacity Management in Interpretation: Efforts, Directionality, and Language Pair Considerations

Catherine Chabasse
chabasse@uni-mainz.de
Johannes Gutenberg University Mainz/Germersheim, Germany

Maren Dingfelder Stone
Dingfel@uni-mainz.de
Johannes Gutenberg University Mainz/Germersheim, Germany

1. Introduction

This article looks at the learning process of conference interpreting as a problem of capacity availability and allocation, and consequently at the teaching of conference interpreting as a challenge to create first an awareness of, and subsequently coping skills for, the difficulties involved in interpreting. It also proposes that such difficulties are contingent upon both language combination and directionality. To substantiate this premise, the first section briefly sets out Daniel Gile's Effort Models as a theoretical basis. This serves as a foundation for an assessment of directionality-dependent differences in capacity allocation, and of language pair-specific considerations (section 2). Section 3 translates these reflections into practical teaching suggestions for the skills underlying each Effort[1], classifying each exercise according to student level, directionality, and the Efforts it affects. The article provides a range of teaching approaches and exercises that target specific interpreting competences in order to complement traditional interpreter training and thus enhance the efficiency of the learning process of interpreting.

---

1   Without capitalisation, the terms effort, production, analysis, memory and such are used in a generic way; when capitalised, they denote operations as set out by Gile's Effort Model.

2. Capacity Allocation in the Interpreting Process: Daniel Gile's Effort Models

If interpreting trainees are to master the complex tasks of simultaneous and consecutive interpreting, they first need the (declarative[2]) knowledge to understand not only the processes that are involved, but also the interactions between them, and the pitfalls these can hold in store. Building on that, they then need to be equipped with learning strategies to develop the (procedural) knowledge for avoiding or managing these pitfalls (ANDERSON 2007: 333f). Models can help beginners visualise and ultimately understand the individual components of the interpreting process, thus allowing them to isolate particular aspects and work towards their automation, an important step for proficiency in interpreting. To this point, there certainly is no shortage of models in Interpreting Studies (see also ANDRES/BEHR/DINGFELDER STONE 2013); the charm and popularity of Gile's Effort Models, however, lies in their succinctness. Over the past decades, Gile has added to and revised his models to reflect new findings and insights in interpreter training, but their basic structure remains unaltered.

Positioning himself in contrast to the Paris School and Danica Seleskovitch's *théorie du sens*, Gile did not consider any aspect of the interpreting process to be effortless and thus unworthy of scholarly or didactic attention when he first drafted his Effort Models in the 1980s; instead, he aimed to provide a textbook for the interpreter and translator classroom that would "explain well-known, recurrent difficulties in interpreting as well as advice given to students to overcome them" (GILE 2009: 188). Gile was the first to openly discuss that mistakes occur regularly, even for highly experienced interpreters with excellent language command: "performance problems arise not only in fast, informationally dense or highly technical speeches, but also in clear, slow speech segments [and] also in the work of seasoned professionals" (GILE 2009: 157). Asked to interpret the same text twice, interpreters furthermore frequently make different mistakes in both interpretations (GILE 2009: 183), which indicates the cause for such errors and omissions goes beyond inadequate knowledge or preparation. These observations form the basis of Gile's

---

2 Declarative knowledge is knowledge of facts or events that can be directly recalled [...]. One kind of nondeclarative knowledge (often termed *implicit* knowledge) is *procedural* knowledge, which underlies skills or procedures and encodes information that cannot be easily described in language. [...] Practice through repetition permits hitherto controlled and conscious procedures to become automatized, through which process the declarative input is transformed into unconscious procedural information and memory (ROSENBLATT 2004: 202f).

Tightrope Hypothesis which proposes that interpreters always work at their saturation limit with regard to both the overall processing capacity and to each individual Effort (GILE 2008: 60). This entails that any obstacle that increases capacity requirements can cause the interpreter to stumble, leading to the above-mentioned mistakes – mistakes which had previously been attributed to insufficient linguistic or extra-linguistic knowledge, but that were now understood in terms of insufficient resource allocation.

To illustrate this hypothesis, and to explain the origin of mistakes occurring within the interpreting process in terms of capacity allocation, Gile developed a set of simple, easily understandable models for simultaneous and consecutive interpreting.[3] According to Gile, simultaneous interpreting (SI) encompasses four distinct, non-automatic Efforts that compete for processing capacity: Listening and Analysis (L), Production (P), Memory (M) and Coordination (C):

$$SI = L + P + M + C$$

Listening includes "all comprehension-oriented operations, from the subconscious analysis of the sound waves [...] through the identification of words to the final decisions about the 'meaning' of the utterance" (GILE 2009: 160). Production, in turn, is defined as ranging from a first mental representation of the message through speech planning to speech performance; it also includes self-monitoring and, where necessary, self-correction (GILE 2009: 163). Memory comprises the successive and/or parallel short-term memory processes required to a) store the beginning of the word until its completion, b) store a component of a sentence until the meaning has become clear, and c) store the source-language information until production in the target language has been completed (GILE 2009: 165). Coordination is characterised as the capacity required to allocate attentional resources to the other Efforts (GILE 2009: 168).

Consecutive interpreting (CI), in turn, entails the reception phase (CI 1) and the reformulation phase (CI 2):

$$CI\ (1) = L + N + M + C$$
$$CI\ (2) = Rem + Read + P + C$$

---

3   Other Effort Models pertain to simultaneous interpreting with text (GILE 2009: 181-182), translation (GILE 2009: 183f), and sight translation (GILE 2009: 179ff).

In CI, Gile holds Listening (L) to be identical to L in simultaneous interpreting. Memory (M) he defines as 'similar'; however, instead of bridging the gap between hearing and speech production, CI (1) Memory stores chunks of information from when they are heard to when they are noted down "or processed mentally and sent on to (long-term) memory" (GILE 2009: 175f). Note-taking (N) revolves around "how to reduce processing capacity and time requirements of note-taking while maintaining the efficiency of notes as memory reinforcers" (GILE 2009: 178). To that end, Gile considers it helpful to have a note-taking system with pre-determined symbols and abbreviations. In phase 2, Rem (Remember) refers to the recall of the information memorised during the first phase of the consecutive interpretation, while Read refers to the deciphering of the notes, both of which combined provide the input for the Production effort (P). The Coordination effort in phase 2 is a recent addition; Gile originally assumed that the interpreter was under no time pressure in the production of a consecutive interpretation, so that capacity shortages simply would not occur in phase two. In the revised 2009 edition, C has been included for this reformulation phase, but Gile still maintains that "in phase two, the interpreter is free to [...] allocate processing capacity to each [Effort] at his/her own pace," so that "only phase one seems to generate potential threats of saturation" (GILE 2009: 176).

Gile then proposes that (finite) processing capacity can be allocated flexibly to the various processes. The interpreting process is successful so long as two conditions are met: all individual Efforts receive the mental processing capacity they must have, and the combination of these individual requirements ('total required processing capacity' TR) does not exceed the maximum capacity available ('total available processing capacity' TA). Interpreting is thus basically defined as a problem of allocating mental resources: if one assumes that interpreting requires a processing capacity which is finite, and that every non-automated element of the interpreting process requires a share of those attentional resources, it stands to reason that a sudden peak in capacity requirements for one Effort would necessitate additional resources to be diverted away from another process. If this happens in an imperfect, uncontrolled manner, performance deteriorates (GILE 2009: 159).

In terms of didactics, this implies two basic consequences. The first didactic conclusion is that students profit from a high level of automation. Gile differentiates between non-automatic operations, which require time and attention capacity, and automatic ones, which do not (GILE 2009: 158f). The more frequently processes are practised, the more they can become automatic: "initial performance is mediated by sequential processes, which with additional practice are transformed into a single direct (automatic) retrieval of the correct response from memory" (ERICSSON et al. 1993: 396). This then frees capacities for other tasks within the interpreting process. A good example of this is the processing of figures: if their recognition in a foreign language has become automatic with practice, those resources no longer needed for processing the acoustic information can be devoted to placing that information more firmly in its textual and semantic context. If in addition, the occurrence of a figure in a consecutive text automatically triggers a discontinuous notation of the figure, preceding completion of the last unit of meaning, this alleviates cognitive pressure downstream due to memory overload. If the figure is then automatically noted down in its context of unit and referent (1 kg of fish), this facilitates the deciphering of the notes in the reproduction phase and thus frees capacities for smoother production, better body language control, or superior output monitoring.

The second didactic consequence relates to the analysis of interpreting errors, or what Gile calls "failure sequences" (GILE 2009: 171) – when trying to ascertain why a mistake was made, one should look beyond the immediate phrase/item to what preceded it. If, for instance, capacity requirements for the Memory effort suddenly peak during simultaneous interpreting (a long, complicated name comes up which the interpreter was unprepared for and which must be remembered), capacities may briefly be diverted away from Listening. This causes the interpreter to miss the beginning of the next sentence, which includes a significant transitional phrase ('However, …'). Without that link, the analysis of the next paragraph requires more attention, which in turn diverts capacity away from the Production effort, leading to a clumsily phrased target-language solution. Didactic feedback that simply looks at, and corrects, the clumsy phrase or sentence structure falls short if it does not also address the origin of the failure sequence, namely the interpreter's inadequate preparation and subsequent capacity misallocation.

Gile's Models are a useful tool; however, some teachers may wish to tweak them so as to reflect more adequately their own teaching emphasis. For instance, a more nuanced, three-tiered model of long-term, short-term and working memory would allow for a more tailored didactic approach as to strategies for information storage and retrieval, without necessarily making the model more confusing or less comprehensible. Likewise, a more explicit highlighting of the presentation aspect as part of the Production effort in consecutive interpreting might be helpful. This could be done in the description of the Efforts, or it might be reflected within the model itself: CI (2) = Rem + Read + P{Lg+Pres}, which reads: Production in the reformulation phase of consecutive interpreting consists of linguistic production and presentation. Nevertheless, even without such adaptations the models can serve to break down the complexity of the task, illustrate the processes involved, and pinpoint the origin of mistakes, especially when placed in the context of directionality and language pair-specific considerations.

3. Shifts in Capacity Allocation: Directionality and Language Pairs

As shown in the previous chapter, Gile's Models emphasise the usefulness of addressing capacity allocation issues within the interpreting class room. Capacity allocation is highly variable; is it impacted not only by situational aspects such as setting, speaker, and topic, but in a more fundamental way by directionality and language pair considerations. Depending on whether one interprets into or from one's mother tongue, the cognitive burden shifts from Listening (for B/C into A)[4] to Production (for A into B), necessitating an adjustment in interpreting and teaching approaches. Syntactic, morphological and cultural differences or similarities between language pairs similarly impact the allocation of resources and require the employment of appropriate strategies. Accordingly, efficient interpreting training should consider both of these aspects in the design of the class.

In order to increase awareness of such capacity allocation shifts, it is immensely valuable if students understand how individual Efforts influence each other, and how they can be influenced by the interpreter in order to overcome problems. For instance, adequate preparation reduces the capacity requirements for Listening (better understanding of the concepts, easier comprehension of lexical units) and thus potentially for Memory (less unknown terminology) as well as for Production (technical terms at one's disposal, understanding of adequate discourse structure). Similarly, a decrease of the décalage

---

4   A language is the interpreter's mother tongue; B language is their foreign active language, while C language is their foreign passive language.

may lower the Memory load while, however, potentially raising the Production effort due to increased syntactic interference and less sentence oversight; expanding the décalage in turn might increase the Memory effort but could benefit Listening (more information available for analysis and hence better comprehension) as well as Production (more room for free reformulation). Only if students understand the interdependencies between Effort, directionality and language pair, can they appraise the significance of the various subprocesses, select appropriate strategies[5], achieve their partial automation and use the freed resources to manage cognitive bottlenecks.

In order to bolster such awareness and enhance students' problem solving skills, teachers should progress "from easy to more difficult, isolating problems and focusing on variables one at a time and, at a later stage, combining them into progressively more intricate structures" (KURZ 1992: 245). Such a structured learning process allows students to gradually develop directionality- and language pair-adequate interpreting skills. To this point, the following segments will first look more closely at questions of directionality and language pairs, before turning to the practical application in the form of teaching suggestions in chapter 3.

3.1 Directionality-Related Considerations

Gile identifies a range of so-called problem triggers (GILE 2009: 192ff). Many of them, such as high density of the source speech, high rate of delivery, and signal vulnerability in low redundancy elements such as numbers or acronyms are comparable for interpreting into the mother tongue as well as into a foreign language[6]. Other factors (unfamiliarity with multi-component names, syntactic differences between source and target language) take on an added degree of

---

5   Strategies are defined as "[…] methods that are potentially conducive to solving particular problems encountered by interpreters or generally facilitating the interpreter's task and preventing potential problems" (BARTŁOMIEJCZYK 2006: 152). Gile himself prefers the use of the term "tactics" as opposed to "strategies" (GILE 2009: 201). For a more detailed discussion of strategies in interpreting, see KADER & SEUBERT in this volume.

6   For the longest time, many interpreter training institutes as well as international organisations (among them the European Union) worked exclusively with the theorem that simultaneous interpreting was possible only into one's mother tongue. The EU expansion policy and its concurrent explosion in language combinations – 24 official languages, which adds up to a total of 522 language combinations – changed this viewpoint. Retour interpreting became accepted as an inevitability. A 2001/2002 study on the acceptance of retour interpreting confirmed that there was no apparent correlation between directionality and user satisfaction (DONOVAN 2004: 207). German universities have, as a rule, always offered an A/B/C combination (partly due to the demands of the German free market), so that retour interpreting has traditionally been part of German conference interpreting curricula.

difficulty when interpreting into the foreign language, which becomes evident when examining the re-allocation of cognitive resources based on directionality.

Each Effort's cognitive load rises or falls dependent on directionality; when interpreting from B into A, the relative unfamiliarity with the linguistic, cultural and nonverbal codes of the source language, for instance, requires additional resources for listening comprehension and analysis and fewer resources for speech production and presentation. Alternatively, an interpretation into the foreign language places a heavier burden on speech production and presentation while freeing mental capacity in listening comprehension and analysis. Explaining this phenomenon requires a brief excursion into information processing theory: when hearing a message in normal unmediated communication (KOHN & KALINA 1996: 123ff), the listener retains not the words, but the content (HÖRMANN 1981: 80, CHABASSE 2009: 67). This is due to the fact that not all features of a term are stored individually, but that they are structured in the form of scenes (FILLMORE 1976: 24). Such scenes are not only linguistic or personal in nature, but may also reflect groups or cultures (RISKU 2009: 336), which means that their storage and retrieval is easier in the mother tongue. Incidentally, this 'advantage' is even more pronounced in consecutive interpreting, since native language syntax and lexicon are more present in simultaneous due to the overlap of hearing and production, which may lead to unidiomatic speech production.

Other impacts of directionality are less obvious but no less significant. When interpreting from an S-O-V into an S-V-O language, for instance, the cognitive burden caused by information storage is more impactful than when interpreting the other direction. Mother tongue input furthermore allows for a quicker and more effortless formation of an A-language based mental representation and storage of the input, lowering the Memory load when interpreting A into B. That same direction comes with a caveat, though: the (subjective) sense of having understood the A-language text in detail may occasionally be problematic, as students might be tempted to interpret 'everything' without proper analysis and filtering of the A-language source text, which would increase the Production load. The heightened need to monitor output when interpreting A into B further adds to that load. For consecutive, A into B indicates a reduced cognitive load for Note-taking, as the latter is facilitated if the mother tongue serves as the source language (VAN DAM 2004: 13). Conversely, however, a consecutive interpretation of B/C into A carries the potential of alleviated cognitive pressure downstream: if the target language is the mother tongue, target language notation becomes more feasible, which facilitates target language production in the reformulation phase of the consecutive.

These observations are summarised in the following figure, which traces the shift in capacity load allocation for each Effort pending on directionality[7]:

---

[7] To illustrate more clearly how the cognitive shift occurs, Analysis and Presentation are listed separately.

Effort	Dir.	Operations	Cogn. Load +/-
L (Listening)	B – A	SI, CI: recognition of B-language structures (lexical, syntactic, idiomatic) not instantaneous SI, CI: less familiarity with regional differences/accents	+
	A – B	SI, CI: native language and culture competence	–
A (Analysis)	B – A	SI, CI: recognition of para- and nonverbal codes not intuitive	+
	A – B	SI, CI: native language and culture competence	–
M (Memory)	B – A	SI: more information storage for syntactically different language structures (S-V-O/S-O-V)	+
	A – B	SI: more information storage for syntactically different language structures (S-V-O/S-O-V) SI, CI: A-language based mental representation SI, CI: easier storage of A-language input	+ –
P (Production)	B – A	SI, CI: easier access to syntax, collocations, register SI, CI: effortless pronunciation SI, CI: less pronounced linguistic perfectionism	– –
	A – B	SI: syntactic interference from A SI, CI: less control over spontaneous, idiomatic, syntactically and lexically correct solutions, speed of deliverance SI, CI: less familiarity with appropriate prosody/intonation SI, CI: over-ambition regarding completeness and exactitude SI, CI: more output control required	+
C (Coordination)	B – A	Capacity allocation managed by central executive	n.a.
	A – B		
N (Note-taking) + Rem	B – A	CI (phase 1) : source language notation hampered (SL ≠ A)	+
		CI (phase 2): target language notation facilitated (TL =A)	–
	A – B	CI: A-language based mental representation of message CI: easier storage of A-language input CI: source language notation facilitated (SL = A)	–
Pres (Presentation)	B – A	CI: familiarity with cultural codes	–
	A – B	CI: less familiarity with appropriate non-/paraverbal signals	+

Fig. 1: Directionality-dependent cognitive load allocation

As the emerging patterns illustrate, cognitive load allocation is at least partly contingent upon directionality. This is confirmed by a study conducted by Magdalena Bartłomiejczyk for the language pair Polish-English (2006). She found that particular strategies such as paraphrase, approximation and compression were used with much higher frequency for simultaneous interpreting A into B, while addition, inferencing, parallel reformulation, repair and anticipation were used more frequently when interpreting B into A. The choices of these strategies indicate that interpreting trainees must rely more on reformulation (approximation, paraphrase) when working into B, presumably because they are not (yet) capable of expressing themselves more efficiently. Interestingly, however, the study also illustrates that students recognise this as a consciously-employed strategy rather than an emergency fall-back option. It follows logically that, if directionality has such an impact on the application of strategies, this must be reflected in teaching approaches and classroom discussions, so that teaching interpreting into the foreign language places different emphases than teaching interpreting into the mother tongue (DONOVAN 2004: 211f).

3.2 Language Pair-Specific Considerations

The Effort Models can not only serve to illustrate the impact of directionality, they also highlight the necessity of language-specific interpreter training: certain language pairs place higher burdens on particular Efforts, and while students can become moderately proficient with a language-independent training structure, "language-specific training is associated with much potential gain and little potential loss" (GILE 2009: 199). Roughly speaking, there are four areas of potential conflict arising from language combinations: problems can occur if the two languages are too diverse; if they are too closely related; if the numerical systems are asymmetrical; and if cultural expectations do not match[8].

When discussing language pair-specific aspects of interpreting, potential repercussions of morpho-syntactically asymmetrical languages have received quite some attention (see, for instance, SEEBER & KERZEL 2011: 1f). And indeed, cognitive load asymmetries surface here most perceptibly. When interpreting from or into German, for instance, compound nouns can drive interpreters to desperation: Kraftfahrzeug-Haftpflichtversicherungsgesetz (act on motor vehicle liability insurance) or Rechtsschutzversicherungsgesellschaften (insurance

---

8   These language-specific considerations draw heavily on the teaching and interpreting experience of the staff at the University of Mainz/Germersheim. We are specifically indebted to Gisela Böhm, Ulrike Endell-Steiert, Nam Hui Kim, and Patrizia Pantaloni for their valuable input.

companies providing legal protection), are perfectly acceptable words, but will need to be restructured completely to be intelligible in most other languages, requiring resources to be allocated to Listening/Analysis and Memory. A similar cognitive burden arises from syntactic differences – good anticipation and/or segmentation skills are crucial for alleviating the Memory load when waiting for the German verb to appear. Other syntactic constructions may be less common or more complex in the target language, requiring significant adaptation. Russian, for instance, features sequential genitive constructions compounded by noun-heavy syntax: Налицо неполноценность сложившейся системы защиты основных прав и свобод человека (roughly: presence non-adequate-beingness of the having-emerged system of the protection of the basic rights and freedoms of a person); the English s-genitive can be used in similarly extensive sequences ("my mother's niece's neighbour's best friend's dog"). In other cases, grammatical structures may exist in a very different form in the target language, necessitating complete rephrasing, as with relative clauses when interpreting into Korean (KIM 2009). Reproducing these constructs in other languages requires finding alternative structures, reversing the sequence, and often rearranging the entire sentence, with a significant load on Memory, Listening and Production.

Asymmetry of figures is particularly challenging; numerical items already place a significant burden on an interpreter (see 4.4 in this article), and translating between language systems where numerals are not developed symmetrically compounds that difficulty. The Russian declension of the numerals, for instance, can be quite challenging for non-native speakers, as can the transposition of the Korean system which counts thirty-five as 'three-ten-five' and one million as 'hundred ten thousand'. But even the simple basic structure of numerals (five-and-thirty in German vs. thirty-five in English) or the French system of quatre-vingt-dix-huit (four-twenty-eighteen, a.k.a. ninety-eight) can result in cognitive overload if comprehension, notation and transfer of such elements have not been adequately practised.

However, language pair-related challenges do not invariably derive from the divergence of the languages involved; sometimes it is their very similarity that causes the problems. When working in a pair of closely related languages, such as Dutch/German or a combination involving Romance languages (e.g. French, Italian, Spanish, Portuguese), one of the main challenges is linguistic interference, i.e. the avoidance of false friends. Interpreters need to be able to recognise such pitfalls instantaneously and shy away from translating the

German 'abmachen' (to arrange) with its Dutch counterpart 'afmaken' (to kill); the French 'demander' (to ask) with the Spanish 'demander' (to sue), or the Italian 'digiunare' (to fast) with the French 'déjeuner' (to eat lunch). Similar difficulties arise with regard to syntax, which becomes especially problematic for students who have not (yet) learned to adjust their décalage. Even under the best of circumstances, an overly short décalage tempts interpreters to follow the syntax of the source language closely at the expense of idiomatically appropriate target language expression. This danger increases significantly if the languages are very similar, and if interpreters have not been sensitised to this danger during their training (see chapter 4 in this article).

Finally, interpreters must be able to translate between culture-specific communication patterns. When interpreting between, for instance, German and languages such as Dutch, English or Italian, the register must be adapted to reflect the less formal approach of the latter cultures. This is compounded by the problem of adequate address when interpreting into German with regard to honorifics; German culture still places great emphasis on the use of appropriate titles and forms of address, and is much slower to proceed to a first name or informal basis. Teachers must also enhance students' awareness of culturally-specific rhetorical patterns and expectations such as emphasis, religious references, or pathos. This is particularly relevant for Russian, where pathos is much more acceptable in a public speaking context, so that students must be careful not to translate terms like бессмертный подвиг (immortal heroic deed), вечная слава (eternal renown) or благородное дело (noble cause) in a way that would arouse ridicule or imply irony. Similar problems occur when dealing with American English speeches, where religious references are common, even expected, and with speeches in an African French context, which tend to be more effusive and flowery. Spanish speeches in turn can be wordier and more redundant than their German or English counterparts (see also NOLAN 2012[2]: 163), so that reduction/expansion strategies must be employed depending on directionality. Korean interpreters must learn to handle similar challenges when confronted with the Korean habit of repeating and reemphasising items that are of particular significance, and transposing the speech into a cultural context where such repetitions are met with little patience.

This collection of examples shows one thing very clearly: language pair-specific considerations must play a role in interpreter training. In order to be able to properly train budding interpreters, interpreting teachers must first be aware of these differences themselves. Only if they have internalised the syntactic, morphological, cultural and idiomatic specificities of the language combination that is to be taught, can they select appropriate training material and thus provide students with the tools and strategies to overcome such problems themselves. The following chapter will propose a variety of teaching suggestions that tackle exactly these difficulties.

4. Capacity Allocation in the Class Room: Teaching Suggestions

As has been shown by the last two chapters, teaching methods are, to a certain extent, contingent upon directionality and language pair. While many apply to both A into B and B/C into A, figure 1 shows clearly that there are directionality-specific shifts in cognitive load allocation; similarly, as has been shown the language pair one is working with also directly impacts strategies and interpreting choices. Flowing from these considerations, the following chapter sets out a broad range of suggestions for the teaching of interpretation. It will continue to be placed in the context of Gile's Effort Models. However, Gile's Efforts typically comprise several competencies, which overlap significantly. Rather than applying the Efforts as chapter structure, and risk tedious repetition or constant referral, the teaching suggestions will therefore be structured to reflect the following competencies: linguistic expertise, technical expertise, presentation skills, analysis, note-taking, and memory. There are no specific exercises to train or isolate a Coordination effort; training of the Coordination effort is an integral part of each of the exercises proposed, as enhanced parallel processing and the partial automation of processes and strategies can all serve to increase momentarily available capacity and allocate resources more efficiently[9]. To maximise applicability, there is, as a rule, no specific mention as to which exercises are to be used for which language pair. It is incumbent upon each teacher individually to assess which methods and exercises might be most beneficial for the structures they are working with.

---

9 Some authors propose split attention exercises, such as Kornakov, who suggests exposing students to "two different verbal messages simultaneously, each message coming in through a different ear," one of which is used as the basis for shadowing or later paraphrase (KORNAKOV 2000: 247). However, the effect of such training on interpreting has never been validated.

This portfolio includes a break-down of the Efforts these competences influence; it differentiates between beginners and advanced students, and it includes supra-directional and directionally-specific considerations, where applicable. As a caveat, it should be pointed out that empirical validation of any, if not all, of these exercises is still outstanding; the exercises assembled here are based on collective teaching experience and scholarly recommendations. All of the exercises can be included either in class, in self-study sessions, or both.

4.1 Linguistic Expertise

Linguistic expertise refers to language proficiency in the broadest term; as such, it influences both the Production effort P and the Listening effort L. Even if the target language is one's mother tongue, this by no means implies that it is used effortlessly. Not only B-language proficiency, but also native language competence can be improved by exercises in speech production which lower the cost of verbal information retrieval. Familiarity with idioms and phrases, as well as with collocations and grammatical structures, facilitates understanding and production significantly and can free capacities for better communication, presentation, and prosody.

Beginning students should learn to use their available knowledge and skills in the best possible way, and begin to expand on them. Exercises that force the student to speak while planning the next utterance, whether in B or A, increase their linguistic agility and train them to control their nonverbal and paraverbal communication, maintain eye contact, and overcome any remnants of shyness or inhibitions concerning public speaking:

- Silent Picture: Students are shown a muted film scene and must verbalise everything that is relevant to understand the scene. Along the same lines, Szabó suggests an impromptu dubbing of a scene with different roles assigned to different students (VOLFORD 2003: 90f). These exercises hone students' descriptive precision; they learn to speak under time pressure, and distinguish core elements of a scene from peripheral information. In addition, such assignments provide a good basis for visualisation of linguistic input.
- Impromptu speech with cues: The student is given one, or a series of, cue cards and must, on the spot, produce a coherent speech integrating the words displayed on them. The level of difficulty can be adjusted based on the words chosen – speeches on one familiar item such

as climate change are easier to improvise than an unusual combination of words – as well as based on the register to be employed, and the speed with which the cues are presented (see CHABASSE in this volume). In addition to enhancing linguistic flexibility, this also improves speed of reaction and presentation skills. Szabó suggests a variation on this exercise: instead of providing additional cue cards throughout the impromptu speech, the teacher announces taboo words that may not be used (VOLFORD 2003: 162). This trains problem-solving, paraphrasing, and monitoring.
- Instruction manual: Students bring a gadget to class (a hair dryer, a toaster, a tablet PC) and, in their B-language, explain in detail its functions and handling. The more advanced the students, the more complex the devices to be explained. This exercise improves precision of expression in a non-narrative, technical field and enhances speech planning under time pressure in the B-language, revealing deficiencies concerning register, collocations or syntax.
- Syntactic variation: A speech is presented in A, and is interpreted simultaneously by the students. After the critique, the students return to the booth with the text, which is then presented to them again, one sentence at a time. For every sentence, the trainer determines the syntactic element with which the interpretation is to begin. The same sentences or paragraphs can (and should) be interpreted repeatedly, starting with different elements. This enhances linguistic flexibility in the B-language, which is crucial for A- and B-languages that are syntactically radically different.

These exercises lay the groundwork for further instruction; when students reach a certain level of competence, they will be abandoned as students no longer profit from them. Other exercises can be used throughout the entire course, provided the level of difficulty is adjusted accordingly:

- Semantic Field Exercises: When introducing a new subject in class, a preceding brain storming can ascertain students' associations and levels of familiarity with the topic, illustrate its interrelations and challenges, and activate students' knowledge. This enables them to form mental representations and expectations which aids listening comprehension and analysis (CHABASSE 2009: 65ff).

- Phraseology: Students should analyse speeches for standard, elegant phrases of welcome, thanks, congratulations, appeals etc. These speech components, if collected and revisited repeatedly, become easily accessible both for listening comprehension and production.
- Active reading/listening: This self-study exercise requires students to read newspapers and magazines or listen to web, radio, or TV programmes, noting all terminology that is new, unfamiliar, or (in their B-language) non-active. These terms should be noted in their context, and should be reviewed and actively used on a regular basis (VOLFORD 2003: 29ff; GILLIES 2004: 16ff). DÉJEAN LE FÉAL suggests that such active reading/listening, "Lecture complete", should also encompass technical texts (DÉJEAN LE FÉAL 1981: 90f), as even bilinguals show fluctuating language dominance for different technical fields (MÜLLER 2007²: 63ff) and must consciously strengthen the weaker language. This is even more crucial for non-bilinguals. The aim is not solely vocabulary competence, but also enhanced understanding of the subject and familiarity with the expert discourse.
- PowerPoint slam: Students are presented with an unfamiliar, complex PowerPoint presentation and, taking turns, have to spontaneously provide a verbalisation of the slides as they appear. For beginners, this can be done in their mother tongue, while advanced students can be presented with slides in their B-language which they are to verbalise in their A-language, or vice versa. This exercise aims at enhancing linguistic flexibility, improvisation, pattern recognition, and stalling.

4.2 Extra-Linguistic Knowledge

A successful interpretation is contingent not only on linguistic competence, but also and particularly on a thorough understanding of the intended message in all its complexity. In addition to language proficiency, this requires cultural competence and a grasp of the technical field under discussion. Hence, extra-linguistic knowledge directly influences L (Listening) through a quicker understanding of what is being said; M (Memory) due to easier recall of re-activated, pre-stored information; and P (Production), because it is easier and quicker to verbalise a familiar vs. an unfamiliar concept. This holds true for N (Note-taking) as well, as capacities can be saved in both CI (1) and CI (2) if the concepts that are noted down are familiar. Several of the exercises mentioned above also include such a component of extra-linguistic knowledge (active reading/listening, phraseology); however, there are other teaching approaches aiming at specifically these skills, all of which can be used throughout the entire interpreting course:

- Free Speech: Students prepare a freely presented speech on a chosen or assigned topic. In preparation for the speech, classmates can be provided with a hand-out, and possibly a glossary, in advance. As a second step, such presentations can then be interpreted by other students. If done as a B-language exercise, this raises students' awareness for the difficulty of transferring a B-language cultural concept into an A-language context (VOLFORD 2003: 35). Highlighting and discussing culture-specific discrepancies boosts the cultural and intercultural competence necessary to perform as a translator/interpreter (WITTE 2003: 345). This exercise can be done in class or in self-study groups and helps students operate more comfortably within their B- or A-language and trains their public speaking skills. As information stays activated through rehearsal (SEEBER & KERZEL 2012: 2), it also broadens or reactivates their general and technical knowledge.
- Wikis: Students collaborate to assemble a wiki or mini presentation, potentially as a video, on a chosen topic. This trains their research competence and their ability to structure complex information, as well as their collaboration and teamwork.

4.3 Presentation

Presentation competence is more obvious in consecutive interpreting, but is no less essential in simultaneous. While in consecutive the focus lies on public speaking skills, eye contact and appropriate nonverbal and paraverbal communication, presentation in simultaneous relates exclusively to the voice: intonation, breathing patterns, pauses, accent. Presentation skills most immediately impact the Production effort P both directly (better presentation means better communication) and indirectly (effortless presentation skills leave more capacities available for verbalisation of the message). Beginners can profit from more mechanical exercises that are discontinued once the student has a stable basis:

- Mimicry: Shadowing news reports, as well as learning by heart and prosodically copying interviews, speeches and stand-up comedians in the B-language helps students develop a more authentic intonation (Gillies 2004: 16ff). This also trains their working memory and helps students' cultural awareness, especially in the case of stand-up comedians as cultural explicators.

Other exercises can be used throughout the entire course:

- Video evaluation: Free speech exercises (see above) and consecutive performances should be videotaped and analysed by the students themselves, as well as by a peer group, to determine a student's conscious and subconscious communicative behaviour. This helps students become aware of their own facial expressions, gestures and prosodic idiosyncrasies, evaluate their appropriateness, and adapt them to the respective communicative situation.

Advanced students with a stable interpreting performance can be challenged by way of the following exercise:

- Distraction: At intervals, students can be exposed to distractions within the interpreting process. Such distractions can be additional noise (tinkering with the original sound, a booth mate's clattering, a loud fan), a distracting situation (taking the class into a crowded area), or repeated interruptions of the presentation, which requires students to pick up again without losing focus. Training to work through such non-ideal circumstances prepares students for the pitfalls of future assignments and forces them to maintain concentration in the face of distraction.

4.4 Analysis

For the purpose of this chapter, analysis has a two-fold meaning: it refers both to the comprehension of content, and to the selection of appropriate interpreting strategies. In terms of Efforts, analysis most obviously influences Listening (L); however, it is equally important for M and P, since both storage and verbalisation of concepts is significantly easier if the structure of the speech and the content of the message have been understood. It also certainly directly impacts N, both in the taking and the reading back of the notes. Analysis is highly culture-specific, and the application of analytical skills are different for B/C into A and A into B. For B/C into A, it is essential to be able to fill lexical gaps by referencing contextual information; for A into B, the emphasis would be on analysing the original speech to such an extent that it can be re-expressed with the limited verbal resources beginners have at their disposal in their B-language.

The second aspect of analysis requires students to apply appropriate strategies, and as a next step, to automate that application process. Purposefully chosen or edited speeches, along with clearly defined learning objectives, can help students automate particular strategies such as segmentation, anticipation, or generalisation (see KADER & SEUBERT in this volume). For instance, texts with highly complex sentence structures can be coupled with the instruction to segment each sentence into smaller parts (see also VOLFORD 2003: 150). Done repeatedly, this becomes automatic and thus effortless.

For beginners, the focus is on the first aspect of analysis, i.e. the comprehension of the content. This is facilitated by the following exercises:

- Paraphrase: An A-language text must be paraphrased aloud, incorporating simplification, generalisation, syntactic shifts, etc., first based on the written text, then later in the booth using oral input. Since the greater linguistic competence in their A-language allows students to grasp the purpose of the exercise more fully, this exercise would begin in the student's mother tongue, before moving on to the B-language. In the advanced stages, oral texts with highly complex sentence structures (or containing many metaphors and idioms) can be paraphrased and simplified into short, simple sentences. Alternatively, speeches with false starts, self-corrections, broken-off sentences etc. can be shadowed, later interpreted, without any of these deficits showing in the production (KALINA 2000: 181). Students can also be required to transform a text from passive into active voice while shadowing, or from direct to indirect speech, or they can be expected to change the register from scientific to popular style and vice versa. These exercises boost awareness and systematic use of strategies such as approximation, compression, syntactic transformation, and thus aid both Production and Listening.

- SynCloze: Students listen to a text where particular words have been replaced by a beep. Without shadowing, the students have to complete the sentences and list as many synonyms as possible for the left-out word (PÖCHHACKER 2011: 113). The aim is two-fold: extracting the necessary information from contextual data boosts analytical thinking, while finding the synonyms enhances linguistic flexibility. For S-O-V languages[10] such as German, anticipation is crucial and can be trained by leaving out all end-position verbs in a speech, with students being required to fill the gaps based on contextual information. For enhancing B-language competence, Viaggio suggests specifically eliminating syntactic connectors such as prepositions; he also proposes that the elimination of subordinate makers such as 'because' or 'although' helps students perfect their anticipation skills (VIAGGIO 1992: 40).

In addition, some exercises can be used throughout the entire interpreting program, either continually or intermittently:

- Consecutive without notes: Students are required to reproduce a text consecutively without taking notes. This can be done at the very beginning of consecutive interpreting instruction, then repeated intermittently throughout the training course. For beginners, the texts can be narrative and anecdotal, whereas advanced students can be exposed to more dense and sophisticated speeches (see DINGFELDER STONE (07) in this volume). This approach helps students mentally structure incoming information, focus on and retain the core elements of a speech, and optimise their memory recall.
- Redundancies: This exercise uses a high-speed original speech. The first, slow reading of the speech by the instructor is interpreted simultaneously; the interpretations are critiqued, paying special attention to redundancies in the original which may even be highlighted in the written text. The students then return to the booth (without the text) and provide a simultaneous for the speech at its original pace, aiming at eliminating such redundancies. As a learning objective, the stu-

---

10 In S-O-V languages, the verb typically follows the object (Dutch, German), while S-V-O languages have the verb preceding the object (French, English, Italian).

dents are to understand that a fast speech does not need to be, and often cannot be, interpreted in a matching pace, but that incoming information must be analysed in order to separate core from peripheral elements. The exercise helps them appreciate that such a communicative approach might serve their clients better than mad dashes to catch up with the speaker at the expense of completeness and coherence.
- Text typology and subtext analysis: Students should develop an awareness for the variety of speech types, and understand the underlying patterns of each type. On such a basis, students develop tailored note-taking and analytical strategies for speeches on the spectrum of appellative (e.g. campaign speech) to informative (e.g. technical conference) or event-based (e.g. anniversary, funeral). Interpreting and analysing speeches with a high subtext content furthermore helps students move beyond the most obvious level of meaning to understand the hidden agenda. This task includes identifying persuasive-manipulative phrases ('Every decent person knows…', 'Only an idiot would doubt that…'), analysing complex argumentation (straw-man attacks, worst-case scenarios, slippery-slope arguments), and decoding contextual settings (venue, audience, date). The more advanced the students are, the more challenging and hidden the agenda can be. Textual analysis and speech typology are props to lower the necessary resources for Listening/Analysis, and allow for a more appropriate rendering of the target speech.

A few exercises should be reserved for advanced students. If confronted with them too early, students might not yet have the mechanisms at their disposal for handling such complex, demanding material, which would not only make the experience frustrating and demotivating, but also might lead to the development of harmful emergency strategies which can be hard to unlearn later:

- Speed interpreting: In the very advanced classes, speeches can occasionally be presented at high speed. This forces students to employ strategies such as compression, generalisation, etc. rather than randomly omitting information due to over-taxation (see KADER & SEUBERT in this volume).

- Figures: Figures are notorious stumbling blocks for interpreters. For advanced students, texts that rely heavily on numbers (balance sheet press conferences, CFO reports etc.) force students to mentally organise and structure the incoming figures, understand their communicative content and pay attention to their point of reference. In time, they learn to round up or down efficiently, or focus on the communicative purpose of the figure over exact preciseness down to the last digit. A mere dictation of numbers without context or reference, while helpful in automating the mechanics of processing numbers, does not seem like an adequate long-term solution, since an excessive focus on figures at the expense of their context and communicative function will hamper rather than help the interpreting effort.

4.5 Note-Taking

Note-taking skills are crucial for both phases of consecutive interpreting: phase (1) due to extra capacities made available through efficient, smooth note-taking, and phase (2) due to the facilitated recall of information based on a well-structured, well-thought out notation (Rem and Read), which again free capacities for Production. When teaching note-taking in a B/C into A vs. an A into B context, the question of the language of the notes is always prominent. In contrast to earlier publications, Interpreting Studies scholars are increasingly moving away from the source language vs. target language dichotomy that used to dominate the debate. Instead, the choice of notation language is seen to result from an interplay of A- vs. B-language, source and target language, and easy notability (SZABÓ 2006: 141f, VAN DAM 2004). Interpreting experience also seems to play a role, which is easily explained in terms of capacity management. Noting in the source language spares capacities for L, which potentially leaves more room for analysis, resulting in better notes and a more structured memory recall. Target language notation, on the other hand, frees capacities in CI phase two, which leaves more capacities for nonverbal and paraverbal communication, and also reduces the risk of linguistic interference in the production of the interpretation (see DINGFELDER STONE (07) in this volume).

There are a multitude of possible exercises to help students develop a stable, reliable and adaptive note-taking technique. Many of these exercises simultaneously also train other skills; in fact, one would be hard pressed to find one that did not positively affect at least one other subset of skills. The article by Dingfelder Stone on the teaching of note-taking in this same publication sets out many of these exercises. Hence, this article shall merely point out two of the most essential elements in teaching note-taking skills for A into B and B/C into A interpretation, both of which can be used throughout the entire course:

- Text typology and phraseology: Students should be familiarised with a wide range of text types, speech acts, and the phrases that typically accompany such speech situations. This will allow them to judge the note-taking strategy that is most appropriate for the occasion: a seminar paper will require attention to details, facts, and figures, but will typically not present hard-to-follow rhetorical arguments or manipulative elements, while a campaign speech would call for a very nuanced noting of rhetoric and style, with close attention to non- and paraverbal communication.
- Mixing it up: In order to enhance the adaptability of a note-taking system, it can be useful to occasionally challenging students' existing automatisms. This can be done by, without previous announcement, requiring students to interpret from their neighbour's notes, by asking them to note while standing up, or by limiting their note-taking space to a post-it note or a filing card. In addition to training their memory, the latter forces them to note sparingly and efficiently, while the former requires them to revisit and verbalise their own note-taking strategies.

4.6 Memory

Short-term memory improvement is limited and no studies have shown a conclusive impact of short-term-memory training on interpreting performance. Timarová's 2008 article, however, provides a convincing examination of different models investigating the various aspects and functions assigned to working memory by a range of authors, and their significance for simultaneous interpreting, and points to a discrepancy between theoretical models of working memory and the empirical studies conducted in the framework of Interpreting Studies (TIMAROVÁ 2008: 21). Memory impacts the Production effort as well, and has direct consequences for Read and Rem in CI (2). Some of the exercises that may prove useful for memory skills have already been discussed: consecutive without notes, already illustrated in the analysis exercises, helps not only analytical skills, but obviously also trains students' memory storage and recall processes, as they must retain the information without being able to 'outsource' anything onto the notepad (see 4.4). Other exercises commonly suggested to improve working memory have a more specific, tailored approach. For beginners, some of these exercises are more mechanical in nature:

- Memorisation: Kornakov suggests memorising poems, prose, or radio news as a way to enhance memory performance. He also recommends regular dictation on figures, names, and measures in one or both of the languages (KORNAKOV 2000: 247, GILLIES 2004: 16ff; see also chapter 4.3 of this article: Presentation/mimicry).
- Board Games (self-study): Board games such as Trivial Pursuit, Pictionary, Taboo, Activity, and Charade in many instances help train working memory. In addition, they may improve linguistic and cultural competence and soft skills such as team work, frustration tolerance, and cultural awareness (GILLIES 2004: 19f).

Advanced students might profit from more challenging tasks that reveal their areas of potential improvement without demotivating and frustrating them:

- Sight translation: Kalina proposes presenting students with a written text, which as a first step is to be read, highlighted, and then (without text consultation) summarised, first in the same, then in a different language; this is then followed by sight interpretation of a succeeding segment (KALINA 2000: 179f).
- Complex texts: The use of texts that are dense or highly rhetorical challenges students to retain more elements of the text's macro structure. A text that traces an argument over the length of several pages, for instance, and continues to refer back to the first stages of the explanation in an abbreviated form, requires that students retain the previous segments and recall the information to correctly interpret the abbreviated references.
- Combination of interpreting modes: To train the initial parallel processing in the booth, Déjean Le Féal suggests beginning with a consecutive piece and then having the students interpret that same segment (plus a little extra) simultaneously. This would then be succeeded by a text on which notes are taken, but instead of providing a consecutive, the students render a simultaneous interpretation (DÉJEAN

LE FÉAL 1997: 168). This combination of interpreting modes is, in fact, a useful tool in a variety of combinations: An initial simultaneous interpretation, for instance, followed by a consecutive summary of the content (without hearing the text again) forces students to pay more attention to the content of their interpretation.

5. Final Thoughts

This article has considered the teaching of conference interpreting in terms of capacity management; more specifically, it has applied Gile's Effort Models to the questions of directionality and language specificity. Aiming to provide interpreting instructors with a hands-on, practical resource for incorporating skill-specific training into their interpreting classes, it provides a range of sample exercises that can be used for that purpose. In order to maximise didactic applicability, these exercises are graded based on skill level, level of difficulty, directionality, and the Efforts they influence.

Despite – or rather because of – their simplicity, Gile's Effort Models continue to be a useful tool in the classroom. Teachers can explain the processes involved in interpreting, identify problem triggers, suggest methods for alleviating cognitive pressure, structure their classes, and provide more individual, useful feedback. Students, on the other hand, can break down the complexity of the task into more manageable chunks; also, a theoretical understanding of the task at hand and the origins of mistakes can help them proceed from declarative to procedural knowledge. The exercises set out here allow teachers and students alike to tackle specific deficits in an efficient, effective manner.

References

ANDRES, Dörte; BEHR, Martina & DINGFELDER STONE, Maren (2013) (eds.): *Dolmetschmodelle: Erfasst, erläutert, erweitert*. Frankfurt a. M.: Peter Lang.

BARTŁOMIEJCZYK, Magdalena (2006): "Strategies of Simultaneous Interpreting and Directionality", *Interpreting* 8(2), 149-174.

CHABASSE, Catherine (2009): *Gibt es eine Begabung für das Simultandolmetschen? Erstellung eines Dolmetscheignungstests*. Berlin: Saxa.

DÉJEAN LE FÉAL, Karla (1981): "L'enseignement des méthodes d'interprétation", *L'enseignement de l'interprétation et de la traduction, Cahiers de traductologie* 4. Ottawa: Editions de l'Université d'Ottawa.

DONOVAN, Clare (2004): "European Masters Project Group: Teaching Simultaneous Interpretation into a B Language – Preliminary Findings", *Interpreting* 6(2), 205-216.

ERICSSON, Anders K.; KRAMPE Ralph Th. & TESCH-ROMER, Clemens (1993): "The Role of Deliberate Practice in the Acquisition of Expert Performance", *Psychological Review* 100(3), 363-406.

FILLMORE, Charles (1976): "Frame Semantics and the Nature of Language". In: HARNARD, J. et al. (eds.): *Origins and Evolution of Language and Speech. Annals of New York Academy of Sciences*. Vol. 280. New York: Academy of Science, 20-32.

GILE, Daniel (2008): "Local Cognitive Load in Simultaneous Interpreting and its Implications for Empirical Research", *Forum* 6(2). 59-77.

GILE, Daniel (1995, r. 2009): *Basic Concepts and Models for Translator and Interpreter Training*. Amsterdam/Philadelphia: John Benjamins.

GILLIES, Andrew (2004): *Conference Interpreting: a new students' companion*. Cracow: Tertium Society for the Promotion of Language Studies.

HÖRMANN, Hans (1981): *Einführung in die Psycholinguistik*. Darmstadt: Wissenschaftliche Buchgesellschaft.

KIM, Nam Hui (2009): *Der Umgang mit deutschen Relativsätzen beim Dolmetschen ins Koreanische*. Berlin: Saxa.

KOHN, Kurt & KALINA, Sylvia (1996): "The Strategic Dimension of Interpreting", *Meta* 41(1), 118-138.

KORNAKOV, Peter (2000): "Five Principles and Five Skills for Training Interpreters", *Meta* 45(2), 241-248.

KURZ, Ingrid (1992): "Shadowing Exercises in Interpreter Training". In: DOLLERUP, Cay & LODDEGAARD, Anne (eds.): *Teaching Translation and Interpreting: Training, Talent, and Expertise*. Amsterdam/Philadelphia: John Benjamins, 245-250.

MÜLLER, Natascha (2007[2]): *Einführung in die Mehrsprachigkeitsforschung: Deutsch, Französisch, Italienisch*. Tübingen: Gunter Narr.

NOLAN, James (2012[2]): *Interpretation: Techniques and Exercises*. Bristol: Multilingual.

PÖCHHACKER, Franz (2011): "Assessing Aptitude for Interpreting: The SynCloze Test", *Interpreting* 13(1), 106-120.

Risku, Hanna (2009): "Was bedeutet es, ein Translationsprofi zu sein? Drei Antworten aus dem Bereich der Kognitionswissenschaft". In: Ahrens, Barbara et al. (eds.): *Translationswissenschaftliches Kolloquium I – Beiträge zur Übersetzungs- und Dolmetschwissenschaft*. Frankfurt a. M.: Peter Lang, 331-347.

Rosenblatt, Allan (2004): "Insight, Working Through, and Practice: The Role of Procedural Knowledge", *Journal of the American Psychoanalytic Association*, 52(1), 189–207.

Seeber, Kilian G. & Kerzel, Dirk (2012): "Cognitive Load in Simultaneous Interpreting: Model Meets Data", *International Journal of Bilingualism* 16(2), 228-242.

Szabó, Csilla (2006): "Language Choice in Note-taking for Consecutive Interpretation: A Topic Revisited", *Interpreting* 8(2), 129-147.

Timarová, Šárka (2008): *Working Memory and Simultaneous Interpreting*. https://www.arts.kuleuven.be/cetra/papers/files/timarova.pdf (07.07.2014).

Van Dam, Helle (2004): "Interpreters' Notes: On the Choice of Language", *Interpreting* 6(1), 3-17.

Viaggio, Sergio (1992): "Cognitive Clozing to Teach them how to Think", *The Interpreters' Newsletter* 4, 40-44.

Volford, Katalin (2003): "The Importance of Cultural Background Knowledge". In: Szabó, Csilla (ed.): *Interpreting from Preparation to Performance. Recipes for Practitioners and Teachers*. Budapest: British Council Hungary, 29-35.

Witte, Heidrun (2003): "Die Rolle der Kulturkompetenz". In: Snell-Hornby, Mary et al. (eds.): *Handbuch Translation*. Stauffenburg: Tübingen, 345-34.

Easy? Medium? Hard?
The Importance of Text Selection in Interpreter Training

DÖRTE ANDRES
andres@uni-mainz.de
Johannes Gutenberg University Mainz/Germersheim, Germany

1. Introduction

"To interpret one must first understand" (SELESKOVITCH 1978: 11). This simplestatement illustrates that the process of understanding is of overarching importance in interpreting (cf. SELESKOVITCH & LEDERER 1989, KOHN & KALINA 1996, KAUTZ 2002). It is therefore somewhat surprising that the analysis of the sourcetext (ST) and hence the evaluation of its difficulty level has not received much attention in interpreting studies (cf. PÖCHHACKER 1994). The difficulty level of a text does not only determine whether it can be interpreted at all; it also defines how this interpretation is to be evaluated (cf. HÖNIG 2003). The quality of the target text (TT) depends on the ST since the interpretation in the target language depends on the ST (cf. KALINA 2011).

Objective evaluation and the successful selection of texts should be an integral component of the theory of interpreter training, because "[i]n interpreter training, and to evaluate quality, we need to know what is easy or difficult in different conditions and situations" (SETTON 2001: 1). Interpreter trainers should be able to select a text that allows the students to acquire the abilities and skills necessary for interpreting step by step (KAUTZ 2002: 145). The selection of overly difficult texts can have negative long-term effects on the students' learning behaviour: "To destroy a trainee's confidence in her ability to understand by badly or arbitrarily chosen speeches will not only impair her performance in this particular instance but in the long run lead to irreparable injuries" (HÖNIG 2003: 71).

The difficulty level of a text results from the interaction of a multitude of factors that impinge upon each other (cf. KUTZ 2010: 415). This complexity may be the reason why so far there has been almost no research done on this topic. Hönig (2003) is one of the few authors who have dealt with the topic in some detail. The interpreting research currently available usually only contains the suggestion to start with easy texts, which is of little use (cf. SEILER DE DUQUE 1997: 112).

What, then, makes a text easy or difficult? This is the problem the article at hand concerns itself with. We begin by exploring how interpreters (must learn to) understand. Next, we discuss parameters of difficulty internal to the text – topic and structure, speech acts and levels of redundancy, cohesion, numbers and proper names, expressive effects such as quotes, Latin idioms, humour as well as culture-specific aspects – followed by presentation-based difficulty parameters: visual aids, para- and nonverbal properties such as speaking velocity, preformulation and accent/dialect as well as speaking style and errors. These parameters are explained individually and summarized in table form at the end of each section. The conclusion illustrates and summarizes the didactic relevance of discussing texts and their difficulty in interpreting.

2. The Process of Understanding

The goal of interpreting is to produce a functioning text:

[…]a target text that is equivalent to the source text in terms of communicative function and overall sense; accurate as to the reformulation of the information content; appropriate in that it overcomes cultural barriers and meets listener-related and event-related requirements; usable, i.e. easily followed and understood by the Listeners. (VIEZZI 2009: 373)

Beyond the purely auditory process of listening to a text, listening to comprehend is the basic prerequisite of interpreting (cf. HEINE 2000: 216). Language comprehension is dealt with in the field of cognitive psychology (cf. ANDERSON 2007[6]: 453f). This field has provided results indicating that comprehension occurs subjectively, selectively and in part on an unconscious-intuitive level. These conclusions have significantly influenced interpreting studies. In the 1980s, interpreting research started exploring which factors influence understanding, how comprehension competence can be developed and which prerequisites make understanding easier. Language skills, world knowledge, intelligence and sociocultural background are considered fundamental factors influencing comprehension in interpreters (cf. GARZONE 2000: 72). Understanding is therefore not only based on decoding linguistic signs, but also on extra-linguistic elements, which are involved in the generation of meaning. Because the input is presented to interpreters in segmented form, they must gather information step by step, for example through logical inferencing. For this purpose, they utilise their knowledge about the world, the speaker, the situation and the target audience. They arrive at a set of expectations based on this knowledge, which helps them understand quickly and holistically.

Like cognitive psychology, psycholinguistics considers the process of understanding a process of meaning generation, which is based on personal experience to a considerable extent. According to the *scenes-and-frames* semantics developed by Charles J. Fillmore, the recipients of a text develop a *scene* in their mind based on the words *(frames)* they read or hear. Scenes are the culturally influenced knowledge of objects, situations and actions represented in the brain. Every *scene* is assigned a specific linguistic encoding, a *frame*. The relationship between *scene* and *frame* is reciprocal, i.e. there is a *scene* for every *frame* and vice versa. The activation of *scenes/frames* only works, however, when it can be linked to "some personally meaningful setting or situation" (FILLMORE 1977: 62). Interpreting difficulties arise when the scenes connected to certain frames differ between cultures (cf. FILLMORE 1977, PRUNČ 2007: 186) and the interpreter does not reflect on the activated scenes. In German, an example is the *frame Kaffeetrinken* (drinking coffee). In German listeners, especially older ones, this frame activates a specific image (*scene*) along with associated social conventions which do not have an equivalent for English-speaking listeners: Sunday afternoon, apple pie with whipped cream, a smartly decorated table, starting around 3:30 pm, lasting about two hours, and the presentation of a small bouquet of flowers to the hostess.

Strategies help the interpreter to understand in an economical way. They can be practiced individually and can be chosen as sub-goals in the units of instruction (see SEUBERT & KADER in this volume). According to Kalina, strategies of comprehension include "[…] segmentation of input, anticipation, inferencing, accessing previously stored knowledge, building relations between stored and new information, in short, mental modelling"(KALINA 2000: 7). In addition, she lists 'global strategies' which support the development of comprehension competence:

Global strategies are of a more general and comprehensive nature; they involve memorizing the input, adapting one's mental model, monitoring one's own output for deficiencies but also that of the text producer for coherence, and repairing errors. (KALINA 2000: 7)

Grasping meaning quickly and economically plays a crucial role in the process of interpreting. Interpreters are comprehension specialists who, according to Hönig, must not "nach den Bäumen, sondern nach dem Wald schauen"[1] (HÖNIG 2011: 270). That is why it is so important for interpreters to understand already during their education how comprehension works and how comprehension techniques can be learned and developed (cf. VIAGGIO 2000: 134).

3. The Text in Interpreter Training

As explained earlier, text comprehension is subjective and to a large extent dependent on an individual's prior knowledge. For this reason, it must be assumed that there is a significant difference between the subjective and the objective difficulty level of a text. The total difficulty of a text therefore cannot be an absolute value (cf. SELESKOVITCH & LEDERER 1989: 182). Nevertheless, discourse and textual analysis as well as descriptive linguistics offer a set of tools enabling us "[…] to make an informed choice of suitable speeches for tests and training" (HÖNIG 2003: 71). Hönig suggests using a framework distinguishing between parameters internal to the text and presentation parameters as well as five other categories as an aid for text analysis. He states that he restricts his consideration to the most important linguistic and paralinguistic aspects in order to keep the model as simple as possible (HÖNIG 2003: 72; cf. also KUTZ 2010: 404). Text-internal parameters include topic and structure, speech acts and levels of redundancy, cohesion and numbers and figures. Presentation based parameters (external to the text) include speaking velocity, visual aids and accents/dialects.

This section presents an extension of this framework. The text-internal parameters are extended by adding proper nouns to the category of numbers. 'Expressive effects' (quotations, Latin idioms, humour) and culture-specific

---

[1] "look at the trees, but at the forest instead"

aspects are added, because interpreting is "by definition an instance of intercultural communication" (KONDO & TEBBLE 1997: 150). Among the presentation-based parameters, the 'visual aids' are discussed first according to Hönig's considerations. This is followed by para- and nonverbal properties as an umbrella term. These can be divided into speaking velocity (according to Hönig) with the added aspect of the degree of preformulation. This is followed – again according to Hönig – by the parameters of accents/dialects. In addition, speaking style and errors are added. The evaluation criteria mentioned are widely accepted difficulty factors in interpreting studies, which can, for example, be explained by Daniel Gile's Effort Model (HÖNIG 2003: 70). According to this model, interpreting consists of various processes. Each of these processes uses a certain percentage of an interpreter's capacities. The available capacities are limited, however. If the demands of a specific *effort* become too high, that is, if there are *problem triggers,* i.e. difficulties in the text, an overload occurs and more capacities are needed than are available. This overload leads to deficits in the TT. By using interpreting strategies, however, errors can be avoided (GILE 2009: 171ff, 191) (see CHABASSE & DINGFELDER STONE in this volume).

'Problem triggers' in the ST are also an indicator of the difficulty of a text. The parameters listed above are understood as potential *problem triggers* and are explained below.

3.1 Difficulty Parameters Internal to the Text

3.1.1   Topic and Structure

The difficulty of a text depends on whether and to what degree the interpreter is familiar with the topic. The more familiar the topic, the easier understanding and interpreting are for the interpreter. This is why preparing for the topic that is to be interpreted is of fundamental importance (KUTZ 2010: 418f).At the beginning of training it is recommended to utilise familiar topics with concrete contents discussed in a comprehensible way, so that students can mobilize the knowledge they possess and can refer back to existing structures (cf. SELESKOVITCH & LEDERER 1989: 67ff). Texts of high information density can impact the interpreting performance negatively. This is also true of texts touching upon many different topics or contentless speech – "stonewalling speech" (JONES 1998: 191) – as well as highly implicit texts, which force the interpreter to constantly 'listen' between the lines (cf. SETTON 2001: 14).

Structure is of equal importance for comprehension. "*Standard ritualized speeches* like e.g. welcoming addresses where both theme and structure follow a stereotype are considered *very easy* because they can be totally anticipated and learned by heart" (HÖNIG 2003: 72, emphasis in original). If a speech is structured chronologically, if its topic and problem statement are discussed at the outset, if it is phrased in an explicit way and stands on its own, then the interpreter will have a good overview of the text that is to be interpreted even if it is abstract or specialised (cf. JONES 1998: 17ff). A clear structure is usually more important than familiarity with the topic (cf. HÖNIG 2003: 73, KUTZ 2010: 406).

3.1.2 Speech Acts and Levels of Redundancy

Speech acts indicate the communicative intention of an utterance (illocution). They can be divided into direct and indirect speech acts. A speaker may connect an utterance directly with a demand (Come over here!) or request an answer to a question (Is it raining?). "Speech organizing illocutions like e.g. *I repeat, I stress, I ask, I submit, I admit* and their indicators highlight the structure of a speech" (HÖNIG 2003: 76, emphasis in original). Direct speech acts, which verbalize the communicative intention of the speaker, ease comprehension. Indirect speech acts, on the other hand, require a higher degree of attention and must be analysed before they can be understood (cf. HÖNIG 2003: 76, KAUTZ 2002: 355), which is why they require more processing capacity than their direct counterparts. A typical example of an indirect speech act is the utterance 'There is a draft in here'. It can be a statement of fact, but in certain situations it could also be interpreted as a request to close a window, without directly voicing the request. If the utterance had been 'Please close the window!' it would have been a direct speech act. Indirect speech acts also include rhetorical questions.

Redundancy, on the other hand, makes comprehension easier. Chernov provides the primary discussion of the topic of redundancy from an interpreting perspective, highlighting its importance in simultaneous interpreting (cf. CHERNOV 2002). At the outset of interpreter training, a high degree of grammatical and thematic redundancy can be helpful. If consecutive interpreting training for beginners does not require the students to constantly process new information but instead repeats it and provides examples, more time remains to analyse and take notes effectively on what is being heard (cf. ARDITO 1999: 180). A low degree of redundancy usually means that many meaningful elements and therefore a high information density (usually in combination with a high speaking velocity) must be processed. In such a case, omissions can quickly lead to incomprehensibility. A high density of information "is probably the most frequent source of interpreting problems" (cf. KAUTZ 2002: 304, GILE 2009: 192, SETTON 2001: 10).

In addition, redundancies facilitate anticipation, which is a highly important strategy in text comprehension and interpreting. Anticipation can take place based on linguistic or content-related factors. Linguistic factors include the language skills of the interpreters, allowing them to anticipate based on their knowledge of the grammatical structures of the source language (syntax, semantics). "[E]xtralinguistic information like general and situational knowledge, and information obtained in the course of translation" (VAN BESIEN 1999: 258) is equally important, however. Information already contained in the text indicates its future direction. However, interpreters can also make use of their situational and world knowledge, i.e. their knowledge of the speaker and the subject at hand (cf. KIRCHHOFF 1976: 64f). The ability to anticipate is a part of interpreting expertise (cf. TIJUS 1997: 41). We can therefore assume that it can be learned or acquired and therefore that it can also be taught. It follows that "[…] anticipation ability is an important goal in the training of interpreters" (VAN BESIEN 1999: 252), because "[…] the more accurately the interpreter is able to anticipate the speaker of the speech, the easier the job becomes" (VAN DAM 1989: 172).

3.1.3 Cohesion

Cohesion is "[…] the most important quality of a well-formed discourse" (HÖNIG 2003: 76). It is defined as "die syntaktisch-semantische Verflechtung der Oberfläche einer Äußerung"[2](KUTZ 2010: 407) – in contrast with coherence, which refers to the logical, content-oriented layer. A cohesive text consists of sentences, which are connected in a meaningful way in order to create a formal relationship (BÜHLER 1989: 131). Cohesive devices, for example, include lexical repetitions (example: *The meeting* will take place tomorrow. An agreement must be reached at *this meeting*), pronouns (example: *The draft* will be completed tomorrow. *It* takes the various remarks into account) and con-

---

2 "syntactic-semantic interweaving of the surface of an utterance"

junctions (example: I know *that* I speak too quickly). Cohesion supports the process of comprehension (cf. HÖNIG 2003: 76).

3.1.4 Numbers/Proper Nouns

Numbers are considered a problem in interpretation studies regardless of mode. They are perceived as "strings of unpredictable or loosely contextualized items [...] that [...] increase the 'density' of the discourse, and place an exceptional burden on the interpreter" (SHLESINGER 2003: 39). They are hard to store and can usually not be anticipated. Fractions, powers or roots as well as numbers with different units require a high processing capacity. Even when interpreted correctly, numbers often produce a trail of overload in their wake as evidenced by an increase in omissions or errors later in the text (cf. GILE 1988: 16f). Interpreting researchers also agree that proper nouns and acronyms require large amounts of attention – especially due to the importance of their correct interpretation (cf. GILE 1984: 79). Unfamiliar proper nouns always mean a lack of coherence for the interpreter. Familiar proper nouns can also cause erroneous interpretations in the case of long acronyms, abbreviations or multi-part names.

3.1.5 Expressive Effects (Quotes/Latin idioms/Humour)

Expressive effects such as quotes, Latin idioms and humour cause similar problems. Rephrasing quotes poses high analytical requirements and therefore consumes significant capacities. This is also true of Latin idioms. If they are well known they can be repeated unchanged (a simple Latin idiom would be: *in vino veritas*). If they are not well known, they are either lost or they require a high level of processing capacity in order to be rephrased (Example: *qui tacet consentire videtur* – one who remains silent appears to agree).

"Humour is difficult to translate and even more difficult to interpret. For a simultaneous interpreter to draw a laugh from the audience at the same time that those hearing the original joke burst into laughter is a rare feat" (NOLAN 2005: 258). Humour, including jokes, puns etc., are definitely among the problem triggers mentioned above. It is frequently strongly influenced by culture but it does not have to be, which is why it will be dealt with elsewhere. If the source language audience is laughing, i.e. if they understand the joke, the target language audience also wants to understand it and laugh (cf. PÖCHHACKER 1994: 210). Humour is frequently used in order to produce a relaxed atmosphere and therefore has a specific communicative intention. It can play an important role in achieving communicative success. The lower the influence of culture on humour, the more likely it is that it can be transferred to the target language with comparable effect. This property should therefore be covered in training by using multiple humorous texts.

3.1.6 Cultural Specificity

Cultural factors can influence the difficulty level and therefore the comprehension of a text in a large number of ways. The speaker's culture becomes visible in the content communicated, in the language used (presentation style and argument structure) (cf. KONDO & TEBBLE 1989: 153, KUTZ 2010: 450ff), but also in para- and nonverbal behaviour. The latter is discussed in Section 2. It includes a description of general parameters deemed of special importance to interpreting. Due to the complexity of the topic, culturally specific aspects cannot be covered in this context (cf. PÖCHHACKER 1994, POYATOS 2002, VIAGGIO 1997, WEALE 1997).

A strong cultural influence, for example through frequent references to culturally specific topics or words without equivalents in the other language, require interpreters to provide potentially time-intensive explanations (cf. JONES 1998: 116, KUTZ 2010: 458) in order to produce an interpretation which satisfies the customer's requirements. In addition, they must determine to what degree the interpretation can be adapted to the culture of the TT (cf. KUTZ 2010: 450). A number of examples of culture-specific aspects are given below. The style of speaking, which is also a part of culture specific factors, is discussed in the section on presentation-based parameters. Culture specific aspects increase the difficulty level of the ST because the interpreter not only has to understand these realia but potentially also has to explain them. This can definitely pose problems as illustrated in the following example:

> No one would understand a direct transfer of a person in the US saying "He just laid down a bunt". In the US, this expression comes from baseball terminology and refers to someone only letting the ball rebound without swinging the bat. In a figurative sense, it is used to describe someone who does not take risks. It can also mean 'cowardly'. Bunting is strategic, i.e. it can also represent a sacrifice, which is needed for the team or for others. There is no German equivalent; just describing the

baseball situation would not help the German listener understand the communicative intent of the speaker. The interpreter first has to know the expression herself, she then has to grasp the figurative sense of the utterance and must then decide to what extent the speaker's use of the expression was judgmental and what effect (positive-appreciative or negative-criticizing) was intended. Based on this, the interpreter must then choose a translation which either only includes the core statement or also explains the culture specific meaning in some way, depending on the given time constraints.

Culture-specific aspects increase the *listening* and *analysis effort*. Less complex concepts can also cause problems when transferring them to the target language. An example is the German word *Professor*. In Germany, this designation is limited to lecturers who have received a call from a university, while every university lecturer can be called 'professor' in the US.

A possible solution for transferring culture specific aspects is to keep the source language term in its unmodified form, potentially with a short comment, for example in the case of terms from the educational system such as the 'habilitation'[3]. This concept does not exist in the US, no one would understand it and it would therefore require an explanation by the interpreter. Texts without culture-specific aspects are certainly easier to interpret than those in which culture specific aspects are extremely important for the text's meaning.

The language combination in which the interpreting is done lies between the text-internal and the presentation-based parameters and plays a significant role in both cases (cf. TAYLOR TORSELLO et al. 1997: 168). It is included in both the text-internal and the text-internal difficulty categories because it has an effect on the language level (transferability of idioms, passive constructions) as well as on the presentation level (speaking velocity and intonation).

---

3 Post-doctoral qualification or 'second book'

Overview of text-internal criteria of difficulty:

More difficult:	Less difficult:
• Unfamiliar/contentless topic • Implicit speeches (listening between the lines) • Abstract/technical topic • Abrupt start of the speech • Unclear references/logic • Digression-riddled structure • High information density (due to fast presentation/a large amount of information) • Indirect speech acts • Numbers/proper nouns/acronyms • Culture specific aspects • Expressive effects (quotations/Latin expressions/humour)	• Well-known/familiar topic • Explicit speeches • Standardized speeches/clear structure • Starts out with empty phrases • Chronological structure • Coherence and cohesion • Redundancies (content- and language-related) • Direct speech acts • 1-2 digit numbers • Familiar concepts • Examples/Explanations

3.2 Presentation-Based Difficulty Parameters

3.2.1 Visual aids

A controversial topic when evaluating the difficulty level of a text is the media-based support of the speech with visual aids. They can be used to complement the auditory input (cf. KAUTZ 2002: 304) but processing them does pose an additional burden (cf. HÖNIG 2003: 79). Visual aids include overhead transparencies and PowerPoint presentations; Pöchhacker also mentions films, graphics and hand-written records (cf. PÖCHHACKER 1994: 113). He sees these instruments of visual expression as "supportive of reception" (PÖCHHACKER 1994: 113). Hönig, on the other hand, states that visual aids can also make comprehension more difficult due to "technical hitches (including the fact that often interpreters cannot see or read captions because of the position of their booths); unprofessionally prepared and presented visual aids; time pressure which forces speakers to hurry through their slides" (HÖNIG 2003: 79). In simultaneous interpreting, the speaker may sometimes already be describing slide 16 while the interpreter is still on slide 15. This problem is even more significant in relay interpreting where the distance from the speaker is even larger (cf. VIEZZI 2009: 368). Easily visible visual aids with a clear structure presented at a moderate pace tend to support comprehension, while unclear material can make comprehension harder.

3.2.2   Para- and Nonverbal Properties

Para- and nonverbal elements (speaking velocity, voice quality, volume, tone of voice, pauses, etc.) are part of the message of the ST and therefore influence the interpreter's comprehension (cf. VIAGGIO 1997, PÖCHHACKER 1994: 114). Correctly interpreting para- and nonverbal signals is not always easy (cf. WEALE 1997: 307). Nonverbal and paralinguistic elements that are used to support the main statement and therefore comprehension are especially useful to the interpreter (cf. VIAGGIO 1997: 285). Correctly employed prosodic elements (intonation, pauses, emphasis) provide the speech with contrast and weighting, facilitate the storage of what is being heard and produce cohesion. A monotonous presentation style, on the other hand, makes comprehension and therefore storage in short term memory more difficult. More mental capacity is required to recall the segment (cf. MAZZETTI 1999: 126, SETTON 2001: 1). These para- and nonverbal properties are explained below on a theoretical level as well as with a number of examples.

3.2.3   Speaking Velocity and Preformulation

The topic of speaking velocity was addressed early in interpretation studies although there are a number of diverse opinions on it (PÖCHHACKER 1994: 113). According to Riccardi, speaking velocity is "the greatest language-independent constraint" (RICCARDI et al. 1998: 95) in interpreting. Multiple experiments have shown that a high speaking velocity can cause problems and lead to a higher number of errors and omissions in the interpretation (cf. GERVER 2002: 62f, GARWOOD 2002: 271, MEULEMAN & VAN BESIEN 2009: 20f). This is especially true if the source language and the target language exhibit large structural differences. The other extreme, a speech presented at very low speed, can also make interpreting more difficult as it delays the completion of a unit of meaning, referred to as 'closure' in simultaneous interpreting (cf. HÖNIG 2003: 78f) and the interpreter's working memory becomes overloaded (cf. KIRCHHOFF

2002: 113). The distinction between free speech and a written text is not always unambiguous and there are also hybrid cases (cf. BÜHLER 1989: 134).

Speaking velocity, in turn, is also influenced by the style of speaking. Whether a text is presented spontaneously, semi-spontaneously or is prepared, that is, whether it is presented or read, affects speaking velocity, but also redundancy and cohesion (cf. PÖCHHACKER 1994: 113). Presentation speed and information density are higher when a manuscript is being read. Such readings also have a level of language and style close to written texts, which, in turn, leads to an "awkward discourse structure" (SETTON 2001: 17). A speech recorded in writing has the advantages of possessing a clear structure and being semantically correct, but does not include "ideation and message planning" (DODDS et al. 1997: 101). This makes the text highly compressed and means it contains very few redundancies. However, it also has complex syntactic structures and usually possesses a higher level of abstraction. This is why speeches read from a manuscript are usually harder to interpret. In contrast, a freely presented speech is usually slower, less formal, more redundant, contains more pauses, contains simpler syntactic structures and has a lower information density. Texts not recorded in written form (*impromptu speech* or *extemporaneous speech* which is planned in advance but presented freely) are considered easier in general, because the interpreter can trace the development of the speaker's thoughts and the spontaneity in free speech leads to more redundancies (cf. ARDITO 1999: 181). An improvised speech can, however, also have shortcomings when it comes to structure and logic, or it may make use of an informal register of speech with syntactic and lexical deviations, which make comprehension more difficult.

3.2.4   Accent/Dialect

Hönig primarily sees regional accents and dialects as well as accents when speaking or presenting in a foreign language as falling into the category of deviations from standard language. The latter is a problem that occurs in practice with increasing frequency (cf. HÖNIG 2003: 79f). A strong foreign-language-based accent increases 'listening effort' and can lead to significant errors in comprehension (cf. GILE 2009: 193, KURZ 2002: 70). Accents from foreign languages are especially problematic because they generally not only deviate from the standard language in pronunciation, but also in syntax, choice of words and prosody (cf. MAZZETTI 1999: 127). These deviations mean that the interpreter must utilise additional capacities for listening and analysing

(GILE 2009: 139). Hönig and Kautz judge slight deviations from the standard language to be compensable and strong deviations as not compensable (cf. HÖNIG 2003: 75, KAUTZ 2002: 354ff).

For these reasons it is advisable to use texts presented by native speakers in the early phases of training (cf. SELESKOVITCH & LEDERER 1989: 69f), even though different language variants should definitely be practiced at a later point in time in order to familiarize the students with different varieties such as African, Eastern European, Indian English, etc. and to allow them to learn to decode and cope with different pronunciations (cf. ALBL-MIKASA 2013: 7), if necessary by using inference.

3.2.5 Speaking Style

A text written by an author with an unusual style of language can cause difficulties if it is unfamiliar to the interpreter (cf. GILE 2009: 193). The more standardized a text is, the easier it is to interpret (cf. SEILER DE DUQUE 1997: 112).

A highly formal or very informal register also present an obstacle for the interpreter – due to the missing familiarity with these linguistic forms but also because a highly formal register often implies a highly complex syntax and choice of words – because the knowledge and use of registers works primarily through intuition (cf. RUCCI 1999: 193). The same is true of speaking styles with a strong cultural influence which might surprise the respective target audience and which may have to be adapted to the equivalent conventions of speaking in the target language. In this context, one has to pose the question of how much an interpreter may and should interfere (cf. KUTZ 2007). Gile therefore also considers 'culture-specific difficulties' to be potential problem triggers: "Taking decisions related to such difficulties entails additional cognitive load and increases the risk of saturation" (GILE 2009: 198).

Speeches underlying strong emotional, poetic, patriotic or religious influences also pose problems when transferring them to the target language (cf. KUTZ 2010: 409). Emotive contents are especially likely to pose problems for the interpreter as they are often communicated via intonation and are therefore not immediately obvious if the interpreter is not familiar with the speaker (cf. BÜLOW MØLLER 2003: 1). Strongly patriotic or religious speeches presented by American politicians may often appear strange to non-Americans. This also raises the question of whether and to what degree the interpreter should adapt the discourse to the target culture. In dealing with student translators, this problem must, in any event, be addressed in preparatory activities prior to the interpreting exercise.

Speeches with large cultural influences are not very common at international conferences. According to Hönig, the international (not culturally influenced) style of speaking can therefore be considered easy, while speaking styles with strong cultural influences fall into the difficult or very difficult categories (cf. KAUTZ 2002: 356).

3.2.6 Errors

Errors include the category of (intentionally or unintentionally) wrong numbers, names or facts as well as slips of the tongue and sentence breaks/restatements. Both categories do not have to lead to errors in the TT but must definitely be considered problem triggers because they usually mean that the interpreter must utilise more capacities in these situations in order to comprehend the ST or to produce a 'correct' target language solution.

Frequent slips or sentence breaks or restatements endanger the coherence of a text, which means the interpreter often requires greater distance from the text in order to give meaning to what is being said. These characteristics frequently occur with inexperienced speakers and are found in conjunction with pauses and sounds of hesitation, which further increase the difficulty of understanding such texts. Occasional slips of the tongue are certainly not a significant problem for language transfer. Frequent slips and sentence breaks can, however, have an aggravating effect. It is universally accepted that interpreters are allowed to intervene by correcting such errors, i.e. by producing a correct text free of slips and sentence breaks. Correcting incorrect numbers, names or facts is more problematic (cf. KUTZ 2007). Making such a decision while interpreting can lead to significant cognitive overload for the interpreter (cf. GILE 2009: 198), especially considering that a clear differentiation of whether an (unintentional) error occurred or not is not always possible. Incorrect numbers can certainly be intended by the speaker in order to provide a more positive impression of an economic situation. An 'incorrect' description of an event can also be intentional, because the event is perceived differently for political reasons. These situations require the interpreter to decide whether to intervene and correct the error or not. This decision consumes capacities and therefore makes the interpretation more difficult.

Overview of Presentation-Based Criteria of Difficulty:

More difficult:	Less difficult:
• Deficient visual aids • Very high/very low speaking velocity • Speech manuscript that is memorized/read out • Non-native language speaker, strong accent/dialect • Monotonous presentation style • Strongly culturally influenced style of speaking • Errors in the ST (incorrect numbers, names or facts as well as slips of the tongue and sentence breaks)	• Visual aids supplementing the contents • Improvised/free speech with redundancies • Native-language speaker, only slight accent • Targeted use of prosodic elements • International style of speaking • Experienced speaker presenting in a fluid way

4. Final Conclusions

"Choosing texts for interpreting practice is a task which faces every instructor" (DODDS et al. 1997: 100). Working with a thought-out choice of practice texts is essential in order to develop interpreting competence in a systematic way. This task poses the following difficulties: On the one hand, it is not possible to analyse every text with respect to all of the difficulty criteria discussed above. On the other hand, the characteristics provided so far allow a characterization of a text as 'difficult', although a text is rarely equally difficult with respect to every characteristic. Each student also evaluates the difficulty of individual characteristics differently.

All in all, besides the interpreter's knowledge and skills, numerous linguistic factors, cultural factors, environmental factors (…) and delivery-

related factors interact in determining interpreting difficulty. This interaction is so complex that it is generally not easy to predict the overall difficulty of a given speech to a particular interpreter, though specific problems (…) can be anticipated. (GILE 2009: 200)

And yet, the source text is a crucial element in interpreter training and must therefore be given more attention in teaching. In this context, 'skill-appropriate progression' is an important principle of teaching (MOSER-MERCER 2005: 65). It is achieved by increasing the difficulty of the chosen text step by step: "[T]he speeches gradually become more difficult, more formal or structured (or indeed, more problematically incoherent), are delivered faster, and in the later stages, are complicated with other input like unfamiliar proper names, complex numbers, written text and slides" (SETTON 2010: 9). The increasing level of difficulty leads to a step-by-step introduction to an appropriate handling of problems in the source text. These problems should be highlighted and practiced using as many different texts and types of texts as possible, thereby also ensuring a high degree of practical relevance. The difficulty of these texts should be consciously adapted in a targeted manner. For example, the possibilities for preparation may be varied: information about the text and/or the type of text is provided early in order to allow the student to engage with the topic, the speaker and the terminology intensively. The following text on the same topic, possibly also by the same speaker, can then be more difficult overall. The information about the text can also be provided in the short term while allowing the group of students to discuss what texts are to be expected, what content it may have and what style it may be presented in. This knowledge provides the students with the impression of not being completely surprised by the text. Replacing difficult, less well-known words with easier, more familiar terms can also modify a text. Varying the form of presentation or using the voice and body in different ways also allows the teacher to vary the text and therefore to control the level of difficulty.

It is crucial to aim towards a learning objective, which is transparent to the students. A text presented at high speed does not have to lead to a frustrating experience if the purpose of the exercise is explained to the students in advance, in this case for example to arrive at a sensible compression of the text. Differentiation between simultaneous and consecutive training is certainly also useful when it comes to selecting texts. Consecutive interpreting contains the additional capacity-consuming factor of note taking which has a strong individual component and requires well-thought out instruction at the beginning of training (cf. GENTILE 1991: 346; see DINGFELDER STONE (07) in this volume). Beginners often have difficulties "mehrere *verschiedene* Schwierigkeiten [...] gleichzeitig unter Kontrolle zu bekommen"[4] (KÖNIGS 1986: 11, emphasis in original). It is therefore all the more important to select texts for beginners in consecutive interpreting "deren lebensweltlicher Hintergrund möglichst problemlos ist, [...] deren Textstruktur relativ einfach und deren Satzkonstruktionen überschaubar sind"[5] (KÖNIGS 1986: 11).

The selection of texts for interpreter training has a major impact on the acquisition of interpreting competencies and strategies. A carefully chosen selection confronts the students with interpreting difficulties and problems in a targeted manner and requires them to develop strategies for solving them. It significantly influences the students' motivation as well as their learning process and success. Text selection is therefore a highly crucial component of interpreter training theory. It is deserving of much more attention than it has received in the past.

Translated from German by Yann Kiraly

---

4 "managing multiple different difficulties at once"
5 "with real-world background that is as unproblematic as possible, in which textual structures are relatively easy and where sentence structure is straightforward"

References

ALBL-MIKASA, Michaela (2013): "Teaching Globish? The Need for an ELF Pedagogy in Interpreter Training", *International Journal of Interpreter Education* 5(1), 3-16.
ANDERSON, John R. (2007[6]): *Kognitive Psychologie*. Heidelberg: Spektrum.
ARDITO, Giuliana (1999): "The Systematic Use of Impromptu Speeches in Training Interpreting Students", *The Interpreters' Newsletter* 9, 177-189.
BÜHLER, Hildegund (1989): "Discourse Analysis and the Spoken Text – a Critical Analysis of Performance of Advanced Interpretation Students". In: GRAN, Laura & DODDS, John (eds.): *The Theoretical and Practical Aspects of Teaching Conference Interpreting*. Udine: Campanotto Editore, 131-135.
BÜLOW MØLLER, Anne-Marie (2003): "Second-Hand Emotion: Interpreting Attitudes", *The Interpreters' Newsletter* 12, 1-36.
CHERNOV, Ghelly V. (2002): "Semantic Aspects of Psycholinguistic Research in Simultaneous Interpretation". In: PÖCHHACKER, Franz & SHLESINGER, Miriam (eds.): *The Interpreting Studies Reader*. London/New York: Routledge, 98-109.
DODDS, John; KATAN, David; AARUP, Hanna; GRINGIANI, Angela; RICCARDI, Alessandra; SCHWEDA NICHOLSON, Nancy & VIAGGIO, Sergio (1997): "The Interaction between Research and Training". In: GAMBIER, Yves; GILE, Daniel & TAYLOR, Christopher (eds.): *Conference Interpreting: Current Trends in Research; Proceedings of the International Conference on 'Interpreting: What Do We Know and How?' (Turku, August 25-27, 1994)*. Amsterdam/Philadelphia: John Benjamins, 89-107.
FILLMORE, Charles J. (1977): "Scenes-and-Frames Semantics". In: ZAMPOLLI, Antonio (ed.): *Linguistic Structures Processing*. Amsterdam: North Holland, 55-81.
GARWOOD, Christopher John (2002): "Autonomy of the Interpreted Text". In: GARZONE, Giuliana & VIEZZI, Maurizio (eds.): *Interpreting in the 21st Century: Challenges and Opportunities; Selected Papers From the 1st Forlì Conference on Interpreting Studies, 9-11 November 2000*. Amsterdam/Philadelphia: John Benjamins, 267-276.
GARZONE, Giuliana (2000): "Textual Analysis and Interpreting Research", *The Interpreters' Newsletter* 10, 69-88.
GENTILE, Adolfo (1991): "The Application of Theoretical Constructs from a Number of Disciplines for the Development of a Methodology of Teaching in Interpreting and Translating", *Meta* 36(2-3), 344-351.
GERVER, David (2002): "The Effect of Source Language Presentation Rate on the Performance of Simultaneous Conference Interpreters". In: PÖCHHACKER, Franz & SHLESINGER, Miriam (eds.): *The Interpreting Studies Reader*. London: Routledge, 53-66.
GILE, Daniel (1984): "Les noms propres en interprétation simultanée", *Multilingua* 3-2, 79-85.
GILE, Daniel (1988): "Le partage de l'attention et le 'modèle d'effort' en interprétation simultanée", *The Interpreters' Newsletter* 1, 4-22.

GILE, Daniel (2009): *Basic Concepts and Models for Interpreter and Translator Training*. Amsterdam/Philadelphia: John Benjamins.

HEINE, Manfred J. (2000): "Effektives Selbststudium – Schlüssel zum Erfolg in der Dolmetscherausbildung". In: KALINA, Sylvia; BUHL, Silke & GERZYMISCH-ARBOGAST, Heidrun (eds.): *Dolmetschen: Theorie – Praxis – Didaktik; mit ausgewählten Beiträgen der Saarbrücker Symposien*. St. Ingbert: Röhrig, 213-230.

Hönig, Hans G. (2003): "Piece of Cake – or Hard to Take?" In: NORD, Britta & SCHMITT, Peter A. (ed.): *Traducta Navis: Festschrift zum 60. Geburtstag von Christiane Nord*. Tübingen: Stauffenburg, 69-82.

HÖNIG, Hans G. (2011) "Sinngebung beim Dolmetschen". In: HAGEMANN, Susanne: *Übersetzen lernt man nicht durch Übersetzen: Translationswissenschaftliche Aufsätze 1976-2004*. Berlin: SAXA, 260-277.

JONES, Roderick (1998): *Conference Interpreting Explained*. Manchester: St. Jerome.

KALINA, Sylvia (2000): "Interpreting Competences as a Basis and a Goal for Teaching", *The Interpreters' Newsletter* 10, 3-32.

KALINA, Sylvia (2011): "Maß für Maß. Eine vergleichende Profilanalyse von Diskursen beim Dolmetschen", *trans-kom* 4(2), 161-175.

KAUTZ, Ulrich (2002): *Handbuch Didaktik des Übersetzens und Dolmetschens*. München: Iudicium/Goethe-Institut.s

KIRCHHOFF, Hella (1976): "Das Simultandolmetschen: Interdependenz der Variablen im Dolmetschprozeß, Dolmetschmodelle und Dolmetschstrategien". In: DRESCHER, Horst W. & SCHEFFZEK, Signe (eds.): *Theorie und Praxis des Übersetzens und Dolmetschens; Referate und Diskussionsbeiträge des internationalen Kolloquiums am Fachbereich Angewandte Sprachwissenschaft der Johannes Gutenberg-Universität Mainz in Germersheim (2.-4. Mai 1975)*. Frankfurt a. M.: Peter Lang, 59-71.

KIRCHHOFF, Hella (2002): "Simultaneous Interpreting: Interdependence of Variables in the Interpreting Process, Interpreting Models and Interpreting Strategies". In: PÖCHHACKER, Franz & SHLESINGER, Miriam (eds.): *The Interpreting Studies Reader*. London: Routledge, 111-119.

KÖNIGS, Frank G. (1986): "Der Vorgang des Übersetzens: Theoretische Modelle und praktischer Vollzug", *Lebende Sprachen* Band 31, Heft 1, 5-12.

KOHN, Kurt & KALINA, Sylvia (1996): "The Strategic Dimension of Interpreting", *Meta* 41(1), 118-138. http://www.erudit.org/revue/meta/1996/v41/n1/003333ar.pdf (20.03.2014)

KONDO, Masaomi & TEBBLE, Helen (1997): "Intercultural Communication, Negotiation and Interpreting". In: GAMBIER, Yves; GILE, Daniel & TAYLOR, Christopher (eds.): *Conference Interpreting: Current Trends in Research*. Amsterdam/Philadelphia: John Benjamins,149-166.

KUTZ, Wladimir (2007): "Korrektives Dolmetschen", *Lebende Sprachen* 2007(1), 18-34. http://www.degruyter.com/view/j/les.2007.52.issue-1/les.2007.18/les.2007.18.xml (29.03.2014).

KUTZ, Wladimir (2010): *Dolmetschkompetenz: Was muss der Dolmetscher wissen und können?* Berlin: Europäischer Universitätsverlag.

MAZZETTI, Andrea (1999): "The Influence of Segmental and Prosodic Deviations on Source-Text Comprehension in Simultaneous Interpretation", *The Interpreters' Newsletter* 9, 125-147.

MEULEMAN, Chris & VAN BESIEN, Fred (2009): "Coping with Extreme Speech Conditions in Simultaneous Interpreting", *Interpreting* 11(1), 20-34.

MOSER-MERCER, Barbara (2005): "Challenges to Interpreter Training". In: MAYER, Felix (ed.): *20 Jahre Transform: Koordinierung von Praxis und Lehre des Dolmetschens und Übersetzens*. Hildesheim: Georg Olms, 61-72.

NOLAN, James (2005): *Interpretation. Techniques and Exercices*. Clevedon: Multilingual Matters Ltd.

PÖCHHACKER, Franz (1994): *Simultandolmetschen als komplexes Handeln*. Tübingen: Gunter Narr.

POYATOS, Fernando (2002): *Nonverbal Communication across Disciplines, Volume 1: Culture, Sensory Interaction, Speech, Conversation*. Amsterdam/New York: John Benjamins.

PRUNČ, Erich (2007): *Entwicklungslinien der Translationswissenschaft. Von den Asymmetrien der Sprachen zu den Asymmetrien der Macht*. Berlin: Frank & Timme.

RICCARDI, Alessandra; MARINUZZI, Guido & ZECCHIN, Stefano (1998): "Interpretation and Stress", *The Interpreters' Newsletter* 8, 93-106.

RUCCI, Marco (1999): "Working with Register in the Classroom: the Spanish Case", *The Interpreters' Newsletter* 9, 191-198.

SEILER DE DUQUE, Dagmar (1997): "Übersetzerische Kompetenz und Textauswahl im Übersetzungsunterricht Deutsch – Spanisch – Deutsch für Anfänger". In: FLEISCHMANN, Eberhard; KUTZ, Wladimir & SCHMITT, Peter A. (eds.): *Translationsdidaktik: Grundfragen der Übersetzungswissenschaft*. Tübingen: Gunter Narr, 109-114.

SELESKOVITCH, Danica (1978): *Interpreting for International Conferences*. [übersetzt aus dem Französischen von Stephanie Dailey und E. Norman McMillan]. Washington, D.C.: Pen and Booth.

SELESKOVITCH, Danica & LEDERER, Marianne (1989): *Pédagogie Raisonnée de l'Interprétation*. Paris: Didier Erudition.

SETTON, Robin (2001): "Deconstructing SI: a Contribution to the Debate on Component Processes", *The Interpreters' Newsletter* 11, 1-26.

SETTON, Robin (2010): "From Practice to Theory and Back in Interpreting: the Pivotal Role of Training", *The Interpreters' Newsletter* 15, 1-18.

SHLESINGER, Miriam (2003): "Effects of Presentation Rate on Working Memory in Simultaneous Interpreting", *The Interpreters' Newsletter* 12, 37-49.

TAYLOR TORSELLO, Carol; GALLINA, Sandra; SIDIROPOULOU, Maria; TAYLOR, Christopher; TEBBLE, Helen & VUORIKOSKI, Anna-Riitta (1997): "Linguistics, Discourse Analysis and Interpretation". In: GAMBIER, Yves; GILE, Daniel & TAYLOR, Christopher (eds.): *Conference Interpreting: Current Trends in Research; Proceedings of the International Conference on 'Interpreting: What Do We Know and How?' (Turku, August 25-27, 1994)*. Amsterdam/Philadelphia: John Benjamins, 167-186.

TIJUS, Charles Albert (1997): "Understanding for Interpreting, Interpreting for Understanding". In: GAMBIER, Yves; GILE, Daniel & TAYLOR, Christopher (eds.): *Conference Interpreting: Current Trends in Research; Proceedings of the International Conference on 'Interpreting: What Do We Know and How?' (Turku, August 25-27, 1994).* Amsterdam/Philadelphia: John Benjamins, 29-48.

VAN BESIEN, Fred (1999): "Anticipation in Simultaneous Interpretation", *Meta* 44(2), 250-259.

VAN DAM, Ine-Marie (1989): "Strategies of Simultaneous Interpretation: A Methodology for the Training of Simultaneous Interpreters". In: GRAN, Laura & DODDS, John (eds.): *The Theoretical and Practical Aspects of Teaching Conference Interpretation.* Udine: Campanotto, 167-176.

VIAGGIO, Sergio (1997): "Kinesics and the simultaneous interpreter: The advantages of listening with one's eyes and speaking with one's body". In: POYATOS, Fernanando (ed.): *Nonverbal Communication and Translation – New Perspectives and Challenges in Literature, Interpretation and the Media.* Amsterdam/Philadelphia: John Benjamins, 283-293.

VIAGGIO, Sergio (2000): "The Overall Importance of the Hermeneutic Package in Teaching Mediated Interlingual Intercultural Communication", *The Interpreters' Newsletter* 10, 129-145.

VIEZZI, Maurizio (2009): "Aspects of Communication Quality in an SI Setting". In: FORSTNER, Martin; LEE-JAHNKE, Hannelore & SCHMITT, Peter A. (eds.): *CIUTI-Forum 2008: Enhancing Translation Quality: Ways, Means, Methods.* Bern: Lang, 365-375.

WEALE, Edna (1997): "From Babel to Brussels: Conference Interpreting and the Art of the Impossible". In: POYATOS, Fernanando (ed.): *Nonverbal Communication and Translation – New Perspectives and Challenges in Literature, Interpretation and the Media.* Amsterdam/Philadelphia: John Benjamins, 295-312.

Anticipation, Segmentation ... Stalling? How to Teach Interpreting Strategies

STEPHANIE KADER
kader@uni-mainz.de
Johannes Gutenberg University Mainz/Germersheim, Germany

SABINE SEUBERT
seubert@uni-mainz.de
Johannes Gutenberg University Mainz/Germersheim, Germany

1. Introduction

The *Oxford Dictionary* 2010 edition defines the term 'strategy' as follows: "A plan of action designed to achieve a longterm or overall aim" (cf. STEVENSON 2010). These elements of planning and goal orientation can also be found in a definition Kalina puts forward for the interpreting context:

A strategy is goal-oriented, so that the goal determines the amount and thoroughness of processing. It may be consciously used but may also have become automatic in so far as the processor will not have to make any cognitive decision. (KALINA 1992: 253)

This definition suggests that the overall interpreting process is made up of individual actions, of which some are performed consciously and others unconsciously. Therefore, in order to be able to interpret successfully, a good awareness of all available individual strategies is crucial.

The overall aim of any interpreting strategy is successful interpretation. This means that it is the interpreter's responsibility to ensure that all communication needs are met: The interpretation has to be appropriate for both the setting and the target audience. To achieve this and maintain a steadily high level of quality throughout their performance, the interpreters need to apply their cognitive resources as efficiently and economically as possible (cf. DONATO 2003: 102). The existence of individual strategies applicable to the interpreting process and therefore also to interpreter training has already been acknowledged in numerous scientific publications (cf. KALINA 1996: 276; cf. NIEMANN 2012). However, amongst these, there has been a marked difference in approach and emphasis (for a general overview see DONATO 2003: 106f; cf. NIEMANN 2012: 6).

Interpreter training does not consist solely of practising with contextualised speeches. What is equally important is to equip students with the skills and tools they need for successful interpretation. This entails imparting declarative knowledge – i.e. about the individual strategies – and enabling students to independently apply this knowledge, thus turning the strategies into procedural knowledge. Declarative knowledge refers to the body of knowledge a person acquires during their lifetime and which they can draw on explicitly and consciously (cf. ANDERSON 2007[6]: 285). According to Anderson, procedural knowledge means that an interpreter needs to know how to perform a task (ANDERSON 2007[6]: 283). Because procedural knowledge has been internalised and is not consciously remembered, accessing this type of knowledge is more difficult than retrieving simple factual knowledge.

The aim of this chapter, therefore, is to compile all the available general interpreting strategies and to show how they are jointly applied during the interpreting process, including by means of graphical representation. In describing the individual strategies, it will be noted where in the overall process and in which mode of interpreting – simultaneous or consecutive – they are particularly relevant. We will also explore the functional relationship between the different strategies. This is followed by a description of the didactic adaptation of the strategies for the three fundamental learning levels in interpreter training.

2. Interpreting Strategies: Strategy Identification and Functional Relationships

The interpreter already starts applying strategies to the interpreting process in the run-up to the interpreting assignment, not just when actually interpreting (cf. KALINA 2011: 163).

2.1 Preparation and Macro-Strategies

The interpreter does preparation and research work ahead of the actual interpreting job, for example by revisiting past assignments on the same topic[1]. In this way, the interpreter prepares for the conference theme and setting, the anticipated speeches and terminology as well as the colleague(s) they will be working with – in a word, the overall context of the assignment[2]. This preparatory work constitutes a key strategic step without which initial planning and expectation management would not be possible (cf. ANDRES 2011: 86). In the diagram below, this stage is represented by the broad arrow on the left feeding into the circle which contains the overall process. Planning and expectations are part of the macro-strategies[3] which determine and form part of the entire interpreting process.

- *Planning,* on a macro-strategic level, means that the interpreter decides on their approach: First regarding the conference itself, and then during the conference regarding the individual speeches. With professional interpreters, this will not just be a result of the preparation done in the run-up to the conference, but also of a certain routine based on previous conference experience.
- *Expectations,* on a macro-strategic level, means that the interpreter is able – due to the above-mentioned routine or their pre-conference preparation work – to anticipate certain topics, speakers and speeches. The knowledge the interpreter has acquired both through previous assignments and specific preparation enables them to come to an inference regarding possible speech topics.
- *Inferencing* thus also falls into the category of macro-strategies to be taught to students in interpreter training. However, inferencing is more of an unconscious process than a teachable strategy[4].
- Continuous *monitoring*, i.e. analysing and checking all plans and expectations for accuracy, allows for adjustments where necessary. For example, if the conference's keynote speech changes because the invited speaker falls ill, the interpreter needs to prepare for a new

---

1 Kalina calls this the "pre-process (pre-process prerequisites)" (KALINA 2009: 177).
2 Pöchhacker calls this the "hypertext" (PÖCHHACKER 1994: 48).
3 For a definition of macro-strategies, cf. e.g. HÖNIG 1993/2011:133.
4 Cf. Hönig's reference to the "uncontrolled workspace" (HÖNIG 1993).

speaker. Insufficient preparation of conference-specific issues and terminology can also lead to skewed expectations which the interpreter will need to correct. These necessary *corrections* can therefore be regarded as learnable and hence teachable macro-strategies.

2.2 Micro-Strategies

When regarding the interpreting process as divided into the subprocesses of understanding the source text, transferring the content and its meaning from one language to another, and producing a target text[5], especially the processes of understanding and language production are linked to so-called micro-strategies, which allow the interpreter to deal with speech-inherent issues. This kind of strategic planning is initially triggered by a text signal, i.e. a lexeme or phrase that is being recognised and so initialises the comprehension process.

Every level of the process consists of bottom-up-processes, i.e. immediate input processing, and top-down-processes (empirical knowledge interacting with new information). (LAUTERBACH 2009: 24; own translation)

The micro-strategies below are applicable to all language pairs:

- *Chunking:* One micro-strategy which students are usually able to grasp quickly and which is easy to teach is *chunking*. This means recognising and translating individual units of meaning contained within a ST sentence in a way that does not adhere to the original sentence structure (cf. e.g. WÖRRLEIN 2007: 34ff; MAŁGORZEWICZ 2003: 127; SEEBER & KERZEL 2012: 231). Chunking is especially useful when dealing with language pairs that are very different syntactically, as it frees up working memory capacity. To practise this strategy, students are asked to reproduce all the information from the original sentence they were able to understand when listening, and to do so in individual sentences. In this way, they also train their rhetorical abilities, or in this case, their ability to paraphrase (see below). Chunking is a useful strategy both for the simultaneous and consecutive modes of interpreting. However, the stage in which this strategy is mainly applied is different for each of the two modes: In consecutive interpreting,

---

5   Hereinafter shortened to 'ST' and 'TT'.

the interpreter uses the comprehension stage to break down complex ideas into single units and to note them down accordingly. In simultaneous interpreting, on the other hand, the production stage is used to produce shorter sentences.

We shall use an example to illustrate this point: The following sentence is taken from the speech Barack Obama gave at the memorial ceremony for Nelson Mandela which took place in Johannesburg[6] in December 2013: "Given the sweep of his life, the scope of his accomplishments, the adoration that he so rightly earned, it's tempting, I think, to remember Nelson Mandela as an icon, smiling and serene, detached from the tawdry affairs of lesser men".

Possible (extreme) chunking: Nelson Mandela led an extraordinary life. He accomplished a lot. He was adored. He earned that adoration. He is seen as an icon. He often appeared detached from daily affairs.

- *Paraphrasing*: This means rephrasing an idea[7] if "[…] the interpreter can't think of a particular target language term or doesn't know the correct expression" (WÖRRLEIN 2007: 51; own translation), or for "syntactic simplification" (WÖRRLEIN 2007: 48; own translation). It is important, however, that the core message remains intact and the linguistic register of the ST is preserved in the paraphrased TT expression. The strategy of paraphrasing is therefore applied exclusively during the production stage, but is equally important both in simultaneous and in consecutive interpreting.[8]

The above sentence might be paraphrased as follows: "Considering his extraordinary life and all the things he accomplished, considering also how the South African people honored him, it's tempting to see him as an icon, always smiling and at peace with the world, as if he had risen above the mundanities of everyday life".

- *Flexible décalage (Ear-Voice-Span, EVS)*: In order to be able to employ the strategies of chunking and paraphrasing, the interpreter first

---

6 All the sample sentences used in this chapter are taken from the speech Barack Obama gave at the memorial ceremony for Nelson Mandela in Johannesburg on December 10, 2013: "What A Magnificent Soul It Was", *Vital Speeches of the Day* 80(2) (2014): Business Source Premier, 30-32.

7 Gile calls this "reformulation tactics" (GILE 2009: 206f).

8 In consecutive interpreting, a paraphrase may also be noted down during the notation stage. However, note-taking strategies will not be covered in this chapter (see DINGFELDER STONE (07) in this volume).

needs to know what has been said. This is where the *Ear-Voice-Span* (EVS) comes in. Being able to vary one's EVS is a key requirement for successful interpretation. For example, complex passages (lists, names, numbers) demand a short EVS, whereas more abstract ideas require a longer EVS. In simultaneous interpreting, the EVS initially applies to the comprehension stage and subsequently ensures the ideal – i.e. most resource-efficient – time delay between the speaker's utterances and the interpreter's output. In consecutive interpreting, the EVS is also a crucial element of the comprehension stage and allows for delayed note-taking. Interpreting students need to be made aware that in simultaneous interpreting, a flexible EVS will enable them to be more in control of their target language production and to use clearer and more idiomatic expressions, whereas in consecutive interpreting, a flexible décalage allows for more sensible note-taking with a view to improved target language production (cf. ANDRES 2002: 183f; see ORLANDO in this volume).

- *Stalling*: This strategy can be applied to moments during which the interpreter is waiting to receive fresh information to be able to continue. Stalling can mean a silent, i.e. nonverbal and nonvocal, pause on behalf of the interpreter, or an instance where neutral[9] expressions are used (see example below) or some facts repeated by the interpreter to fill the pause while waiting for the next crucial bit of information (cf. DONATO 2003: 106; cf. SEEBER & KERZEL 2012: 229ff; cf. SEEBER 2011: 193). In simultaneous interpreting, verbal stalling can make sense so as to avoid a longer pause which might unsettle one's listeners.

    Example: "There is a word in South Africa – Ubuntu – [this, Ladies and Gentlemen, is] a word that captures Mandela's greatest gift: his recognition that we are all bound together in ways that are invisible to the eye [...]" The exclamation in square brackets might be used as 'padding' in simultaneous interpreting while the interpreter waits for the word 'Ubuntu' to be explained.

    However, stalling might also be used by the interpreter as an "emergency strategy" (KALINA 1998: 119) if they haven't been able to

---

9   This has been described as e.g. "stalling by neutral material" (DONATO 2003: 110) or "producing neutral padding" (SEEBER & KERZEL 2012: 231).

grasp the next message quickly enough. In consecutive interpreting, verbal or nonverbal stalling is used consciously – or to make up for a deficit – in the production stage, when the interpreter encounters problems in reading their notes or finding the right expression.

- *Generalising:* Generalising as a sensible and conscious strategy can be resorted to in both modes of interpreting whenever the interpreter wants to boil down complex and detailed ideas to a more general message. Often, however, generalisation is used when the interpreter sees no other way to cope with a particular lexical or semantic problem (cf. WÖRRLEIN 2007: 51). If this strategy is used excessively during the production stage, the interpretation risks being watered down.

  Example: "There is a word in South Africa – Ubuntu – a word that captures Mandela's greatest gift: his recognition that we are all bound together in ways that are invisible to the eye; that there is a oneness to humanity; that we achieve ourselves by sharing ourselves with others, and caring for those around us". This sentence might be generalised as follows: "There is a word in South Africa which describes the fact that we are all connected and that we achieve that connection by caring for one another".

- *Simplification:* Simplification is a more extreme form of generalisation. It can be used as a legitimate strategy in both modes of interpreting if, for example, the interpreter can tell from the listeners' reactions that they would no longer be able follow a presentation if it were to be translated using the same level of technical terminology or the same style as the ST (cf. KALINA 1998: 120).

  Example: "But we remember the gestures, large and small – introducing his jailers as honored guests at his inauguration; taking a pitch in a Springbok uniform; turning his family's heartbreak into a call to confront HIV/AIDS – that revealed the depth of his empathy and his understanding". A simplified version might be: "But we remember how he reached out to his political opponents and we remember his efforts in the fight for equality and against HIV/AIDS".

  However, simplification might also be employed as an emergency or erroneous strategy if the interpreter is unable to translate what is being said in sufficient detail because of a comprehension deficit. This deficit could be rooted in either a language or content comprehension problem.

- *Approximation:* Approximation is another form of simplification. If the interpreter is not immediately able to recall the correct target language term, they can make use of approximation, i.e. employ a semantically related term until they can remember the exact expression to use in their interpretation (cf. KALINA 1998: 120; RICCARDI 1996: 221). This could also mean referring to general quantities rather than specific numbers. This strategy can apply to the production stage of both modes of interpreting.

  Example: If, in the sample sentence above, the interpreter cannot think of the target language equivalents for 'inauguration' and 'uniform', they might use the expressions 'when he took office' or 'when he became the President of South Africa' and 'shirt' or 'jersey' etc. as approximations. This can also be regarded as another example of paraphrasing (see above).

- *Transcoding:* This concept was developed by Seleskovitch when interpreting studies were still fairly young (cf. SELESKOVITCH 1975: 9). As with the ones above, the interpreter must be careful to apply this strategy in a way that is acceptable. It can be reasonably applied in simultaneous interpreting or during note-taking in consecutive interpreting in order to ensure the quick rendering of a proper noun, a place name or a number without semantic processing (cf. KALINA 1998: 118; MAŁGORZEWICZ 2003: 127f; GILE 2009: 208).

  Example: "But like other early giants of the ANC – the Sisulus and Tambos – Madiba disciplined his anger and channeled his desire to fight into organization, and platforms, and strategies for action […]". Depending on their general knowledge, interpreting students can repeat the acronym *ANC* or the proper names *Sisulu* and *Tambo* phonetically.

  If, on the other hand, an entire syntactic structure is being transcoded, or an unknown word reproduced onomatopoeically (i.e. repeated in the target language (TL) in exactly the same way it was uttered in the source language (SL)), then this strategy isn't being properly employed. In this case, it no longer aids comprehension but leads to clumsy or even unintelligible expressions and to syntactic and semantic distortions (cf. e.g. GILE 2009: 164f)

- *Expanding:* This strategy may be employed during the production stage of both modes of interpreting. Additional – content- or culture-related – information is being added by the interpreter to make it easier for the audience to understand certain points (cf. DONATO 2003: 107).

Example: In the sample sentence above, the abbreviation *ANC* could be turned into *African National Congress,* whereas *Sisulu* and *Tambo* might be supplemented with their respective first names *Walter* and *Oliver*, or elaborated on by explaining that they were "a fellow inmate on Robben Island for many years" and "the former ANC president" respectively.

In simultaneous interpreting, the application of this strategy depends to a large extent on the time factor, i.e. the pace set by the speaker – much more so than in consecutive interpreting. Expanding as a sensible part of note-taking strategy can consist of, for example, the interpreter noting down an addition in the relevant place, such as a humorous interjection, a change of speakers, and so on, which can then be formulated during the production stage.

- *Completion:* After hearing a certain bit of information, the interpreter memorises and stores it, only to retrieve and vocalise it later (cf. WÖRRLEIN 2007: 53). The information is added in a different place than in the original speech, and this is accomplished through the interpreter's working memory or echoic memory[10]. Strategic completion can be applied during the production stage both in simultaneous and consecutive interpreting and shows advanced interpreting skills.
- *Condensing:* With this strategy, one also needs to be careful to differentiate between employing it deliberately and using it as an emergency strategy to make up for a deficit (cf. e.g. KALINA 1998: 119; WÖRRLEIN 2007: 49). Deliberate condensing means picking up redundancies in the ST in the comprehension process, filtering them out during the transfer of content and meaning from one language to another – or, in consecutive interpreting, during note-taking – and consciously not repeating them at the production stage. What cannot be considered sensible condensing, however, is the omission of meaningful ST elements because of the interpreter's inability to cope, if such omissions lead to an incomplete and incoherent TT and thus to unsuccessful interpretation.

---

10 The echoic memory enables the storing of acoustic and phonetic information for several seconds.

Example: "We know that, like South Africa, the United States had to overcome centuries of racial subjugation. As was true here, it took sacrifice – the sacrifice of countless people, known and unknown, to see the dawn of a new day". A condensed version might be: "We know that both our countries had to overcome racial subjugation. Sacrifices were made by many to bring that change about".

- *Prioritising:* When confronted with a fast speaker or a presentation that is rapidly read off a manuscript, the interpreter might have to opt for a sensible way of condensing the information, i.e. focussing on the most important messages and leaving out redundancies as well as less crucial ideas and phrases. This requires a filtering mechanism to sort important messages from less important ones (cf. KALINA 1998: 120; WÖRRLEIN 2007: 49f). This filtering mechanism is called *prioritising,* and the strategy therefore applies to the comprehension stage. It allows the interpreter to boil the received information down to its key components, i.e. the meaningful elements of a particular statement, in order to convey the message as intended by the speaker and to maintain general coherence and maximum completeness of content. In consecutive interpreting, applying this strategy is easier than in simultaneous interpreting, for two reasons and in two stages: During the note-taking stage, the interpreter can work with a suitable *décalage* (see above) and may subsequently choose not to take down any redundancies or less important elements – or else to mark them directly on the note pad with a view to leaving them out of the interpretation. As regards the production stage, employing this strategy is also easier in consecutive interpreting because the interpreter has already reviewed the text and therefore knows of any potential elements to be left out. Though the simultaneous interpreter will not have received the whole of the speech yet, prioritising can nonetheless be a sensible strategy: The core messages are condensed and translated while keeping the loss of substance to a minimum.

Example: "And because he was not only a leader of a movement but a skillful politician, the Constitution for South Africa that emerged was worthy of this multiracial democracy, true to his vision of laws that protect minority as well as majority rights, and the precious freedoms of every South African". Focussing on the key bits of information, a possible interpretation might be: "Due to his skills as a

political leader, he was able to negotiate a constitution which protects the rights of every South African".
- *Anticipating/Inferencing:* Word order in German tends to be a complex issue (SVO sentence structure, multi-clause sentences, etc.), which is why the strategy of *anticipating* is discussed as an important one in many relevant publications (c.p. e.g. SELESKOVITCH 1975: 128; ILG 1978: 85; WILSS 1978: 346; KALINA 1998: 117; MAŁGORZEWICZ 2003: 131; SCHREIBER 2004: 90; GILE 2009: 173; NIEMANN 2012: 3). Because of interpreters' linguistic competence, certain grammatical signals are all they need to anticipate and complete the word order (cf. GILE 2009: 173) or e.g. separable compound verbs in German. This anticipation according to linguistic signals involves a bottom-up process.

In addition to this kind of linguistic anticipation, there is another form of anticipation, which is based not on language, but on content: inferencing from one's world and contextual knowledge.

Besides so-called 'linguistic anticipation' good knowledge of the conference situation, of the subject and of the speaker and good understanding of the unfolding statements often make it possible to anticipate ideas and information expressed in speeches. (GILE 2009: 174)

Gile calls this kind of inferencing "extralinguistic anticipation" (GILE 2009: 174), and Kalina and Kautz add another dimension to it, which is the correction of acoustic interference and the completion of sentences left unfinished by the speaker (cf. KALINA 1998: 116; KAUTZ 2002: 325)[11]. This is a compensation strategy used both in simultaneous and consecutive interpreting. Kalina describes this as anticipation via the "formation of hypotheses":

Based on inferences they have reached and other text-bound and text-independent indicators, the interpreter is able (via mental modelling) to form hypotheses and anticipate certain utterances even before they are expressed by the speaker. [...] A form of anticipation which is specific to simultaneous interpreting is active TT production on the basis

---

11 Inferencing of missing information happens as a top-down process during the comprehension stage. The information is then added in the production stage.

of the formation of hypotheses, taking place even before the equivalent ST element has been uttered. (KALINA 1998: 117, emphasis in original; own translation)

We shall take one of the sentences used above as an example for inferencing: "Given the sweep of his life, the scope of his accomplishments, the adoration that he so rightly earned, it's tempting I think to remember Nelson Mandela as an icon, smiling and serene, detached from the tawdry affairs of lesser men. But Madiba himself strongly resisted such a lifeless portrait. Instead, Madiba insisted on sharing with us his doubts and his fears; his miscalculations along with his victories". The expression "it's tempting to think" already suggests a subsequent qualification of the statement. This is indeed what happens, the qualification being introduced by a 'but' and explained further in a sentence starting with 'instead'. Through inferencing, i.e. drawing on empirical knowledge, the interpreter concludes that 'Madiba' is Nelson Mandela's traditional Xhosa clan name.

Examples of the above-mentioned lexical semantic signals are the following passages: "It was precisely because he could admit to imperfection […] that we loved him so". "He tells us what is possible not just in the pages of history books, but in our own lives as well". Because of their language skills, the interpreter knows that the expression 'precisely because' is always followed by a proposition starting with 'that' and that the phrase 'not just' will necessarily be followed by 'but', and therefore anticipates this sentence structure.

- *Monitoring/Output Control:* Quite apart from the above-mentioned monitoring at the macro-strategic level, the interpreter also undertakes continuous *monitoring* at the micro-strategic level in the sense of language- and content-related *output control.* This means the interpreter checks their language for grammatical correctness as well as cohesion and coherence, and their translated content for plausibility and accuracy. If this *monitoring* throws up a problem or deficit, the interpreter can and should correct themselves.
- *Correction,* therefore, is another strategy, which needs to be brought to the students' attention. In simultaneous interpreting, correction happens at the production stage, for example to remedy so-called *false starts* (cf. WÖRRLEIN 2007: 53). In consecutive interpreting, by

contrast, the interpreter might make corrections as early as the note-taking stage, when an increasingly clearer understanding of a presentation necessitates an adjustment to the notes they took earlier on (cf. KALINA 1998: 120).

Whilst these micro-strategies can be applied to any and all language pairs, it is important to mention that there are also those micro-strategies which can only be applied when working with specific language pairs. For target languages which rely heavily on nominalisation, like e.g. German, the interpreter needs to turn source language infinitive and participial constructions as well as relative clauses etc. into nominal phrases and/or compound words for the target audience. Conversely, German nominal phrases can be broken down in the target language, e.g. by turning them into verbal constructions, if necessary by using relative, participial or infinitive constructions[12].

2.3 Strategies: Interplay and Interdependencies

The figure below graphically depicts the interplay of the different macro- and micro-strategies. This diagram can be used to make students aware that the act of interpreting is not a linear process but a complex structure based on synergies between all the different subprocesses and strategies.

---

[12] For more information on unique language characteristics as well as structural differences between languages (using the language pairs French-German and English-German) (cf. NIEMANN 2012: 31ff). For more information on teaching interpreting out of or into a foreign language see CHABASSE & DINGFELDER STONE in this volume.

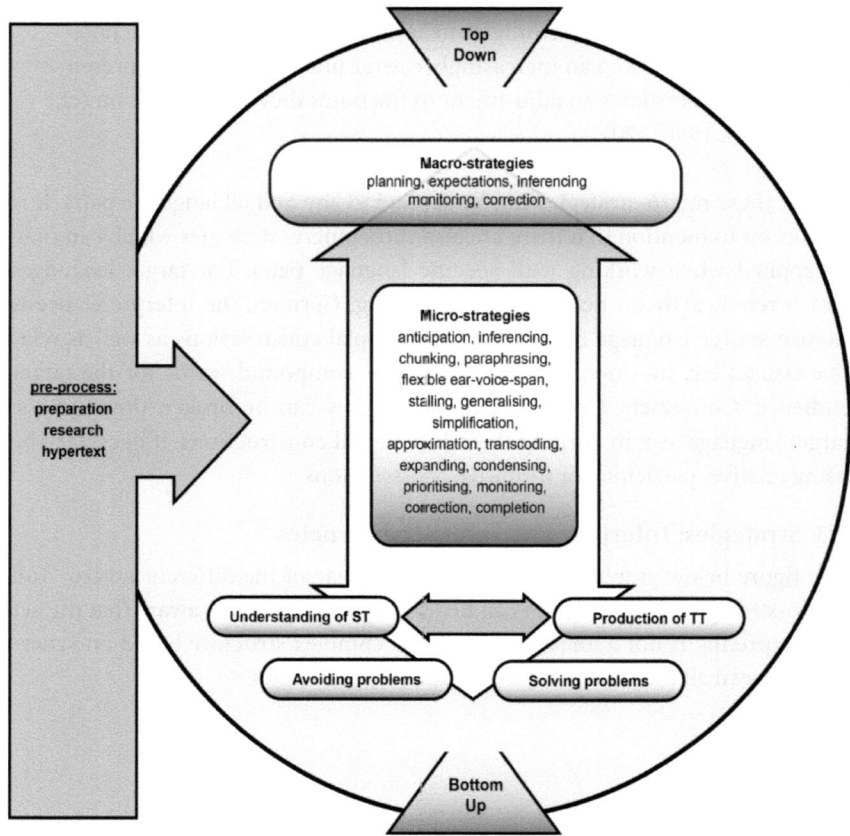

Fig. 1: A model of interpreting strategies

The figure is designed to illustrate the interdependency and interplay of all the different strategies during the interpreting process (outer circle). Every interpreting process consists of understanding the source text and producing an accurate target text by skilfully managing one's cognitive resources, while at the same time continuously memorising and processing the additional ST input. This is illustrated by the horizontal double-headed arrow in the lower half of the diagram.

The macro-strategies enable the interpreter to prepare for individual concepts or speakers they might be familiar with from previous interpreting assignments, and to activate the relevant micro-strategies. If, however, during the interpretation the interpreter can no longer reach inferences based on their knowledge, they will be forced to revise their expectations and perhaps do more research during the conference in order to be better prepared for the rest of the event. As laid out in the definitions of the individual macro-strategies, they enable the interpreter to quickly grasp source language concepts. If the interpreter can no longer follow what is being said, it means that they initially developed insufficient expectations or false premises on the macro-strategic level. Therefore, expectations and planning need to be adjusted according to the current situation.

Correct implementation of all macro-strategies ideally leads to the avoidance or at least the mitigation of risk before the actual interpreting process has even started so as to minimise the likelihood of problems during interpretation. However, if the interpreter does encounter a problem, they can immediately start the problem-solving process by making the necessary adjustments at the macro-strategic level.

Similar processes are happening at the micro-strategic level: Having internalised all of the micro-strategies, the interpreter can always employ one of the other available strategies to solve sporadic problems and to avoid making the same mistake twice when faced with the same problem, utilizing what Gile calls "coping tactics" (GILE 2009: 191f). In other words: Continuous macro- and micro-strategic monitoring helps the interpreter avoid, solve and repeatedly tackle problems in ST understanding during the entire interpreting assignment.

As the definitions of the micro-strategies have shown, linguistic anticipation and inferencing from empirical knowledge can not only directly kick-start the comprehension process but also, thanks to acquired automatisms, lead to correct interpretation: While the macro-strategies can ensure accurate interpretation in terms of audience and situation, the skilful implementation of all available micro-strategies enables linguistically adequate and correct TT production. If the interpreter realises through their output control that they need to switch to a different micro-strategy to ensure adequate TT production, they can do this, while their macro-strategic monitoring continues to ensure that their TT production remains true to the contents and the speaker.

Smart strategy application can ultimately free up the interpreter's capacity for listening and understanding, if they manage to keep content- and language-related problems at bay from the start. Such rapid input processing will allow them to continue interpreting without too many worries and to either nip further problems in the bud or solve them immediately and adequately. Once a problem is solved, this frees up additional cognitive resources, which in turn enables the interpreter to focus on understanding the next bit of ST. This clearly illustrates the extent of the interdependencies: The above strategies for problem avoidance immediately lead to better TT production. Fluent, complete and accurate TT production in turn frees up cognitive resources which can be used to focus on understanding the ST.

3. Didactic Adaptation of the Strategies

The strategies described in this chapter can prove didactically useful in two ways. For one thing, they can be used as a diagnostic tool. With the aid of these strategies, the reasons for successful or failed interpretation can be pinpointed. For another thing, students are handed a tool through which they can purposefully and gradually improve their interpreting skills according to their learning level, by consistently finding or being made aware of strategy-based problem-solving approaches. At the same time, failed or emergency strategies can be spotted, identified and pointed out to the students: For example, excessive generalising by using a lot of uncalled-for modal particles ('actually', 'approximately', 'perhaps') or the qualification of statements due to a lack of confidence on the part of the interpreter can be regarded as failed strategies (cf. KALINA 1998: 120). It is important to avoid failed strategies from the start, as well as other mistakes often arising from cognitive overload. This includes the usage of incorrect connectors (e.g. 'so' despite the lack of a causal relationship, 'and' without there being a direct link, etc.) as they could result in inconsistencies. Slow speech tempo peppered by sounds of hesitation as well as interferences due to "a lack of contrast between the two languages" (KALINA 1998: 124; own translation) are also issues which the audience might find objectionable.

The first learning level (*Beginners*) is about identifying possible strategies[13] and illustrating them by means of sample sentences. In this first stage of learning, single-language text materials may be used. If the students succeed in applying a particular strategy, actual interpretation could be the next stage within this

---

13 This is about the teaching of declarative knowledge, which Chesterman calls "strategy exemplification" (CHESTERMAN 2000: 83).

learning level. Explaining the strategies by means of sample sentences and texts can, of course, be done either in one language only or in two languages involving a specific language pair. The aim of the lesson might be the application of one or several of the strategies, whereby the students get to practice with suitable speeches or text passages. It can be a good idea to have students interpret a text they know and have prepared several times, asking them to consciously employ a different strategy every time (cf. CHESTERMAN 2000: 84). This is good training for their paraphrasing and rhetorical abilities. By the end of this first learning level, students should be able to identify the strategies they or their peers have been using during interpretation ("strategy recognition" or "strategy analysis" (CHESTERMAN 2000: 83)).

At the second learning level (*Intermediate*), students are expected to be able to convert this declarative knowledge into procedural knowledge (cf. WÖRRLEIN 2007: 41) and, through further practice, master not only individual strategies but also apply them collectively and automatise their usage. Since they know all about the individual strategies, they are able to find their own solutions to certain interpreting issues. The teacher helps out by identifying persisting problems and suggesting exercises to overcome them. Whereas in a beginners' course, the aim of the lesson is usually determined by the teacher, intermediates are able to set their own personal goals as they become aware of their weaknesses and can try and tackle them specifically with the help of the right strategy or strategy combination. This also allows for an increasingly self-determined and independent way of studying.

At the third learning level (*Advanced*), students are expected to have increasingly automatised the strategies, i.e. to be able to apply them almost automatically (cf. CHESTERMAN 2000: 78) and combine them in various and flexible ways during interpretation (cf. CHESTERMAN 2000: 84). This applies to speeches of greater linguistic and textual complexity as well as speakers with a faster speech tempo. If, at this level, the students fail to independently find solutions to interpreting issues and do not succeed at interpreting, the teacher is tasked with identifying the relevant deficits, or having the students diagnose them themselves ("strategy justification" (CHESTERMAN 2000: 84)). These deficits might include insufficient language skills or empirical knowledge as well as poor strategy automatisation or inadequate and therefore resource-intensive application of strategies. This helps motivate students (see ANDRES et al. and BEHR in this volume) and highlights further training possibilities.

4. Concluding Remarks

Part of the didactic mission in interpreter training is to communicate the numerous individual strategies to the students in a way that initially enables them to deliberately practise these strategies in class and for themselves. As the students progress through the various learning levels, they are increasingly able to automatise their strategy usage and to combine these strategies ever more flexibly, whilst minimising the strain on their cognitive resources – over the whole of the interpreting process. Though the various interpreting strategies are explained separately in this chapter, they should be regarded very much as an entity made up of individual strategies all working together. This interplay should be pointed out to students from the very beginning. The aim is for students to not only know all the macro- and micro-strategies, but to have them at their fingertips and be able to recall them automatically, so that different strategies can be flexibly combined. This ensures interpretation at the highest level because it enables the interpreter to keep their cognitive load as light as possible (cf. KALINA 1998: 121; WÖRRLEIN 2007: 27; SEEBER 2011: 190). The resources available to the interpreter during the whole of the interpreting assignment ideally ensure optimal handling of any challenges they may face during the interpreting process (cf. KAUTZ 2002: 325). If the teacher succeeds in preparing their students to master these challenges, Chesterman regards their didactic mission as accomplished:

A good teacher of expertise might then be defined as an expert who normally exercises a given skill at the level of expertise, but who can access his or her conscious rationality at will, *when asked, and verbalise about his or her performance, thus making it accessible to the consciousness of trainees.* (CHESTERMAN 2000: 79, emphasis in original)

Translated from German by Alexandra Reuer

References

ANDERSON, John R. (2007⁶): *Kognitive Psychologie*. Berlin/Heidelberg: Springer.
ANDRES, Dörte (2002): *Konsekutivdolmetschen und Notation*. FASK Publikationen des Fachbereichs Angewandte Sprach- und Kulturwissenschaft der Johannes Gutenberg-Universität Mainz in Germersheim. Frankfurt a. M.: Peter Lang.
ANDRES, Dörte (2011): "Dolmetschwissenschaft zu Beginn des 21. Jahrhunderts: Ein integrativ konzipiertes Dolmetschprozessmodell", *StudiaUniversitatisBabeș-Bolyai. Philologia, 56(1)*, 81-103.
CHESTERMAN, Andrew (2000): "Teaching Strategies for Emancipatory Translation". In: SCHÄFFNER, Christina & ADAB, Beverly (eds.): *Developing Translation Competence*. Amsterdam/Philadelphia: John Benjamins, 77-89.
DONATO, Valentina (2003): "Strategies Adopted by Student Interpreters in SI: A Comparison between the English-Italian and the German-Italian Language-Pairs", *The Interpreters' Newsletter* 12, 101-134.
GILE, Daniel (2009): *Basic Concepts and Models for Interpreter and Translator Training* (Revised Edition). Amsterdam/Philadelphia: John Benjamins.
HÖNIG, Hans G. (1993): "Vom Selbst-Bewusstsein des Übersetzers". In: HÖNIG, Hans G. & HAGEMANN, Susanne (eds.) (2011): *Übersetzen lernt man nicht durch Übersetzen. Translationswissenschaftliche Aufsätze 1976-2004*. Berlin: Saxa, 128-141.
ILG, Gérard (1978): "L'apprentissage de l'interprétation simultanée de l'allemand vers le français", *Parallèles* 1. Cahiers de l'École de Traduction et d'interprétation. Université de Genève, 69-99.
KALINA, Sylvia (1992): "Discourse Processing and Interpreting Strategies – An Approach to the Teaching of Interpreting". In: DOLLERUP, Cay & LODDEGAARD, Anne (eds.): *Teaching Translation and Interpreting. Training, Talent and Experience. Papers from the First Language International Conference, Elsinore, Denmark, 31 May – 2 June 1991* (Copenhagen Studies in Translation). Amsterdam/Philadelphia: John Benjamins, 251-257.
KALINA, Sylvia (1996): "Zum Erwerb strategischer Verhaltensweisen beim Dolmetschen". In: LAUER, Angelika; GERZYMISCH-ARBOGAST, Heidrun; HALLER, Johann & STEINER, Erich (eds.): *Übersetzungswissenschaft im Umbruch. Festschrift für Wolfram Wilss zum 70. Geburtstag*. Tübingen: Gunter Narr, 271-279.
KALINA, Sylvia (1998): *Strategische Prozesse beim Dolmetschen. Theoretische Grundlagen, empirische Fallstudien, didaktische Konsequenzen*. Tübingen: Gunter Narr.
KALINA, Sylvia (2009): "Die Qualität von Dolmetschleistungen aus der Perspektive von Forschung und Kommunikationspartnern". In: AHRENS, Barbara; ČERNÝ, Lothar; KREIN-KÜHLE, Monika & SCHREIBER, Michael (eds.): *Translationswissenschaftliches Kolloquium I. Beiträge zur Übersetzungs- und Dolmetschwissenschaft* (Cologne/Germersheim). FASK Publikationen des Fachbereichs Angewandte Sprach- und Kulturwissenschaft der Johannes Gutenberg-Universität Mainz in Germersheim. Frankfurt a. M.: Peter Lang, 167-191.

KALINA, Sylvia (2011): "Maß für Maß. Eine vergleichende Profilanalyse von Diskursen beim Dolmetschen", *trans-kom* 4(2), 161-175.

KAUTZ, Ulrich (2002): *Handbuch Didaktik des Übersetzens und Dolmetschens*. München: Iudicium/Goethe-Institut.

LAUTERBACH, Eike (2009): *Sprechfehler und Interferenzprozesse beim Dolmetschen*. Frankfurt a. M.: Peter Lang.

MAŁGORZEWICZ, Anna (2003): *Prozessorientierte Dolmetschdidaktik*. Wrocław: Oficyna Wydawnicza ATUT Wrocławskie Wydawnictwo Oświatowe.

NIEMANN, Anja Jane (2012): *Sprachstrukturelle Unterschiede und Strategien im Simultandolmetschen. Eine Untersuchung anhand der Sprachenpaare Französisch-Deutsch und Englisch-Deutsch*. Frankfurt a. M.: Peter Lang.

PÖCHHACKER, Franz (1994): *Simultandolmetschen als komplexes Handeln*. Tübingen: Gunter Narr.

RICCARDI, Alessandra (1996): "Language-specific Strategies in Simultaneous Interpreting". In: DOLLERUP, Cay & APPEL, Vibeke (eds.): *Teaching Translation and Interpreting 3. New Horizons. Papers from the Third Language International Conference. Elsinore, Denmark 9-11 June 1995*. Amsterdam/Philadelphia: John Benjamins, 213-222.

SCHREIBER, Michael (2004): "Kontrastive Linguistik und sprachenpaarbezogene Translationswissenschaft". In: HANSEN, Gyde; MALMKJÆR, Kirsten & GILE, Daniel (eds.): *Claims, Changes and Challenges in Translation Studies. Selected contributions from the EST Congress, Copenhagen 2001*. Amsterdam/Philadelphia: John Benjamins, 83-98.

SEEBER, Kilian G. (2011): "Cognitive load in simultaneous interpreting. Existing theories – new models", *Interpreting* 13(2), 176-204.

SEEBER, Kilian G. & KERZEL, Dirk (2012): "Cognitive load in simultaneous interpreting: model meets data", *International Journal of Bilingualism* 16(2), 228-242.

SELESKOVITCH, Danica (1975): *Language, langues et mémoire*. Paris: Minard.

STEVENSON, Angus (2010): *Oxford Dictionary*. New York: Oxford University Press.

WILSS, Wolfram (1978): "Syntactic Anticipation in German-English Simultaneous Interpreting". In: GERVER, David & SINAIKO, H. Wallace (eds.): *Language Interpretation and Communication*. New York/London: Plenum Press, 343-352.

WÖRRLEIN, Marion (2007): *Der Simultandolmetschprozess. Eine empirische Untersuchung*. München: Martin Meidenbauer.

Speeches:

OBAMA, Barack: What A Magnificent Soul It Was. Language: English. Memorial ceremony for Nelson Mandela, Johannesburg, South Africa. 10.12.2013. (*Vital Speeches of the Day* 80(2) (2014): Business Source Premier, 30-32).

The Theory and Practice of Teaching Note-Taking

MAREN DINGFELDER STONE
dingfel@uni-mainz.de
Johannes Gutenberg University Mainz/Germersheim, Germany

1. Introduction

Few topics have been addressed as regularly in Interpreting Studies as note-taking for consecutive interpretation – and it is here that the debate often became particularly heated. This article traces the debate on note-taking through sixty years of research and publications, and takes these publications as a basis for outlining recommendations for the teaching of note-taking. To this point, it first provides a brief overview of the scholarly discussion; it then sketches the most significant principles of note-taking as a consensus emerging from empirical research and observation, before offering recommendations on teaching note-taking as part of an interpreting programme.

2. The Note-Taking Debate in the Interpreting Studies Community

The credit of being the first to put note-taking on the agenda of teaching approaches and didactic conclusions will forever be Jean Herbert's. Even before the publication of his *Interpreter's Handbook* (*Manuel de l'interprète* 1952), note-taking for consecutive had been discussed as part of the ILO-interpreting training in the 1930s (PÖCHHACKER 2004: 28); Herbert, however, became the first to address, in the form of a publication for teachers and students, a broad range of teaching considerations, among them the question of note-taking. Many of the principles he advocated are echoed still in contemporary note-taking recommendations: he stressed the importance of a structural analysis of the original text, the visual character of the notes, and the need for one-glance rapid comprehensibility. Herbert regarded notes as an essential element of the consecutive interpretation technique that could make or break a performance and required extensive, systematic practice (1952: 36). However, while adamant about the significance of note-taking, he was also convinced that the notes themselves remained essentially unteachable – in fact, he famously compared the copying of someone else's notes to a sick patient filing another person's prescription in hope of getting better – and thus limited his remarks to general, comprehensive recommendations.

The specifics were delivered a few years later by his Geneva colleague Jean-François Rozan in his *Note-Taking in Consecutive Interpreting* (1956), whose influence on modern-day note-taking can hardly be overemphasised (GILLIES & WALICZEK 2004). Rozan's expressed aim was to "put forward a note-taking system which could easily be adopted by all, regardless of the languages from and into which they will have to work" (2004: "Introduction"); an intention which stood in opposition to the wide-spread belief that note-taking was too personal a system to be taught and learnt. Throughout his book, Rozan referred back to Herbert, taking Herbert's more general recommendations and translating them into a textbook full of specific, practical examples. His basic principles can still be discerned in contemporary note-taking classes: focussing on the idea, rather than the word; abbreviating consciously and unambiguously; noting links, negations and emphasis in a systematic way; abandoning a horizontal for a vertical note structure. Rozan also included specific training exercises for student interpreters, and the explanations for his model notes remain an outstanding example of textual analysis and reflection. However, he was adamant that the number of symbols should be minimal, lest "[r]eading back your notes [becomes] an exercise in deciphering; if that were so, we might as well use short-hand" (2004: 25). Accordingly, he propagated a maximum of twenty symbols, of which he regarded only the first ten as "absolutely essential" (2004: 31).

The years after Herbert's and Rozan's publications saw a rise in the use of simultaneous interpretation, but also a shift within the profession itself. Increasingly, interpreting was regarded as a profession adopted not only by extraordinarily skilled interpreter superstars, but by normal, linguistically gifted individuals who were taught the skills required to perform their exacting task in special university training courses (KALINA 2000a: 8; MATYSSEK 1989: V-VI). This prompted a lively debate within the interpreting community as to the content and structure of such training courses, and increased the level of scholarly attention directed at interpreting as a field of scientific study (VAN

HOOF 1962, KADE 1963, WILLETT 1974, HENDERSON 1976, KIRCHHOFF 1979).[1] Not all publications, however, were objective and scientifically validated, as personal experience was "lifted up to the level of a theoretical framework, without assumptions made being reviewed by any scientific standards. […] The result of such an individual approach was a highly prescriptive teaching theory and a rather dogmatic approach by those that had developed it" (KALINA 2000a: 10). Wilfried Becker's 1972 text on note-taking, for example, aimed at providing the students with a more comprehensive pool of model symbols, but his accompanying remarks read more like a lecture transcript than a text book, and his sometimes questionable recommendations are proposed with a maximum of peremptoriness (1972: 20). However, the 1970s also saw the first scientific investigations of note-taking and the teaching of it, notably by Danica Seleskovitch and the Paris School (SELESKOVITCH 1975; 2002). To shed light on the role of notes, she conducted an experimental study where professional interpreters provided a consecutive interpretation and subsequently commented on their notes. Pivotal in her *théorie du sens* was that the sense, rather than the words, be noted, which in itself was nothing new. Seleskovitch, however, maintained that in order for notes not to divert attention from comprehension, they must be highly minimalistic; so minimalistic in fact, that if the text were properly analysed and the memory sufficiently well-trained, there would be little need to consult notes in the production phase at all. Viewing speech production to be automated and thus effortless, and notes to be a highly individualised, transient memorisation strategy, she was vehemently opposed to the teaching of any system of note-taking (SELESKOVITCH & LEDERER 1989: 31).

This was a proposition with which many others did not concur. Heinz Matyssek (1989), for instance, was convinced that, particularly for interpreting talents rather than geniuses, a reliable consecutive interpretation would prove all but impossible without having systematically studied and developed a note-takingtechnique (1989: VI). In marked contrast to the teachings of the Paris School, Matyssek put forward an elaborate, highly complex symbol-based system of note-taking. His basic principles echo the teachings of Herbert and Rozan, though these in his eyes fell short in not providing students with a systematically outlined path towards the acquisition of both reliable note-taking skills and a meticulously developed pool of symbols (1989: 156). Matyssek expanded Rozan's seven basic rules to a total of twenty-three, and

---

[1] For a more comprehensive list, see ANDRES 57.

substantiated this claim by means of a comparative assessment of students' notes based on their transcribed interpretations, thus providing one of the first studies of consecutive note-taking to track cognitive processes in the brain. His system for developing notes, if practised until automated, may indeed allow the interpreter to note nuances and details with greater ease. As evidenced by his 300-page glossary, it also, however, requires a significant forward investment to master to a point where it becomes effortless.

Despite their attempts to establish a scientifically sound(er) base for the study of interpreting, Matyssek and Seleskovitch still argued largely based on personal experience – not unusual in the heated debates within Interpreting Studies publications up to the 1980s. However, over the next years it became increasingly obvious that even the most contrary publications shared some common ground. As Sylvia Kalina points out, even those who considered note-taking a side-product unworthy of scholarly attention still wrote about it, providing recommendations, warnings and instructions which were often passionately defended: "So entstandenpräskriptiveDogmen und Polarisierungen, woeigentlich die Meinungen gar nicht so weitauseinanderliegen" (1998: 254). In the 1990s, authors such as Roderick Jones aimed to move beyond such doctrinaire didactics. Positioning himself very clearly as a practitioner and teacher, rather than as an academic or researcher, Jones's *Conference Interpreting Explained* did not champion any one particular note-taking system; instead, his work is utterly practical in nature. Note-taking constituting only one of many chapters in his ambitious attempt to explain the profession of conference interpreting in all its complexity, he does not, however, get down to the nitty-gritty of the note-taking process, nor does he embed his recommendations into any scientific framework of reference. There is little to no validation of his theories; and it is precisely this lack of scientific validation which became more and more glaring in Interpreting Studies and led to calls by researchers such as Daniel Gile for more scientifically sound, well-researched, and empirically validated literature on note-taking: "We believe that proper scientific research is required, because too many widely accepted ideas are based solely on intuitive personal speculation" (1994: 49).

This call was answered by Kalina in 1998, and by Dörte Andres in 2002. Kalina's original aim was to structure her own interpreting classes in a more systematic way. Basing her conclusions on a thorough and very comprehensive study of the theoretical approaches within Interpreting Studies, she proceeded to identify the strategies that were used to resolve difficulties arising within an interpreting situation, such as inferencing, anticipation, and segmentation (see SEUBERT & KADER in this volume). To validate her theories, Kalina drew on a broad spectrum of empirical data, including analysed notes, questionnaires, and recorded interpretations. Her findings cemented the significance of systematic, clear note-taking:

In den oben beschriebenen Versuchen basierten [...] fehlerlose KD-Leistungen grundsätzlich auf systematischen, eindeutigen Notationen, die detailliert und verlässlich waren, die Makrostruktur erkennen ließen und in starkem Maß Verwendung von Symbolen und individuellen Abkürzungen aufzeigten. (KALINA 1998: 182)

Kalina thus concluded that teaching note-taking was not only possible, but essential, and that – provided the students' notes were concise and structured – this should provide them with a solid basis for understanding their individual note-taking needs and tailoring their technique to suiting them (1998: 246).

These conclusions resonated in Andres's study, too. She aimed at empirically ascertaining capacity allocation bottlenecks during the reception phase, and identifying successful note-taking strategies to alleviate such cognitive pressure. To this end, she compared the (time-coded) notes of professionals to those of students, and related them to transcribed video-recordings of their consecutive performance. This allowed her to draw conclusions not only on the type of notes that yielded the best results, but also on the décalage in the note-taking phase as a fluctuating value providing clues as to capacity management problems. As her sample group included students from three different universities, her study also allowed some measure of comparison of the different systems of note-taking. Interestingly, she found that many of the most heated controversies regarding the language of notes, the number of symbols or the perfect décalage were entirely beside the point (2002: 249). Instead, she proposed that teachers focus on impressing particular truths on their students: that an unambiguous note-taking system with clear rules for abbreviation and a set of symbols saves time, which can be devoted to other processes such as comprehension and analysis; that noting verbs and tenses is an essential factor for a good consecutive; that structuring information aids comprehension; that a conscious structuring of the notes facilitates the correct recall of information; that discontinuing note-taking may help to better structure the information on the page; and finally, that rhetorical features are more frequently incorporated in the target text if noted down (2002: 249-250).

Andres's research is valuable for teachers in designing their note-taking curriculum; it did not, however, lend itself to being used as a student resource independent of a note-taking course. This function was aptly fulfilled by Andrew Gillies's *Note-taking for Consecutive Interpreting* (2005). Aiming to present a "consistent, simple to learn, adaptable and efficient" system of note-taking (2005: 5), Gillies provided a comprehensive, hands-on student manual: "like it or not, you will have to take notes when interpreting consecutively and the way you take those notes will have an enormous impact on the success of your interpretation" (2005: 5). Although he, too, did not explicitly reference other authors, he did incorporate prior research on note-taking, such as theories on automisation, macro-thinking and bottom-up processes. Most importantly, he structured the manual to literally present a week-by-week note-taking training course, and to this end included an abundance of practice materials and suggested exercises. Proposing a very strict structure, he was adamant that no steps be skipped and highlighted the significance of practice:

[…] practice is an essential part of learning to become an interpreter, and the same applies to learning how to take notes in consecutive interpreting. Repeating chapters, practicing regularly with colleagues and alone several times a week, if not every day, is the only way to internalize these techniques so that they become a reflex. (GILLIES 2005: 14)

In the 21st century, research on note-taking has become both simpler and more complex. It is simpler in that new technologies like the Digital Pen [see ORLANDO in this volume] greatly reduce the time investment required to do meaningful research into note-taking; simpler also in that publications and information on curricula and best practices are at everyone's fingertips. It is more complex, however, in that research topics have become more challenging and standards are higher; researchers like Michaela Albl-Mikasa (2007) have taken the study of note-taking to a much more theoretical level, applying relevance-theoretic, cognitive, and linguistic means to investigate 'notation' as a language and text system rather than as a technique. The debates of the past decades have yielded broad areas of common ground on which to base not only future research, but also the teaching of note-taking in a contemporary class room.

3. Core Elements of Note-taking Systems

As the past chapter has demonstrated, consensus within the Interpreting Studies community has not come easily. However, at least the question of 'whether' to teach note-taking seems settled: abundant research has shown the benefit of a structured, systematic manner of noting down the essential elements of a properly analysed source text as a means for retrieving information and reconstructing the target text. As to the 'how', some basic principles have by now become all but universal (although the jury is still out on some of the finer points). These elements are outlined in the following eight points:

3.1 Dig Deeper: Noting the Sense Behind the Words

One element virtually all authors agree on is the need to move away from the level of words to the level of meaning. While few authors are as radical as Seleskovitch, no one disputes the importance of deverbalisation:

[A]successful note-taking technique [...] calls for a method of reducing words to ideas and putting the ideas into symbols that can then be re-expressed in another language. An interpreter must not try to write down word for word everything the speaker says because a hundred words may contain a single idea, while one word may imply several ideas. (NOLAN 2012^2: 278).

This is achieved in a two-fold way. Firstly, notes (or symbols) denote concepts, rather than words (GILLIES 2005: 99). Thus, instead of using separate signs to represent, for instance, aid, support, promote, assist, service and help, one (often supralingual) symbol encompasses the entirety of the concept 'to contribute to the fulfilment of a need or effort'. Secondly, notes are understood as the result of a process of analysis and understanding, where the core of what the speaker wants to convey is grasped in its complexity of verbal, non-verbal and para-verbal information and then noted accordingly, drawing on general knowledge, empathy, analytical expertise and thorough preparation.

3.2 Listen First, Note Later: Noting Only the Minimum

If notes are to reflect the essence of the speech, it is essential that note-taking does not come at the expense of listening, analysis, and memory, and that the impulse to scribble down as much information as possible lest it be forever lost in the realms of memory is firmly controlled. This proposition was taken to its extreme by Becker's recommendation to note a 15-minute dinner speech by means of five elements, and to recreate the rest through improvisation (1972: 24). While this suggestion hardly holds water, the underlying idea – that note-taking take a backseat to understanding, analysis, and re-expression – is unassailable: "If these are not done correctly, the best notes in the world will not make you a good interpreter" (JONES 1998: 43, see also GILLIES 2005: 112, ALEXIEVA 1993: 202, ILG & LAMBERT 1996: 79). Not only does excessive note-taking carry the risk of staying too close to the original linguistic structure (JONES 1998: 43), it also drains capacity away from listening and analysis. This was corroborated by Gile who found that students were significantly better at accurately reproducing names and figures if they were not distracted by the taking of full notes during the listening stage (2009: 178).

3.3 Mix and Match: Noting a Mixture of Symbols, Abbreviations, and Full Words

Under the caveat of individuality, many authors advocate the use of a mixed system of symbols, abbreviations, structural elements and full words. The elements constituting the note-taking system vary, as do the shares authors attribute to each individual group, though practically all scholars agree that mere stenography is an inadequate solution (e.g. BECKER 1972: 7, MATYSSEK 1989: 164). Recommendations as to the ideal number of symbols range from Rozan'sten(ish) and Becker's hundred(ish) to Matyssek's "pictorial Esperanto" (ILG & LAMBERT 1996: 71-72). This elusiveness stems partly from the fact that not everyone's brain is wired the same way: "Some individuals have a predominantly verbal memory, others are more visual. This ought to be respected when trying out strategies to improve retention and recall" (ILG & LAMBERT 1996: 75). Research does indicate, though, that a healthy mixture might be the way to go:

Zusammenfassend lässt sich zu diesem Teil der Analyse sagen, dass sich im 'wie' des Notierens von der Rubrik schlecht zur Rubrik gut eine Tendenz hin zu einer Mischform aus Symbolen, ausgeschriebenen und abgekürzten Wörtern unter verstärktem Rückgriff auf Pfeile erkennen lässt. (ANDRES 2002: 95)

Also, studies point to the danger of noting predominantly nouns (ILG & LAMBERT 1996), recommending instead to focus on verbs, especially modal verbs, without which the reconstruction of a speaker's communicative intent has been found to be practically impossible even for professional interpreters (ANDRES 2002: 136). There is a broad consensus that tenses, emphasis and negation should be noted in a systematic manner, as should link words and grammatical information such as subject and perspective. Jones points out that the interpreter should also indicate incomplete notes, whether these are due to cognitive overload (an element in a list that was dropped), or by conscious choice (for instance in case of an anecdote or joke): "Sometimes an interpreter is aware of what the speaker has said and has fully registered it intellectually but does not have the time to note it down […] they can indicate the existence of the point by including a parenthesis in their notes" (1998: 63).

3.4 Keep it Sweet and Simple: Noting Unambiguously and Efficiently

Whichever system is adopted, symbols must be clearly assigned and identifiable, and must never be improvised (GILLIES 2005: 103). The system of abbreviation must be coherent and avoid any ambiguity (JONES 1998: 45); words that cannot be deverbalised or abbreviated (names, technical term, unfamiliar vocabulary) must be noted down for transcoding. Ilg and Lambert summarise the consensus by stating that "any system [of note-taking] should be highly individual but based on common-sense rules of *efficiency* and *economy*" (1996: 78, emphasis in original). As complicated, over-developed symbols bear the risk of misinterpreting a statement or overtaxing the brain with the extra burden of assembling and drawing/writing, Gillies considers three strokes to be the limit for an efficient symbol (2005: 103). The effort of deciphering notes may impede the interpreter's communicative capacity, resulting in reduced eye-contact or insufficient body language monitoring (JONES 1998: 45); therefore, the postulate of unambiguousness, efficiency and brevity is to ensure that maximum capacities are available for other processes in both the reception and the production phase.

3.5 Structure Determines Content: Noting Vertically, Diagonally Or Circular

Looking at Herbert's notes, his style of note-taking was still largely horizontal. Rozan, on the other hand, had already moved away from that structure and considered a verticality of notes, along with what he called the shift, the backbone of his system (2004: 20): "Shift means writing notes in the place on a lower line where they would have appeared had the text on the line above been repeated" (2004: 22).More recent publications tend to favour a diagonal notation: "The diagonal form offers a natural movement for one's eyes to move from left to right and from top to bottom of a page when reading" (JONES 1998: 50). In addition, diagonal notes bring out more clearly the structure of the speech, and minimise syntactic interference (GILLIES 2005: 44). The space available should be used to clearly relay the hierarchy of ideas, with the location of the sign on the page indicating parallelism, cause-effect, precedence, etc. Kalina's analysis of students' notes determined clearly that notes that were vertically oriented, structured the elements based on their relation to one another, and separated units of meaning, increased students' performances in the reproduction phase (1998: 182-187). For this purpose, the notepad should be large enough to easily accommodate such structuring, while not being so large as to be unwieldy or tempt the student to over-note. While Becker propagates the use of a miniature notepad simply to dazzle the client (1972: 22)[2]; few interpreters are inclined to devote mental capacities to such prestidigitation. Instead, the consensus is that the page structure should be clearly discernible from a moderate distance, so as to facilitate the reading of the notes during the reproduction phase, and that notes should be spread out over the page far enough to allow the discontinuous addition of notes (ANDRES 2002: 250).[3]

3.6 Pick a Language, any Language: Noting in Whatever Language is Most Efficient

Similar to the heated debate on the use, non-use or over-use of symbols, the language of notes, too, has been the subject of academic dispute. Herbert (1952: 39), Rozan (2004: 16), Seleskovitch & Lederer (1989: 31), Karla Déjean Le Féal (1981: 83) and James Nolan (2012[2]: 279), among others, insist on target language notes. Matyssek maintains that notes should be language-independent, with the mother tongue as a fall-back option (1989:136). Wilhelm Weber maintains that it "does not matter what language the notes are taken in, since notes are only symbols that contain a message" but in practice expects a pro-

---

2 "Sie können einen [kleinen Block…] sehr leicht in der Handfläche versteckt halten. [… So] können Sie Ihrem Publikum vorspielen, Sie rezitierten die ganze Rede aus dem Kopf" (BECKER 1972: 22).

3 This linear style of note-taking, while by far the most wide-spread, is not the only option; however, noting by means of mind-mapping, or 'patterned' note-taking, has attracted little scholarly attention. Ilg and Lambert include a brief description of Linda Norton's application of the mind map approach to note-taking, which structures notes around a central argument noted in the middle of the page from which the associated concepts radiate outward. This is meant to more accurately represent the way the human mind processes information (ILG & LAMBERT 1996: 86).

gression from source-language note (for untrained students) to target-language notes (for more experienced interpreters) (1984: 36). Alexieva, on the other hand, is convinced of the merits of noting in the source-language to free resources during the critical listening phase (1993: 205), a viewpoint also adopted by Gile, who adds that in times of low cognitive pressure, the interpreter could use those extra resources for target-language notation (2009: 175). A mixed system is also favoured by, for instance, Henri van Hoof (1962: 71) and Christopher Thiéry (1981: 110). Each method has its merits. Noting in the source language spares capacities for listening and analysis, which may allow for more structured notes and hence for a better recall of the information. Also, without knowledge of the subsequent context, the interpreter may commit to a (potentially erroneous) target language choice too soon, thus losing a significant advantage of consecutive over simultaneous (ALEXIEVA 1993: 205). On the other hand, noting in the target language frees capacities for presentation and information recall, minimises syntactic and linguistic interference, and forces the interpreter to move beyond the surface form of incoming speech (VAN DAM 2004: 4).

Helle van Dam's 2004 study indicates that this debate might be missing the mark; she argues that the status of the language in the personal combination seems to be much more significant than the status of the language in the interpreting situation. Not broad enough to provide a reliable basis for generalisation, Van Dam's study nevertheless suggests a preference for A-language and source language: "A-language and source language are likely to be the competing parameters in note-taking, whereas B-language and target language are theoretically less attractive choices" (13). The reason for that is simple: "In a general attempt to minimise efforts […] interpreters are likely to take notes in whichever language is easier and therefore faster. Other things being equal, writing in one's first language, i.e. A-language, is likely to be easier/faster than writing in one's B-language" (13).[4] This also explains why many interpreters include third- or even fourth-language elements in their notes, and it accounts

---

4 Notation in the mother tongue was already advocated by Minjar-Beloruček in 1969 (MATYSSEK 1989: 135). Interestingly, though, in a study replicating Van Dam's setup with the language combination Hungarian-English, Csilla Szabó found that her subjects took notes overwhelmingly in English (their B-language), irrespective of source or target language considerations. Despite her limited sample selection, Szabó's suggestion - that the interpreters might have turned to English as the morphologically less complex language for simple convenience (2006: 141f) - raises an interesting point and merits further investigation. Marta Abuín González (2012) draws from her study with English-Spanish the conclusion that the choice of language is influenced by three interlinked factors, namely source/target language, A/B-language and interpreting experience/inexperience.

for the shift from source- to target-language notation that seems to come with interpreting experience (ANDRES 2002: 102, ALBUÍN 2012: 66): once the note-taking process has been sufficiently automated, namely in professional interpreters, capacities can be spared for noting in the target language even if that is *not* one's mother tongue.

3.7 Unburden your Memory: Noting Names, Figures, and Lists

In addition to helping the interpreter analyse the speech, recreate it based on the structure of the notes, and retrieve additional information on nuances and logic, notes can also serve as an external storage mechanism allowing the brain to empty its buffer and free resources for the more important tasks of analysing and listening. Names, numbers, dates and lists "are not integral to the grammar of the sentence nor the causality of the ideas and therefore very difficult to remember without notes. It is a good idea to note them immediately, interrupting whatever you are noting […] and then return to where you left off" (GILLIES 2005: 120). Experimental research by Christopher Taylor confirmed such elements were among the most frequently left out in student interpretations (1989: 180). This underlines the role of the notes for memory relief, but incidentally also for memory training, which can reduce the reliance on notes, in Taylor's eyes to the point where a properly trained memory might actually eliminate the need for notes altogether (1989: 183), and also help the interpreter cope with the extra working memory load caused by discontinuous notation.

3.8 Chronology and Décalage: Noting the Right Item at the Right Time

The question of décalage has traditionally been answered by stating vaguely that students should note only after they have understood, but that they also should not wait too long. Part of the vagueness may be attributable to the fact that ascertaining the exact décalage between when an item is heard and when it is noted was time-consuming, if not impossible, without a time-coded video recording not only of the reproduction but also of the note-taking phase. Once applied, however, such an approach clearly indicated that poorer student performance resulted from insufficient strategies for note-taking and décalage reduction. It also determined that décalage is not a fixed value but that it can and may, even must, fluctuate, depending on the momentary demands of the source text, although a permanent décalage of seven or more seconds leads to poorer results due to omissions (ANDRES 2002: 250). Andres's research stressed the close links between (working and long-term) memory and décalage. She found that good professional interpreters were distinguished by their ability to consciously reduce a looming décalage excess by deliberately omitting or minimising familiar concepts in their notes (2002: 184), and by using redundancies or pauses to complete stump notes, add elements to clarify, and/or adjust the chronology of their notes (2002: 160f).

4. The Pragmatics of Teaching Note-Taking: Suggestions for a Syllabus

While the theory of how notes may aid memory recall and analysis has thus been set out, the question remains how to best impart such knowledge for the benefit of interpreting trainees. Teachers in interpreting settings are faced with a diverse set of students in terms of proficiency, linguistic competence, and cognitive preferences. A note-taking class must build on this premise, structure of the course facilitating a gradual, systematic expansion of students' skills: ask too much of them too early, and they might develop bad habits which can be hard to break (WILLETT 1974: 101). Teaching note-taking as a separate monolingual course eliminates the challenges of linguistic transfer and allows students to focus solely on the demands of note-taking to acquire a sound basis for the seminal analysis and listening skills required in subsequent consecutive classes. This might alleviate the danger of untrained students focusing too much on their notes and not enough on listening, analysis and memory skills which has been pointed out by so many authors (SCHWEDA NICHOLSON 1985: 150, TAYLOR 1989: 178, WILLETT 1974: 101, KALINA 1998: 246, WEBER 1984: 35). In addition, it is paramount that students first learn to perceive notes as a prop, rather than a means in and of themselves, and as a prompter for memory, rather than a replacement (HERBERT 1952: 36, ROZAN 2004: 27, MATYSSEK 1989: 41, JONES 1998: 43f). Some students struggle with internalising this concept: while they may rationally accept its logic, when faced with an overload in the consecutive listening phase panic takes over and they scribble down half-caught fragments, disregarding structure, tone, or analysis. Controlling that panic mode, and emerging from such an overload situation by means of extra listening/analysis and conscious reduction/omission strategies, rather than extra note-taking, takes a great deal of practice and may well be among the most difficult skills for a student to master. Thus, an initial discussion of décalage and discontinuous notation, as well as the significance of unambiguous and legible notes (JONES 1998: 45) in relation to capacity management in consecutive interpretation, lays a sound foundation for the development of a personal note-taking system.

Once these premises have been established, a segue into practical issues can cover the basics: the advantages of one-sided over double-sided notes (maximising control); the problem of loose paper (minimising chaos); the advantage of plain pages (moving away from horizontal writing); the size of the note-pad (JONES 1998: 44, GILLIES 2005: 16). Having students note a few simple sentences (e.g. welcoming them to the class and explaining what note-taking is), and then asking them to compare their instinctive, presumably horizontal and word-based short-hand with a model notation, can be an eye-opener and can serve as a basis for explaining many of the more obvious yet seminal parts of the note-taking system, such as the diagonality of the notes, the structuring of the items based on their interrelation, and the mixture of notation elements. If applied with the caveat of critically adapting what is presented based on language combination, mental processing, and memory preferences, such model notations can provide students with a helpful guideline for first visualising, and later fine-tuning, their own note-taking system. Building on this foundation, each subsequent note-taking class can focus on a separate challenge (figures, rhetoric, structure, etc.), combining appropriate source texts with strategy suggestions and practical exercises.

In teaching the structuring of the notes, it is essential that students understand that the "location on the page [...] should in itself convey some additional meaning (parallelism, precedence, subordination, anteriority-posteriority, cause-effect, origin-destination, active-passive)" (ILG & LAMBERT 1996: 82). To this point, it helps to let students practise without the added pressure of time constraint or auditory processing, providing them with a written text as a basis for their notes: "By practicing note-taking from the written word you will learn the techniques of note-taking without the time pressure or multi-tasking that is involved when we have to listen to a speech and take notes at the same time" (GILLIES 2005: 11). The students are then required to analyse the text and relay as much information through the structuring of the notes as possible. The difficulty of the texts can be gradually adjusted, arriving ultimately at a dense, insufficiently structured text as a way of automating the analysis component of note-taking in terms of core ideas vs. add-on thoughts. As part of this teaching unit, students should be sensitised to the noting of semantic-syntactic link words such as 'on the one hand/on the other hand', 'not only/but also', 'either/or' and 'neither/nor', etc. Also, they should at this point have understood how to systematically position their notes to reflect the structure of the source text, by, for instance, the use the margin, the separation of ideas, and the clear marking of the text's ending.

Textual analysis can also take the form of summarisation. Ahrens suggests that using content-rich, narrative texts, followed by redundant texts loaded with empty phrases, improves analysis of the speech's argumentation, helps students identify redundancy and trains them to focus on the core elements of the text. These practice texts can progress from familiar concepts to new, difficult topics, or from summarising in several sentences to mere headlines (2001: 231). If based on written texts, students can also be required to provide summary notes for each paragraph (KALINA 2000b: 180). Having moved on to the spoken word, speeches or speech segments can be noted minimally, to be reproduced as a summary in the production phase. Text analysis and note structuring may be advanced by taking notes on the same text repeatedly. Rozan suggests that this allows students to incrementally adapt and optimise their notes for verticality, layout, etc. (2004: 59). As an added benefit, such text analysis enhances the students' ability to mentally pre-structure a text, thus facilitating information retrieval by segmenting ideas before submitting them to memory: "semantic chunking of input for storage in LTM [long-term memory] and the use of efficient retrieval cues" are essential in consecutive interpreting (PÖCHHACKER 2004: 124).

A separate class can focus on discussing the various sources for symbols, signs or pictorials students can draw on to develop their own note-taking system. If dogmatic decrees are rarely helpful, neither is leaving students to develop symbols entirely on their own. Instead, students should be provided with enough input to assemble their own system based on what works best for them. There is no set ratio of 'symbols to abbreviations to written words;' that remains contingent upon the individual interpreter's inclinations and the needs of the situation. However, if students develop a habit of analysing their own notes after class, they may determine failure patterns that indicate where a symbol for a particular concept is missing or suboptimal, and make a conscious choice on how to attack that concept in the future, be that through an abbreviation, a different language word, or a symbol. To find that symbol, they can turn to glossaries such as the ones provided by Becker, Nolan and (to a certain degree) Matyssek, question teachers or fellow students, or develop their own symbol. Symbols can, very roughly, be separated into two basic categories. The first set of symbols draws on a written system, which may be an alphabet (Latin, Greek, Russian, etc.), or a system like stenography, mathematics, science or music. The second group comprises graphic symbols developed as pictorial devices, either familiar (♀, ☺, →) or developed specifically for the purpose of note-taking (⬜ for country). These symbols are then built upon, so that ⬜→ becomes 'import', →⬜ becomes 'export', and so on. Gillies refers to such symbol families as 'organic' symbols, in the sense that a group of symbols "will grow from a common root [to] reinforce your recognition of the symbols you know and by having a smaller number of 'basic' symbols you will tax your memory less" (2005: 104).

It is essential, however, that students understand that symbols are not an end in themselves – they only serve a purpose if they are quicker and easier to write then a word, so students must keep in mind the mechanics of writing and drawing. As for what to note, students should be trained as early as possible to note verbs and mark them as such (for instance by adding an ^{n}). This is especially true for modal verbs, where the development of automatisms in note-taking can be crucial. Also, students should develop a means of distinguishing singular from plural, for instance by adding an ^{s} to the symbol in case of multiple objects. They can practise these early skills on short, simple speeches chosen to minimise secondary cognitive requirements such as analysis (through clear structure, or a familiar subject), memory (through narrative form), and listening (through slow and clear reading). As the students become more confident about the use and structuring of symbols, those texts can get longer, denser, more complicated, more technical, and faster, depending on which note-taking strategy is prioritised in the session to achieve a particular learning objective. If students are routinely provided with fully verbalised model notations to compare to their own notes, they can identify unsuccessful strategies in their own notes and are provided with suggestions for potential improvements.

Another training session might prioritise abbreviations. As ambiguous abbreviations or stump words can be the downfall of an accurate reproduction of the original ideas, it is useful to provide students with a structured way of abbreviating. To sensitise students for this pitfall, they can be confronted with a speech (segment) that includes a variety of very similar word beginnings (in English, such a segment might contain commission, committee, communication, communal, compromise, commercial, and competence; or partner, party, parliament, particularly and participation). Once the students have come to appreciate the potential for misunderstanding that un- or semi-conscious abbreviations entail, they can develop strategies to avoid such pitfalls: by adding a signifying element to the abbreviation (com^{ss} for *commission* vs. com^{TT} for *committee*), by integrating a symbol into it (C"om for *communication*), by moving away from the word level (using the symbol ☉ for *commercial*, or underlining for *particularly*), by assigning letter combinations to certain concepts (PA for *parliament*), or by using different scripts (P for *partner*).

Text typology should be an essential element of a note-taking syllabus. If students are exposed to a variety of different speech settings and purposes, they can discern which texts and text segments they can more easily remember (narrative vs. technical, concrete vs. abstract), and understand how different types of speech necessitate an adaptation of their note-taking. A factual speech at a seminar or expert conference is prone to be less redundant (VIAGGIO 1992: 55); while burdening the memory with an abundance of technical terms and figures, it would not necessarily require the interpreter to pay much attention to rhetorical verbal and non-verbal features, complicated reasoning etc. A persuasive text with an appeal function, on the other hand, might be better served if the interpreters dedicate their resources to tracking the logical structuring and to capturing and recreating the rhetorical effect of the speech, rather than to noting every figure down to the last digit. If students are further advanced, selecting a speech which remains purposefully vague and ambiguous challenges them to re-think their automatic inferences and re-impresses the need to remain faithful to the speaker's intentions, even (and especially) if those intentions are to *not* say anything. Obviously, these exercises should also entail the analysis of linguistic devices: "public speaking conventions and rhetorical devices have to be analysed and internalised before students know how to apply them in specific settings (eulogies, toasts, after-dinner oratory)" (ILG & LAMBERT 1996: 75).

Text typology can thus be linked to phraseology. Not only can capacities be saved in the production phase by recalling appropriate stock phrases from a pre-existing storage pile, as well as in the reception phase when identifying and comprehending such phrases effortlessly (ILG & LAMBERT 1996: 75), great benefits also lie in being able to *note* such phrases with ease (HENDERSON 1976: 110). This is often done in a reduced form that includes the appropriate level of formality but leaves mental capacities available for handling the names, titles and functions that often accompany standard phrases of welcome or thanks. To this point, students can be required to gather (or, if the teacher is so inclined, can be provided with) a pool of stock phrases and then asked to develop the most efficient way of noting them. If revisited and practised regularly, this notation will eventually become automatic.

One segment of the note-taking syllabus should be dedicated to the concept of noting figures. A stumbling stone for interpreters, figures do not lend themselves to being analysed and deducted from the context, and thus place an extra burden on the memory effort. The recognition and writing down of numbers can (as a very first step) be practised by simply listening to, and noting down, lists of figures (AHRENS 2001: 232, HENDERSON 1976: 113). That alone will never suffice, though; it is the embedding of the number in its textual context, the *how* of the notes, that determines the success of the interpretation. After all, it is an enormous difference whether something has been developed over the last ten years (and will be used as of today) or whether it was developed ten years ago (and has been in use for all this time). Yet, inexperienced interpreters may simply note *10y,* or worse, just *10*. Students must be taught strategies for managing the cognitive bottleneck that numbers invariably bring about by, for instance, writing down a figure as soon as they hear it (discontinuous notation) while consciously, later automatically, embedding it in its context of unit and reference. In addition, they should adopt a system for noting down larger numbers, whether they follow Herbert's recommendation of adding a '-' per three zero's (so 1- would be 1000 and 1= would be 1,000,000) or work with pre-assigned abbreviations such as t (thousand), mio (million) and bio (billion). Most importantly, though, they must learn to appreciate the function of the figure, which may be more crucial than the figure itself: 'Almost 1000!' is quite different from 'Not even 1000!', so merely noting the figure will do nothing to help recreate the nuances of the original. The students should be given the opportunity to practise these suggestions by noting speeches that rely heavily on figures; using statistics can furthermore train them to detect patterns in rows of numbers (AHRENS 2001: 232). Such texts may also enhance their ability to structure incoming information in the form of clusters, which are then stored in the short-term or working memory in chunks rather than individually, to optimise memory capacities (VIAGGIO 1992: 46).

In order to maximise active listening and revisit the role of memory already outlined at the beginning of this chapter, it is helpful to include intermittent training sessions requiring students to reproduce speeches relying entirely upon their memory. In one such exercise, the students might first reproduce segments of a speech entirely without notes; the second part of the speech would be reproduced based on minimal notes taken *after* the reading of the entire segment, and the final segment of the speech is noted traditionally, but in line with the learning objective of the class – to rely as little as possible on notes and as much as possible on memory and analysis. To boost students' self-confidence, and to encourage them to trust their memory skills, Kornakov suggests using "interesting or funny data […] in order to demonstrate to students that they can easily remember quite complicated data so long as it is *important* or *interesting* to them" (2000: 243, emphasis in original). Such assignments, if done regularly, may help to automate the interaction between memory and note-taking. That optimisation of this interaction is indeed possible has emerged from Kalina's and Andres's research, both of whom point to a significantly higher degree of automation for the more advanced students/professionals. Part of this class should be a discussion on the fluctuating volume of notes (WILLETT 1974: 100), depending on internal factors (such as general knowledge, preparation, concentration and memory capacity) and external factors (text type, text density, speed of presentation, and rhetorical capabilities of the speaker).

In the discussion on teaching note-taking, little attention has been paid to the question of verbal vs. non-verbal rhetorical features. Speaking about body language, Sergio Viaggio points out: "The students should be made aware that when we speak, we have all our body, vocal chords, facial muscles, fingers, etc. at our disposal. Thus, lots of information is carried para-linguistically" (1992: 45). Students who exclusively focus on their notepad in the listening phase are prone to miss all that additional and often essential information, which is another reason to note sparingly:"writing is a strong distractor in face-to-face communication" (ALEXIEVA 1993: 202). Non-verbal and para-verbal information can complement or emphasise the speaker's message, facilitating analysis and understanding for the interpreter; it can also, however, change the emphasis or contradict the verbal message completely – in which case it is essential that the interpreter not only understand that subtext, but also mark it in the notes. This is especially important in the case of humour to ensure that what is meant as friendly teasing is not translated as a reprimand, or that what is ironic is not understood as serious criticism. Kalina points out that in some instances, the *how* has become more important than the *what*:

Aspects of presentation have gained priority over content in public speaking in many instances (a point which is most apparent in multimedia events or when interpreting for TV) [...This] has specific consequences for interpreters, who can no longer rely on meaning alone. (KALINA 2000a: 9, see also WILLETT 1974: 98).

Linguistic devices carry their own set of problems. Some of the rhetorical or stylistic features (such as parenthesis, anaphora, epanorthosis, climax, rhetorical question) can be reflected in the structuring of the notes and can thus be reproduced with relative ease. Other elements such as hedging ('it could be argued...'/'it seems to me...') or the positioning of the speaker (I/we/you/they) are less obvious but must by all means be reproduced in notes and translation. Linguistic devices such as alliterations that are strongly linked to the source language, however, will often bind too much capacity when trying to recreate them in the target language, making it more appropriate for the interpreter to focus on content rather than form. In order for students to adequately handle these features, they first must be able to recognise and identify them, which requires training in text analysis, rhetoric, and non-verbal/para-verbal communication. They must then be able to quickly identify and adopt the appropriate strategy for handling the item. When teaching advanced students to adequately note and reproduce the non-and para-verbal features and the rhetorical intent of the speaker, video recordings of the consecutive allow students to ascertain for themselves where they failed or succeeded. Also, speeches that call for emotional engagement (e.g. memorial services) lend themselves to this teaching objective, as do and witty, humorous speeches. It is helpful to expose students to interpreting situations where the speakers aim to present a particular image of themselves as, for instance, approachable, trustworthy, indignant, or intimidating, and to challenge the students to reproduce that effect.

And finally: students should be encouraged to experiment, to adapt their system when necessary and not to become too static – occasionally challenging them ensures that the developing automatisms are both effective and efficient. There are many exercises that can gently force students to review their technique: by having the students take notes but then unexpectedly reproduce the speech based on their neighbour's notes, which not only exposes them to someone else's notes but also requires them verbalise and explain their own choices and strategies; by having students take notes but then interpret without consulting them (WILLET 1974: 101), which reminds them of the importance of their memory and reveals a potential overreliance on notes; by limiting their note-taking space to a single A5 sheet, or even a filing card or post-it note, which strengthens their abstraction, trains their memory and forces them into conscious, efficient notes; by exposing them to noise, distractions, etc., which reveals where the extra capacities to maintain concentration are deducted. Such experimentation comes with a caveat, though. If it is to be consequential and beneficial, the students should already have internalised the underlying principles of note-taking and consecutive interpretation: "Picasso did not draw square faces simply because he could not manage to draw them round: our students will acquire the right to bend the rules only once they have fully mastered them" (VIAGGIO 1992: 59). Once they have a stable foundation for note-taking, students should be able to adapt flexibly to different constraints and situations without falling prey to the pitfalls of semi-conscious, unstructured, and excessive note-taking.

5. Conclusion

The above discussion, but mostly the decades of research it builds upon, has made it abundantly clear that students can and will profit from a structured, conscious and systematic introduction into note-taking as a seminal skill in consecutive interpretation. However, that does not mean that the debates shall end – nor should they. Especially in such a highly individual domain, dogmatic tenets should be approached with a healthy amount of common sense, followed, ideally, by empirical research. The research opportunities in this field are ample enough to keep the next generation(s) of Interpreting Studies scholars well occupied. For instance, an empirical validation of the multitude of exercises recommended in literature on the teaching of consecutive and note-taking (including many that are listed in this article) would be immensely valuable. Similarly, it might be useful to test the limits of the holy grail of teaching interpreting, the development of automated strategies to alleviate cognitive pressure.[5] Despite the limited number of users, research into the

---

5 Andres's research indicates that it is precisely the high level of automated processes that may lead professional interpreters astray: "Es gibt andererseits bei den Professionellen zahlreiche Beispiele dafür, daß die Automatisiertheit der Notizen, die sofortige Verfügbarkeit von Kurzformen und Symbolen, zum Mitschreiben verleitet und damit zu Lasten von Informationsstrukturierung- und gewichtung [sic] gehen" (ANDRES 2002: 111).

mind-mapping style of note-taking might yield fascinating results about information processing and memory recall. New technological features, such as the Digital Pen, will facilitate research significantly, doing away with the painstaking time-coding of the notes and looking at the note-taking process rather than the end result. The findings from such research will certainly be put to good use in making the teaching of note-taking even more effective and efficient.

References

AHRENS, Barbara (2001): "Einige Überlegungen zur Didaktik der Notizentechnik". In: KELLETAT, Andreas (ed.): *Dolmetschen: Beiträge aus Forschung, Lehre und Praxis*. Frankfurt a. M.: Lang, 227-241.

ALBL-MIKASA, Michaela (2007): *Notationssprache und Notationstext*. Tübingen: Gunter Narr.

ALBUÍN GONZÁLEZ, Marta (2012): "The Language of Consecutive Interpreters' Notes: Differences Across Levels of Expertise", *Interpreting* 14(1), 55-72.

ALEXIEVA, Bistra (1993): "On Teaching Note-Taking in Consecutive Interpreting". In: DOLLERUP, Cay & LODDEGAARD, Anne (eds.): *Teaching Translation and Interpreting 2: Insights, Aims, Visions*. Amsterdam/Philadelphia: John Benjamins, 199–206.

ANDRES, Dörte (2002): *Konsekutivdolmetschen und Notation*. Frankfurt a. M.: Lang.

BECKER, Wilfried (1972): *Notizentechnik*. BBK Germersheim.

DÉJEAN LE FÉAL, Karla (1981): "L'enseignement des méthodes d'interprétation". In: DELISLE, Jean (ed.): *L'enseignement de la traduction et de l'interprétation. De la théorie à la pédagogie*. Ottawa: Éditions de l'Université d'Ottawa, 75–98.

GILE, Daniel (1994): "Methodological aspects of interpretation and translation research". In: LAMBERT, Sylvie & MOSER-MERCER, Barbara (eds.): *Bridging the Gap: Empirical Research in Simultaneous Interpretation*. Amsterdam/Philadelphia: John Benjamins, 39-56.

GILE, Daniel (1995, rev. ed. 2009): *Basic Concepts and Models for Translator and Interpreter Training*. Amsterdam/Philadelphia: John Benjamins.

GILLIES, Andrew & WALICZEK, Bartosz (rpt. 2004): "Foreword". In: ROZAN, Jean François: *Note-Taking in Consecutive Interpretation*. English and Polish Translation by Andrew Gillies and Bartosz Waliczek. Krakow: Tertium.

GILLIES, Andrew (2005): *Note-Taking for Consecutive Interpreting: A Short Course*. Manchester: St. Jerome.

HENDERSON, John (1976): "Note-Taking for consecutive interpreting", *Babel* XXII (3), 107-116.

HERBERT, Jean (1952): *Handbuch des Dolmetschers*. Genf: Georg.

ILG, Gérard & LAMBERT, Sylvie (1996): "Teaching Consecutive Note-taking", *Interpreting* 1(1), 69-99.

JONES, Roderick (1998): *Conference Interpreting Explained*. Manchester: St. Jerome.

KADE, Otto (1963): "Der Dolmetschvorgang und die Notation. Bedeutung und Aufgaben der Notizentechnik und des Notiersystems beim konsekutiven Dolmetschen", *Fremdsprachen* 7(1), 12-20.

KALINA, Sylvia (1998): "Strategische Prozesse beim Dolmetschen. Theoretische Grundlagen, empirische Untersuchungen, didaktische Konsequenzen", *Language in Performance* 18. Tübingen: Gunter Narr.

KALINA, Sylvia (2000a): "Interpreting Competences as a Basis and a Goal for Teaching", *The Interpreters' Newsletter* 10, 3-32.

KALINA, Sylvia (2000b): "Zu den Grundlagen einer Didaktik des Dolmetschens". In: KALINA, Sylvia; BUHL, Silke & GERZYMISCH-ARBOGAST, Heidrun (eds.): *Dolmetschen: Theorie, Praxis, Didaktik*. St. Ingbert: Röhrig. 161-189.

KIRCHHOFF, Hella (1979): "Die Notationssprache als Hilfsmittel des Konferenzdolmetschers im Konsekutivvorgang". In: MAIR, Walter & SALLAGER, Edgar (eds.): *Sprachtheorie und Sprachenpraxis*. Tübingen: Gunter Narr, 72-93.

KORNAKOV, Peter (2000): "Five Principles and Five Skills for Interpreter Training", *Meta* 45(2), 241-248.

LONGLEY, Patricia (1989): "The Use of Aptitude Testing in the Selection of Students for Conference Interpretation Training". In: GRAN, Laura & DODDS, John (eds.): *The Theoretical and Practical Aspects of Teaching Conference Interpretation*. Udine: Campanotto, 105-108.

MATYSSEK, Heinz (1989): *Handbuch der Notizentechnik für Dolmetscher*. Heidelberg: Julius Groos.

NOLAN, James (2012^2): *Interpretation: Techniques and Exercises*. Bristol: Multilingual.

PÖCHHACKER, Franz (2004): *Introducing Interpreting Studies*. London: Routledge.

ROZAN, Jean François (1956, rev. ed. 2004): *Note-Taking in Consecutive Interpretation*. English and Polish Translation by Andrew Gillies and Bartosz Waliczek. Krakow: Tertium.

SCHWEDA NICHOLSON, Nancy (1985): "English Consecutive Interpretation Training: Videotapes in the Classroom", *Meta* 30(2), 148-154.

SELESKOVITCH, Danica & LEDERER Marianne (1989): *A Systematic Approach to Teaching Interpretation*. Paris: Didier Erudition.

SELESKOVITCH, Danica (2002): "Language and Memory: A Study of Note-Taking in Consecutive Interpreting". In: PÖCHHACKER, Franz & SHLESINGER, Miriam (eds.): *Interpreting Studies Reader*. London: Routledge, 121-129.

SELESKOVITCH, Danica (1975): *Langage, langue et mémoire. Étude de la prise de notes en interprétation consécutive*. Paris: Minard.

SZABÓ, Csilla (2006): "Language Choice in Note-Taking for Consecutive Interpretation: A Topic Revisited", *Interpreting* 8(2), 129-147.

TAYLOR, Christopher (1989): "Textual Memory and the Teaching of Consecutive Interpretation". In: GRAN, Laura & DODDS, John (eds.) *The Theoretical and Practical Aspects of Teaching Conference Interpretation*. Udine: Campanotto, 177-184.

THIÉRY, Christopher (1981): "L'enseignement de la prise de notes en interprétation consécutive : un faux problème?" In: DELISLE, Jean (ed.): *L'enseignement de l'interprétation et de la traduction – de la théorie à la pédagogie. Cahiers de traductologie 4*. Ottawa: University of Ottawa Press, 99-112.

VAN DAM, Helle (2004): "Interpreters' Notes: On the Choice of Language", *Interpreting* 6 (1), 3-17.

VAN HOOF, Henri (1962): *Théorie et pratique de l'interprétation*. München: Hueber.

VIAGGIO, Sergio (1992): "Teaching Beginners to Shut Up and Listen", *The Interpreter's Newsletter* 4, 45-58.

WEBER, Wilhelm K. (1984): *Training Translators and Conference Interpreters*. Orlando: Harcourt.
WILLETT, Ruth (1974): "Die Ausbildung zum Konferenzdolmetscher". In: KAPP, Volker (ed.): *Übersetzer und Dolmetscher*. Heidelberg: Quelle & Meyer, 87-109.

Implementing Digital Pen Technology in the Consecutive Interpreting Classroom

MARC ORLANDO
marc.orlando@monash.edu
Monash University

1. Introduction

In interpreter training, great strides are being made in the provision of teaching materials and capture of trainees' performance. Audio and video-recording now have an established status in interpreter training as a means to provide aural and video + audio texts independent of the trainer and as a means to capture trainees' performance for the benefit of trainees themselves or for evaluation and testing purposes for trainers and examiners (KUNZ 2002). General language laboratories which feature audio playback and recording facilities are a standard feature of most interpreting training programmes which facilitate guided as well as independent training. *Sanako* Language Laboratories, produced by *Tandberg Educational,* and *Robotel Language Lab Solutions*, are two examples of technology which now offer guided or independent interaction with visual + audio texts with audio and sometimes audiovisual recording facilities (HANSEN & SHLESINGER 2007). Software packages such as *Melissi's Black Box* offer annotated text, simultaneous recording with audio or video sources, Unicode word processor, graphical display of speech waveforms for simultaneous, liaison and consecutive interpretation with transcriptions of source and target speech (HANSEN & SHLESINGER 2007). Worldwide many university training facilities are now investing in digital interpreting laboratories which emulate real-life interpreting situations: interpretation booths, conference interpretation facilities, digital audio and video recording of interpretations, computer translation facilities for the translation of electronically received source speeches etc. In the context of these advances in the pedagogy of interpreting, digital pens are currently used in the development of note-taking systems (ORLANDO 2010).

This chapter will explore and discuss the implementation of digital pen technology in the consecutive interpreting classroom, especially when it is used in relation to the development of note-taking conventions. Starting from the idea that educators in consecutive interpreting who develop exercises in note-taking generally face the impossibility to have easy access to the process of notes being taken by their students, and consequently cannot provide them with adequate remediation strategies, I will propose that the use of digital pen technology helps solving such issues and provides both students and educators with unexplored insights into the relation between comprehension, analysis and memorisation of a source speech and the process of note-taking.

The chapter will first discuss in general terms note-taking as one of the essential and necessary skills to be developed when teaching consecutive interpreting, and then present the *Livescribe Smartpen* technology and how it is currently perceived and used in the profession. In the following sections, I will discuss the didactic rationale and present pedagogical sequences that have been developed and implemented in the programme where I teach (Monash University, Melbourne), as well as focus on responses and opinions on the usability of the pen from students and educators from two different universities' master programmes. The respondents were questioned about the technology and its features, its effects on note-taking analysis, as well as on the overall benefit to the development of good note-taking conventions including cross-student feedback. The final section will briefly introduce another currently trialled application of the digital pen which could have a significant impact on interpreter training: the possible development of a new hybrid mode of interpreting that has attributes of both conventional modes of interpreting – consecutive and simultaneous – due to the immediate recording and play-back functions that the new digital pen technology contains.

2. Consecutive Interpreting and Note-Taking Training

It is generally well understood in the interpreting profession that a good consecutive interpretation depends on various interdependent factors. As discussed by many educators and researchers (GENTILE 1991, GILE 1991, ALEXIEVA 1994, ILG & LAMBERT 1996), teaching consecutive interpreting implies therefore teaching certain sets and subsets of skills (see DINGFELDER STONE (07) in this volume). Trainees should be taught through any curriculum that performing in consecutive interpreting requires the development of a personal note-taking system, but that this skill is only one of those proper to this mode. Indeed, there are too many variables in a speech interpretation to limit its quality to merely good or bad notes. I have already discussed and proposed a breakdown of such skills under four main sets (ORLANDO 2010: 73-75), encouraging the implementation in curricula of various exercises reinforcing sub-sets of skills important in consecutive interpreting: listening comprehension, analysis and memorisation; importance of structure, coherence and *skopos;* note-taking and public speaking. Beyond the various pedagogical activities that can be proposed to develop efficiently each set of skills, I also pointed out that a too important focus on note-taking during training was often what was detrimental to natural and quality interpretations. Trainees must understand that consecutive interpreting is not limited to note-taking which can become an ally but also their worst enemy. Trying to note down nearly everything is simply impossible and useless as it generally entails the Nose-in-the-Notes-Syndrome during the interpretation, and an incoherent production, both contrary to and incompatible with the act of communication an interpreter is supposed to perform.

When educators want to assess an interpretation, it is generally the quality of the consecutive interpretation (based on criteria to evaluate the linguistic accuracy, as well as their expression and presentation) and the final notes (the product) which allow them to give feedback and evaluate the performance. Such a *product* evaluation of the interpretation is generally made without being able to clearly distinguish the memorisation qualities/deficiencies and the note-taking qualities/deficiencies of the interpreter. As already mentioned (ORLANDO 2010: 76), various possibilities have been tried to capture the 'live' process of note-taking (use of OHPs, videos) but all have shortcomings and are judged much too time-consuming for educators to use them.

3. Digital Pen Technology

3.1 Description of the *Livescribe Smartpen*

This new generation of digital pens, belonging to the category of mobile computing platforms, offer advanced processing power, audio and visual feedback, as well as memory for handwriting capture, audio recording, and additional applications. The Smartpen consists of a microphone, a built-in speaker, 3D recording headsets, and an infrared camera. It is used to take notes – it has a normal ink cartridge and is held as a 'normal' pen – and to capture data on a micro-chipped paper. Thanks to the built-in microphone and speaker and the infrared camera, an application synchronises what is being filmed as handwriting with the audio recording. In a nutshell, the tool allows the simultaneous capture of what is said in a room and the notes being taken at that same time.

Thanks to the *dot-paper* technology that enables interactive 'live' capture using plain paper printed with microdots, and to a function called Paper Replay, the user of the pen can playback the speech from the notes taken on paper at any time. One simply needs to tap on a word on the page of the notebook to hear the part of the speech related to that same word or a phrase played directly from the pen. For a better comfort in listening, the flow of the audio playback can also be slowed down or sped up as required.

It is possible to connect the first generations of Smartpens to a computer through a normal USB port so that both audio and video data can be uploaded and played on the computer. This allows users to backup, search, and replay notes from their computer. Users can also upload and convert notes to interactive Flash movies or PDF files which can then be shared. The latest model of the Smartpen is wireless enabling instant transfer of what has been written down to any playback device, e.g. computer, tablet, iPad.

A variety of other approaches and technologies have been developed to help trainees to take and review notes during the learning process. However, they all have shortcomings. For example, other technologies exist that permit the recording and rehearing of speeches/lectures in relation to notes, but the audio segments and notes are not synchronised. This synchronicity can exist with Tablet PCs with audio recording capability, but Tablet PCs are more expensive and less portable than a pen and a notepad. iPads too are currently used in training programs or by professionals but they rarely offer the same precision in handwriting capture as with a pen.

Beyond its digital features enabling simultaneous audio-video capture, the *Livescribe Smartpen* is still used as normal pen and paper, an important asset in the world of interpreters. If used along sound pedagogical activities, this digital technology provides a universal platform for improving note-taking learning among students, and offers the ideal tool for classroom visual activities and immediate individual and collective feedback where students can easily learn from others.

3.2 Use in Institutions and in the Profession

This technology and its potential merits for interpreting research, training and practice has now been around for about 5 years, and when one tries to locate academic publications or instances of its practical use online, several interesting examples show up. In the academic field, it seems that master's theses have been dedicated to some possible uses of the digital *Livescribe Smartpen* (HIEBL 2011) or some research conducted using the digital tool (KOSTAL 2011), and others are currently being written. Even if not that many articles on its pedagogical use have been published, several colleagues in various institutions are trialling the pen for various research or training projects which should lead to publications in the close future (Franz Pöchhacker, University of Vienna; Heidi Salaets, KU Leuven; Michael Jin, Newcastle University). In the professional field, several practitioners report of their using this technology or others in their practice. The examples of instances mentioned below are certainly not the only ones one would find online, and I do not intend or claim here to give a full and exhaustive list of such fora, but they are relevant to what some professional interpreters know about and think of the use of digital pen technology.

On the blog *Endless Possibilities Talks,* for example, one can follow among other things a videorecorded session on "Technology options for interpreting" (Endless Possibilities Talks 2012) where various practitioners from different countries (e.g. UK, USA, Germany and Spain) share ideas and explain how they use digital technology to perform "a better job when interpreting" and to also "reduce costs and incidental elements". In particular, Esther Navarro-Hall, a US-based conference and court interpreter and instructor at the Monterey Institute of International Studies, and Martin Esposito, a conference interpreter based in the UK and Italy, focus on the use of the *Livescribe Smartpen*, which they are both using in their practice. They show its numerous advantages and benefits during practical assignments, in comparison to more traditional digital recorders or Mp3 players. Navarro-Hall also organises workshops on the hybrid *SimConsec* mode in the USA, where trainees are introduced to "an exciting combination of two interpreting skills + portable technology, which is quickly becoming the technique of choice for today's interpreter" (NAVARRO-HALL 2012).

On another blog, *Interpreting.info,* practitioners' questions about this new mode and digital tools are discussed, and even if some doubts are expressed by some, others clearly point out that those in the profession who are not aware of digital devices like the Smartpen somehow "choose to be left behind" (Interpreting.info 2012).

Another interesting online initiative for interpreters to share ideas is the *#IntJC,* the Interpreting Journal Club, led from Japan by professional interpreter Lionel Dersot, which organises Tweetchats, a free web-based service. One of the Club's sessions was dedicated to "Digital Pen and Note-taking" (#IntJC the Interpreting Journal Club 2012). The script of the session, available online in their archive section, clearly shows interest in the use of the Smartpen from researchers and trainers like Heidi Salaets from KU Leuven, Belgium, who reports using the Smartpen for research and training purposes, or also Barry Olsen from the Monterey Institute of International Studies, as well as from different practitioners who already use the pen during missions or plan to.

On these various fora, many different conclusions and opinions are expressed by users, but the fact remains that whether they are positive or negative, digital technology cannot be ignored. Alexander Drechsel, a European Commission interpreter who has been writing for some time on the relation between interpreters and technology, recently concluded one of his web-based articles with these words: "Interpreters today stand right in the middle of a 'tsunami' of technological and social change. We must act and 'understand the wave' to be able to ride it and not drown" (DRECHSEL 2013). To be able to understand and master the wave, it appears obvious that practitioners, researchers and trainers need to collaborate to identify and recommend what works, what does not, what requires particular training, etc.

For more information on the status and trends of digital pen technology and interpreting research, training and practice, one could consult Orlando 2014 and Orlando 2015.

4. Pedagogical Applications of Digital Pen Technology for Consecutive Interpreting

It is my belief that teaching must be seen as an interactive formative activity where the gradual disappearance of the educator and the gradual autonomy of the trainee should always be aimed at, through a range of problem solving strategies and metacognitive activities. One way to achieve such an objective is to design and implement student-centred activities early in the training and to make both students and educators aware of concepts of metacognition.

In any institution training future professionals, no one would contest the benefit of evaluating students against various professional standards. Our programme, for example, is approved by the *National Accreditation Authority for Translators and Interpreters* (NAATI) and is therefore subject to monitoring and controls aiming at ensuring that our evaluation principles follow and comply with NAATI professionally-oriented standards and principles. And it is a good thing to focus on product, professional-oriented assessment objectives, especially towards the end of the training period. However, as pointed out by Choi (2006), such professional focus and evaluation also runs the risk of defeating the purpose of evaluation and assessment from a pedagogical standpoint. Therefore, it is important for assessment to be studied also from the student's perspective. Self-assessment and metacognition play an important part when one wants to give students the possibility to reflect on their progress, to 'learn how to learn' and to become actors in their own learning process. As defined by Choi, "metacognition in learning can be described as the awareness of the learning process and the ability to adapt to challenges that occur during this process through effective strategies, thereby helping learners improve their learning capacity"(CHOI 2006: 277). Feedback is at the centre of any metacognitive approach (see BEHR in this volume). As explained by Veenman (2006), any process of skills acquisition takes time and effort, and teaching and learning activities should be organised around metacognitive skills (as opposed to metacognitive knowledge) which "have a feedback mechanism built-in" (VEENMAN et al. 2006: 5). Collective and individual assessment and feedback activities should therefore be planned in any curriculum.

As I already discussed in the 2010 article, as far as the learning process of note-taking is concerned, research suggests that the use of text-to-speech technology and effective note-taking activities, coupled with review, can aid learning and understanding and therefore enhance the comprehension, fluency, accuracy, speed, endurance, and concentration of individuals (TRAN & LAWSON 2001; LINDSTROM 2007). One can thus consider that if the taking of notes is too demanding on a student's working memory to permit the student to carry out generative processing in real time – and, in the case of interpreting students, leads to a poor performance – the needed generative processing of the content is still capable of occurring during the follow-up review of notes. Given the difficulties many students face when reading their own notes, the synchronised juxtaposition of text and audio provided by this digital pen technology should induce greater learning from the students reading, reviewing and self-evaluating their own notes during assessment activities. Moreover, during these self, peer or class assessment activities, such technology offers the possibility for students and instructors to work together closely and clearly observe and/or show what can be noted down or not, what notes are useful or not, what is detrimental to the restitution, etc. It allows all the participants to make an objective evaluation of what constitute notes based on *efficiency* and *economy* (ILG & LAMBERT 1996: 78, emphasis in original).

In 2010, I started using the Smartpen in the classroom for consecutive interpreting exercises as a tool to assess note-taking skills during consecutive interpretations. It was trialled as a resource to facilitate students' evaluation of their own note-taking conventions, and was introduced in the second semester of a three-semester, post-graduate Masters programme, at a point where trainees had already established a foundation and gained a clear understanding of the nature of consecutive interpretation and at a point where they had also developed their own system of note-taking. Information on the nature of these initial experiments with the digital pen and the design of activities and pedagogical sequences (class activities A, B and C) are contained in Orlando (2010: 80). Since then, and in order to collect data on students' progress and feedback on the assessment of notes using the captured handwriting and speech, the following steps have been undertaken to ensure that all students and educators had the same exposure to the digital pen in the classroom. They were requested to follow the sequence described below when working on the consecutive interpretation of speeches. The sequence was set up for a group class activity (up to 6 students). Each student in the group was provided with a Smartpen. The instructor used a video camera to film the students' performance.

4.1 Class activity

STEP 1:
The speech to be interpreted is played or read to students who take notes with their digital pen (the speech is audio recorded and the notes are filmed thanks to the pen's infrared camera).
STEP 2:
The instructor asks the students one after the other to provide their interpretation of one part of the speech and video records them.
STEP 3:
One student's filmed interpretation is video projected and assessed by the group in terms of communication quality (body language, voice, style etc.) and

accuracy (the written version of the source speech is provided to the students and missing or misinterpreted elements are noted and listed down).

STEP 4:

The information recorded by this student's pen (speech and notes) is played on a computer, a laptop or an iPad and is projected to the class. The instructor and students focus on the 'live' filmed notes and on the list of misinterpreted or missing elements, and try to identify potential reasons in the process of note-taking to explain the deficiencies. This step is repeated for each student and each part of the speech.

STEP 5:

A general discussion is conducted by the instructor, stressing the importance of a collective evaluation and of cross-student feedback about the different performances and note-taking conventions. Comments and ideas are shared based on the notes assessed during the session.

As the collected data can be turned into a flash movie or a PDF document, students were invited to upload their notes at the end of each workshop for further use. Alternatively, they could ask their instructor to send it to them by email, for further self-assessment. At the end of the semester a questionnaire was distributed to all students. The main objective of the questionnaire was to check how students perceive the impact of the digital pen on their note-taking conventions, and to record their views on the use of the Smartpen during their training in consecutive interpreting. Based on the responses of students and educators (see next section), it is my belief that the treatment and review of all data on a weekly basis added to the assessment of the interpreter's performance either by the instructor, by a peer, or on a self-assessment basis, undoubtedly helps to identify patterns useful to define personal remedial strategies in the learning process.

5. Implementing the Digital Tool in a Training Institution: a Comparative Case Study Monash University – Mainz/Germersheim University

This section focuses on initial opinions of respondents to a questionnaire on the general usability of the pen and on the play-back functions and effects on note-taking analysis, and the overall benefit to the development of good note-taking conventions including cross-student feedback.

In June 2013, I was the recipient of the Gutenberg Teaching Council grant from the University of Mainz/Germersheim and was invited for two teaching weeks there to assist the Interpreting Studies staff to implement the digital pen technology in their programme. Most activities consisted of information sessions for staff and students and of workshops where data could be collected along the class activity above-mentioned, and was projected and discussed. Two different questionnaires were sent to students and staff later that year to find out what their views and opinions on the technology were.

It was a great opportunity for me to use the digital pen technology and discuss its merits with staff and students who operate in a different country and a different training institution and context. I had so far only collated data from Monash colleagues and students, and having a fresh objective view on the tool was immensely positive.

Responses from Mainz/Germersheim were analysed and compared with responses to the same questionnaires from students and staff from Monash University. The responses from Monash students and staff were respectively collected in 2012 and 2013.

5.1 Responses from students

The following responses were obtained in 2012 from twenty informants enrolled in the master of Interpreting and Translation Studies at Monash University (in their second semester of training), and in 2013 from eight students from the master of Conference Interpreting at the University of Mainz/Germersheim (two in their third semester of study and six in the fourth). The data presented here relate to respondents' selections to responses provided by the author in an anonymously distributed electronic questionnaire. Informants were not required to provide personal details and responses were provided anonymously. Each table footer contains the (verbatim) question that was put to the informants:

Response	Number of informants from Monash	Percentage of informants from Monash	Number of informants from Germersheim	Percentage of informants from Germersheim
Yes	4	20%	1	12.5%
No	16	80%	7	87.5%

Table 1: Had you heard of or used digital pens before?

Clearly, the Smartpen is still not well-known or used by students, whether studying in Australia or in Germany.

Response	Number of informants from Monash	Percentage of informants from Monash	Number of informants from Germersheim	Percentage of informants from Germersheim
Same as normal pen and paper/easy to use	14	70%	4	50%
Different/too many functions to activate/bigger and heavier	6	30%	4	50%

Table 2: Was using the pen similar or different to conventional note-taking with pen and paper?

The pen is not really difficult or different to use even if it is a bit bigger and heavier and if the different functions to be activated can be a problem for some students. [Note that both the Pulse or the Echo model was used, and Pulse is indeed a bit bigger and heavier].

Response	Number of informants from Monash	Percentage of informants from Monash	Number of informants from Germersheim	Percentage of informants from Germersheim
Nothing that I did not know	1	5%	-	-
I start too early/I write too much or useless notes	10	50%	1	12.5%
I can better see the time lag between speech and notes	12	60%	6	75%
I better see what is not memorised or understood	10	50%	3	37.5%
My notes are not well-organised/absence of links	7	35%	-	-
I am good at noting only ideas/key words	4	20%	2	25%
I am good at not writing immediately/too soon	4	20%	2	25%
I have no consistency in using language A or B	2	10%	1	12.5%

Table 3: The digital pen technology enables the playback of recorded notes and accompanying source text. What were you able to observe/learn about your note-taking conventions through the recording and play-back function? (Multiple responses were permitted.)

Despite the fact they have already been taking notes for a semester or more, and that some problems have already been identified and discussed with them, many students still discovered issues with their notes when using the pen and playing back their notes, but can also see some positive elements. The possibility offered to observe the lag/*décalage* between the speech and the notes in real-time is by far the most appreciated, followed by a clear identification of what they do not understand or memorise properly. Students are therefore really aware of the necessity to have access to the process of notes being taken in order to identify their personal defects and determine personified remediation strategies.

Response: "I need to..."	Number of informants from Monash	Percentage of informants from Monash	Number of informants from Germersheim	Percentage of informants from Germersheim
listen more carefully	8	40%	4	50%
write more quickly	4	20%	2	25%
write less	9	45%	7	87.5%
standardise layout and symbols better/find a more efficient system	8	40%	3	37.5%

Table 4: Are there features of your note-taking conventions that you believe you need to address or change, after viewing playbacks of your performance? What are they?

Using the pen and viewing playbacks also makes some of them aware of necessary changes and possible areas of improvement. In both groups, the fact they need to write less and to listen more carefully when listening to a speech will be of interest to many educators who keep on telling that same thing to students in their note-taking classrooms.

Response	Number of informants from Monash	Percentage of informants from Monash	Number of informants from Germersheim	Percentage of informants from Germersheim
Yes	15	75%	7	87.5%
No	5	25%	1	12.5%

Table 5: You were able to view playbacks of recorded notes from other students. Did the ability to see how others take notes influence your understanding and performance of note-taking?

Using the pen and viewing playbacks of other students is judged profitable by 75% to 87.5% of informants. Most of them mentioned getting better ideas and tips from others for symbols, layout, and links.

Response		Number of informants from Monash	Percentage of informants from Monash	Number of informants from Germersheim	Percentage of informants from Germersheim
There is no difference to me		2	10%	-	-
Advantages	Sharing ideas/better analysis and remediation/Clearly see the time lag/raises awareness	13	65%	8	100%
Disadvantages	Specific paper/non recyclable	3	15%	4	50%
	A more expensive resource	2	10%	2	25%
	A few more steps than with conventional (need to get used to it)	3	15%	-	-

Table 6: In previous semesters, note-taking strategies were taught in a conventional way and you all started developing your system of notes. Do you think digital pen technology has advantages or disadvantages in comparison to conventional note-taking training?

Globally, students find advantages in using the pen during their workshops, especially in having the possibility to see and better analyse problems. 100% of students in Germersheim found this feature useful for remediation and analysis. What was also reported by many in class activities was that they benefited greatly from the cross-fertilisation that the sequential and visual representation of not only their own, but also others' notes facilitated (see table 5). Students were thus able to follow what kinds of symbols, acronyms, abbreviations and other layout conventions were employed by others and at which point they employed them in their notes. Disadvantages have been noted too, like the nature and price of the micro-chipped paper compared to 'normal' paper, as well as the need to get used to the different steps to start recording and using the commands at the bottom of the page.

Response	Number of informants from Monash	Percentage of informants from Monash	Number of informants from Germersheim	Percentage of informants from Germersheim
Yes, I am sure it has	8	40%	-	-
Yes, it may have	5	25%	7	87.5%
No, not necessarily	4	20%	1	12.5%
No, I don't think so	3	15%		

Table 7: Do you think that using the digital pen technology this semester has helped you to develop a satisfying and more efficient note-taking system and to perform better in consecutive interpreting exercises? Tick one of the following.

These selected responses confirm what was already put forward after previous informal experiments: there is merit in introducing the use of the digital pen in the classroom at some stage in the training curriculum, as part of a meta-cognitive strategy. The Smartpen's features enable students to visualise and identify better their own qualities or deficiencies, to share ideas and get inspiration from other students, to understand better and analyse what can go wrong if they take excessive or disorganised notes.

What has emerged from my observations and from students' responses collected in the last three years is that, at each stage of the students' training, the audio-visual evaluation, either by an instructor, a peer or as a self-directed exercise, should impact on the student's performance and note-taking skill development.

5.2 Responses From Educators

The following responses were collected from 8 Germersheim and 5 Monash educators. All respondents are both practitioners and educators. They all teach consecutive interpreting and offer comment on their students' note-taking conventions during their classes.

The data presented here is valuable insofar as educators from different backgrounds, different ages, with different teaching experience, who are practising and teaching in different contexts, have expressed their view on the use of digital pen in the classroom, its advantages and disadvantages. In several tables the responses related to the same idea or concept have been aggregated when possible.

	Respondents	Gender		Age			Years of interpreting practice				
		F	M	30+	40+	50+	1-5	6-10	11-15	16-20	20+
Germers-heim	8	8	-	3	-	5	2	1	-	1	4
Monash	5	2	3	3	2	-	2	2		1	

Table 8: Profiles of respondents

5.2.1 Questionnaire

1. Had you heard of digital pens before they were presented at your university?

	Yes	No
Germersheim	6	2
Monash	4	1

2. Had you heard of digital pens being used in interpreting training before they were presented at your university?

	Yes	No
Germersheim	2	6
Monash	2	3

3. How long have you been teaching consecutive interpreting and note-taking?

	1-5 years	6-10	11-15	16-20	20+
Germersheim	1	3	-	1	3
Monash	3	2	-	-	-

4. a) If any, what are the main problems you have faced in teaching note-taking?

	Germersheim Number of answers (in %)	Monash
Students focus too much on notes and symbols, not enough on comprehension and analysis. They do not listen properly. They write too much.	6 (75%)	4 (80%)
No possibility for trainers to identify WHEN something is noted down in relation to the source speech (no access to the process but only the product)/only a 'guess' approach	5 (62.5%)	3 (60%)
No possibility to show how *décalage* is related to comprehension/students' problems in consecutive are due to comprehension and analysis problems	4 (50%)	2 (40%)
No holistic approach/not enough focus on the macro-structure of texts/the notes are often too linear/the notes are too often illegible or ineffective	4 (50%)	4 (80%)
The use of the black/white board or an overhead projector in the classroom to see notes being taken, which is unrealistic and not comfortable.	2 (25%)	1 (20%)

b) How do you remediate these issues?

	Germersheim	Monash
Focus more on listening comprehension and speech analysis	4 (50%)	2 (40%)
Consecutive exercises without notes (to focus more on listening comprehension)	2 (25%)	2 (40%)
Specific exercises from the same source speech to learn how to take 'effective' (semantically loaded) notes/work on several chunks of the text several times in a row aiming at noting less and more effectively	2 (25%)	2 (40%)

5. How do you usually comment on your students' note-taking conventions in relation to the source speech?

	Germers-heim	Mo-nash
I use a black board/overhead projector to see 'live' notes and to identify and discuss issues (structure, intentions, links…)/I reproduce efficient notes on the board for the benefit of the whole class	4 (50%)	3 (60%)
I check the notes of a student after a performance to see what they noted and to discuss in relation to their performance (accurate units of meaning, links, logical flow)/I comment on the volume of notes not only the content	6 (75%)	5 (100%)
I tell them and show them that structure, coherence and sense prevails/I tell them to focus on links and semantically loaded markers (e.g. modals in English)	4 (50%)	3 (60%)
I play the recording of a performance to the whole class and ask them to follow their own notes and to comment/discuss in relation to what they can hear	2 (25%)	1 (20%)
I don't. Notes are secondary. I only discuss their performance in terms of comprehension and memorisation	1 (12.5%)	-

6. In the presentation you attended you were shown that digital pen technology enables the synchronised playing back of recorded notes and accompanying source text. What do you think of this feature?

	Germers-heim	Monash
Great (x5)! Wonderful (x3)! Excellent feature! (x4) Very useful (x5)!	7 (87.5%)	5 (100%)
It allows to show *décalage*/what is understood or not/the link between notes and comprehension/the moment something is written down or a mistake is made	7 (87.5%)	5 (100%)
It would help students to see they need to wait longer before noting/to trace back their mistakes/to see they need to take some distance with the textual elements	4 (50%)	3 (60%)
It is a brilliant way to have access to the process of notes and not only the product/to see how students digest and understand a speech	3 (37.5%)	2 (40%)
It is an extremely useful feature for students to self-assess their work 'actively' and to analyse the decisions/choices they consciously or unconsciously made.	1	1
I am not sure it actually has any added value	1	-

7. The digital pen allows showing students several playbacks of recorded notes from other trainees. Do you think the ability to see how others take notes can influence your students' understanding and performance of note-taking?

	Germers-heim	Monash
Yes	6 (75%)	5 (100%)
Yes, but … We do not need the digital pen to do so What prevails is the analysis, not the notes	2 (25%)	-
No	-	-
It allows new ideas/to be inspired by others We often learn more from others/ Note-taking is an individual process, this allows multiple sources of knowledge and different perspectives	6 (75%)	5 (100%)
Peer feedback is often more valuable than teacher feedback/it is excellent to make students work together/good student-focussed approach	3 (37.5%)	2 (40%)

8. From the presentation you attended, do you think digital pen technology has advantages or disadvantages in comparison to conventional note-taking training? Explain.

The table below sums up the different answers from the respondents of both institutions and are presented as they were expressed in the questionnaire. Similar answers have been aggregated.

ADVANTAGES: The Smartpen allows…

- To show the relation between comprehension and *décalage*;
- To have evidence and no longer use a 'guess' approach;
- To spot problems in the process of note-taking more easily, to have a better diagnosis of what works or not;
- To see 'live' HOW and WHEN things are written down;
- To establish a cross-fertilisation process in the classroom whereby students learn from each other and not only from the instructor;
- To show why individual systems of notes work or not;

- To shake up didactic practises of teaching and assessing and be more student-focussed;
- To be more efficient in what we want to teach as the projected data can perfectly illustrate what we tell students;
- To give feedback to students anytime (you can send the recordings and videos to them by email or put them on a USB at the end of the class)
- Students to engage in self-directed note-taking independently to a greater degree than they would otherwise engage in;
- Interactive and live peer-evaluation and self-evaluation

DISADVANTAGES:
- It takes time to set up the equipment in each classroom for each class;
- Retrieving data and pass it on (send it) to students is more time-consuming than giving feedback the usual way;
- Instructors should be careful not to give the impression that good note-taking is more important than memorisation and analysis;
- The digital pen and the micro-chipped paper are expensive;
- The digital pen is a bit different to use than a normal pen and the notepads have side spiral binding, whereas students are taught to use top spiral binding.

9. Do you think that using the digital pen technology could help you to develop a satisfying and more efficient way of teaching note-taking systems for your students to perform better in consecutive interpreting exercises? Please explain.

	Germersheim	Monash
Yes	7 (87.5%)	5 (100%)
No	1	-
If it is used in a systematic way along scaffolding strategies with special objectives at different stages of the training	3 (37.5%)	3 (60%)
Students should be encouraged to acquire one or use those available at university for regular self-assessment exercises	2 (25%)	2 (40%)
It should be used as a diagnosis tool especially at the beginning of the training in note-taking/consecutive interpreting, when we focus on the process.	5 (62.5%)	3 (60%)

10. Will you be using digital pen technology during your note-taking classes?

	Germersheim	Monash
Yes	8 (100%)	5 (100%)
No	-	-

11. Why?

- To show them my notes;
- To give it a try and explore the possibilities;
- To compare the evolution of their notes and note-taking techniques at different stages of training;
- To develop new pedagogical resources;
- To better diagnose students' qualities or deficiencies;
- To set up group/peer activities;
- To show students the technology exists and encourage them to use it;

12. Would you recommend the use of digital pen technology to other trainers?

	Germersheim	Monash
Yes	7 (87.5%)	5 (100%)
No	1	-

13. Do you have any other comment on the use of this technology for note-taking training?

> - The technology is available so this is something that we should introduce to the students and allow them to trial.
> - It would be great to have the possibility to show two different 'live' sets of notes at the same time, instead of one only.
> - It seems to be more useful for research and data collection than for training
> - I'd be interested in the aspect of allowing consec/simul (the hybrid mode of interpreting) and the way that the pens can allow students to transition between the two traditional modes.[1]

5.3 Discussion

Most of the responses provided by the educators are in line with the views of all other trainers who have tried using the pen for pedagogical reasons and with whom I have had the opportunity to exchange informally. With this sample of 13 educators, no specific difference relative to their respective institutions belonging can be pointed out. Most of them face the same issues when teaching consecutive interpreting and note-taking: students focus too much on their systems of notes and write too much; they do not listen to and analyse the source speech enough; it is impossible to show the 'live' process of notes being taken or how comprehension and *décalage* relate unless using impracti-

---

[1] During the presentation on the use of the Smartpen in the note-taking/consecutive interpreting classroom, I also presented another possible application allowed by the pen: the possibility to interpret in a hybrid mode of interpreting, labelled Consec-simul with notes, whereby the interpreter records the source speech with the pen and takes notes, and then plays back the recording through ear sets and provides a simultaneous interpretation with still the possibility to use their notes. See 6 below.

cal solutions (OHPs, black boards); students are too linear in their note-taking and do not work enough at the macro-level of the speech. Responses show that all the surveyed educators are interested in using the digital pen with their students; nearly all of them would recommend the tool to other trainers; the high majority of them think that using the pen could help them to be more efficient in their teaching and would provide them with a better diagnosis of their students' qualities and deficiencies. The large majority thinks that establishing a cross-fertilisation process in note-taking assessment in their classroom would benefit all students and that the digital pen would help peer-assessment and group work. Positive feedback was reported in relation to the Smartpen's ability to track the sequence of notes taken throughout a speech, to clearly show how *décalage* and comprehension are related, to locate examples of unclear notes, notes that are too copious for the content contained in the speech, as well as gaps where notes could or should have been made, usually due to lack of clarity of the source speech or in its comprehension. The main questions asked and the caveats put forward by the respondents are about the time to introduce the pen and install the equipment in their classroom; the time required to retrieve the data and send feedback to students; or the costs related to its purchase and its use (pens, micro-dotted paper). But overall no one really doubts the relevance, the usefulness and the significance of the tool. Many of the respondents however insisted on the fact that a good consecutive interpretation does not depend on good note-taking skills only, and that enough time should be dedicated to work on listening comprehension and analysis. I too reiterate here that, indeed, training in this mode should encapsulate several sub-sets of skills.

6. Digital Pen Technology and Interpreting in a Hybrid Mode

The Smartpen is currently also being trialled as a means of offering a hybrid mode of interpreting, *Consec-simul with notes*. The hybrid mode allows an interpretation which is both consecutive and simultaneous. In a context where consecutive interpreting is required, the digital pen offers the possibility to record the source speech and to immediately play it back, from the micro-chipped paper to the interpreter who, using the pen's ear sets, can give a simultaneous interpretation while listening to the source text for a second time and reading from her/his notes. The possibility to slow down or speed up the playback also adds some comfort during the interpretation.

I conducted a comparative study on this topic in 2012, with professional NAATI accredited interpreters. The study analysed and assessed their interpreting performances in the traditional consecutive mode and the hybrid mode (using the *Livescribe Smartpen)* in terms of accuracy, fluency and communicative behaviour. One of the objectives was also to test the viability of the hybrid mode with the pen and the professionals' view about using it in professional settings. The detailed methodology and results of the study can be found in Orlando 2014, but the general conclusion was a recommendation to consider introducing training in the hybrid mode in interpreter training curricula.

Given these results and the necessity to train interpreters in how to operate the pen if they wanted to use it in such a mode, we decided to develop and implement a few training activities in the course of the master degree curriculum at Monash University.

In the hybrid *Consec-simul* mode, the advantage is that the interpreter already knows the content of the speech when (s)he starts interpreting, can use the notes (s)he has taken in anticipation or backup, and can also slow down the playback if necessary. Even if the simultaneous interpretation is facilitated, the difficulty of working in this mode lies in the various tasks to be completed simultaneously: starting the playback, listening and understanding, speaking, reading the notes, and operating the pen if necessary. That is why performing in this unorthodox mode requires specific training, as for the two other modes.

Over the three semesters of their training, our interpreting students are trained in consecutive interpreting (long and short) during the whole first, second and third semester. Simultaneous interpreting is introduced little by little in the second semester only and fully in the third. They are introduced to the Smartpen for their note-taking exercises in the second semester. This is also when they are exposed to some cognitive activities to prepare them to simultaneous interpreting, and especially to listen and speak at the same time. That is why it was decided to start working in the hybrid mode in the second half of that semester, when students know how to use the pen and have already experienced split attention exercises.

As for the first experiments, the activities implemented were calqued on the training in consecutive or in simultaneous: easy speeches to start with (personal narratives, speeches with logical arguments, etc.), which were delivered at an easy pace while students took notes with the digital pen which was recording the speech. Then, they were taught to trigger the speech playback, to use the ear set and start interpreting simultaneously.

Research would be needed to determine what moment would be best to start training in this mode, but it appeared convenient to start between consecutive and simultaneous, seeing the hybrid mode as maybe a step to simultaneous interpreting. As we started training in *Consec-simul* in second semester 2013, I do not have much distance yet to comment on the experiment and it is difficult to see what works or not, but future developments and projects will help determine sound pedagogical strategies. The fact is that beyond the 'technical' steps used in operating the pen, there was apparently nothing very different between learning to work in this mode or the two others. And even after just a few weeks of work in *Consec-simul,* students were very enthusiastic in adopting the mode. This is already a very encouraging sign which might lead to the future adoption of a new mode of interpreting in training institutions.

7. Conclusion

This chapter aimed at presenting digital pen technology and at discussing its potential implementation in the consecutive interpreting classroom, especially in the development of note-taking conventions. The comparative case study of two distinct institutions where the technology has been implemented, through the responses from students and educators, provides insightful data on the relevance and usefulness of such a tool.

Even if note-taking conventions and systems are by nature individual and subjective, their development throughout training should be guided by the need to be economic and effective. To diagnose qualities and deficiencies in their students' systems and to provide them with feedback and remediation strategies, as well as to teach them to develop meaning-bearing and semantically loaded notes, educators teaching note-taking need to access the process of notes being taken 'live' with a technology that permits instant evaluation and feedback. Very few tools allow such a possibility and responses to the questionnaires clearly indicate that the *Livescribe Smartpen* digital technology offers an ideal solution. If used in specific didactic sequences and along clear pedagogical objectives and clear metacognitive strategies, digital pen technology should establish itself as a 'must have' in interpreter training institutions.

Students from the two institutions surveyed clearly indicate that using the pen on a regular basis in their note-taking workshops would help them identify and correct some issues in their note-taking conventions. They are also positive that having the possibility to see other students' notes inspires them and that seeing their notes unfold on screen gave them a better understanding of what they should focus on while listening to the source speech. Most students also acknowledged the fact that having access to the process of their notes being taken and being given the possibility to assess them would help them to improve their systems of notes.

Despite some caveats related to the price of the equipment and the time needed for the installation and operation of the pen, as well as for collating data to be discussed with students, educators were all positive that digital pen technology is worth being used in their classroom. They reckon it would assist them greatly in their teaching, that it is a 'wonderful, very useful tool', whether used as a diagnosis tool or as a way to capture *décalage* and show to students that very often 'an important lag is necessary' if one wants to understand the source speech and provide a faithful and complete rendering. The majority is also interested in the possibility to project students' notes to the whole class so that everyone gets inspiration from others and that either peer-assessment or self-assessment activities can be conducted.

The last section of the chapter is dedicated to the presentation of a hybrid mode of interpreting whereby the interpreter can, in a consecutive interpreting context, provide a simultaneous interpretation thanks to the pen's feature which allows note-taking as well as recording and playback of the source speech to be interpreted. Research and training about the *Consec-simul* with notes mode is still budding but early studies show interesting results which, should they be confirmed by larger investigations, would obviously have an impact on the way we train interpreters in the 21st century.

From the different posts one can find on the subject online, there is little doubt that the profession and industry is ready to take digital pen technology onboard. Whether it is in relation to note-taking training or to the possibility to see a new interpreting mode being developed in the coming years, practitioners, students and educators seem open-minded to technology and innovation. What they all point out is the need to be properly trained to use the promising features of such technology. The ball is now on the side of interpreter training institutions.

Note

Disclaimer: The author of this article declares hereby that he does not have any commercial relation or partnership with *Livescribe*, the manufacturer of the Smartpen, that he is not the beneficiary of any financial, research or other remuneration from this company. Information provided on the product here reflects the views of the author and not those of the company.

References

For more information on the digital pen, visit www.livescribe.com

ALEXIEVA, Bistra (1994): "On teaching note-taking in consecutive interpreting". In: DOLLERUP, Cay & LINDEGAARD, Annette (eds.): *Teaching Translation and Interpreting 2*. Amsterdam/Philadelphia: John Benjamins, 199-206.

CHOI, Jung Yoon (2006): "Metacognitive evaluation method in consecutive interpretation for novice learners", *Meta* 51(2), 273-283.

DRECHSEL, Alexander (2013): *Interpreters vs. Technology: Reflections on a difficult relationship*: https://vkdblog.wordpress.com/tag/ibm/ (14.12.2013).

Endless Possibilities Talks (2012): *Technology options for interpreting – 28 March 2012*: http://endlesspossibilitiestalks.blogspot.co.uk (28.03.2013).

GENTILE, Adolfo (1991): "The application of theoretical constructs from a number of disciplines for the development of a methodology of teaching in interpreting and translating", *Meta* 36(2-3), 344-351.

GILE, Daniel (1991): "Prise de notes et attention en début d'apprentissage de l'interprétation consécutive – une expérience – démonstration de sensibilisation", *Meta* 36(2-3), 431-439.

HANSEN, Inge & SHLESINGER, Miriam (2007): "The silver lining. Technology and self-study in the interpreting classroom", *Interpreting* 9(1), 95-118.

HIEBL, Bettina (2011): *Simultanes Konsekutivdolmetschen mit dem Livescribe™ Echo™ Smartpen*. Masterarbeit, Universität Wien. Zentrum für Translationswissenschaft: http://othes.univie.ac.at/14608 (20.09.2013).

ILG, Gérard & LAMBERT, Sylvie (1996): "Teaching consecutive interpreting", *Interpreting* 1(1), 69-99.

Interpreting.info (2012): *What do you think about simultaneous consecutive?*: http://interpreting.info/questions/1448/what-do-you-think-about-simultaneous-consecutive (15.03.2013).

KOSTAL, Nina (2011): *Die Rolle der Notizentechnik beim Konsekutivdolmetschen*. Masterarbeit, Universität Wien. Zentrum für Translationswissenschaft: http://othes.univie.ac.at/16658/ (17.06.2014).

KUNZ, Ingrid (2002): "Interpreting training programmes. The benefits of co-ordination, co-operation and modern technology". In: HUNG, Eva (ed.): *Teaching translation and interpreting 4*. Amsterdam/Philadelphia: John Benjamins, 65-72.

LINDSTROM, Jennifer. H. (2007): "Determining appropriate accommodations for post-secondary students with reading and written expression disorders", *Learning Disabilities Research and Practice* 22(4), 229-236.

NAVARRO-HALL, Esther (2012): *An introduction to sim-consec*. http://1culture.net/1culture/anintroduction-to-sim-consec (19.04.2013).

ORLANDO, Marc (2010): "Digital Pen Technology and Consecutive Interpreting: Another Dimension in Note-Taking Training and Assessment", *The Interpreters' Newsletter* 15, 71-86.

ORLANDO, Marc (2014): "A study on the amenability of digital pen technology in a hybrid mode of interpreting: Consec-simul with notes", *International Journal of Translation and Interpreting Research*. Vol. 6(2), 39-54 (http://www.trans-int.org/index.php/transint).

ORLANDO, Marc (2015): "Digital pen technology and interpreting training, practice and research: status and trends". In: EHRLICH, Suzanne & NAPIER, Jemina (eds.): *Interpreter Education in the Digital Age: Innovation, Access and Change*. Washington: Gallaudet University Press.

Tran, Tu Anh T. & LAWSON, Mike (2001): "Students' procedures for reviewing lecture notes", International Education Journal: Educational Research Conference 2001 Special Issue 1(4), 278-293.

VEENMAN, Marcel V. J.; VAN HOUT-WOLTERS, Bernadette H. A. M. & AFFLERBACH, Peter. (2006): "Metacognition and learning: conceptual and methodological considerations", *Metacognition and Learning* 1, 3-14.

#IntJC The Interpreting Journal Club (2012): Session 17 – 06/09/2012. Digital Pen and Note-Taking, https://sites.google.com/site/interpretjc/home/archive (12.04.2013).

How to Back The Students – Quality, Assessment & Feedback

MARTINA BEHR
behrmart@uni-mainz.de
Johannes Gutenberg University Mainz/Germersheim, Germany
m.behr@mx.uni-saarland.de
Saarland University, Germany

1. Introduction

Quality, assessment[1], and feedback are three aspects that are closely intertwined in conference interpreting training as well as in conference interpreting practice. To become a good or potentially an excellent interpreter not only depends on the student's talent and motivation but also on the didactic and pedagogical skills of the student's trainer. The more the latter knows, the better they can efficiently accompany the learning process of the student. This ensures – by shaping best-qualified future interpreters – the fulfilment of the high quality standards required in conference interpreting.

The first part of this article is a brief overview of the main results of research into quality in interpreting in order to give a brief theoretical background. This may help the trainer a) to identify the different approaches to quality and therefore to concretise particular learning goals in the classroom and b) to focus gradually on the development of different interpreting strategies for real life situations in front of a respective audience.

Since interpreting assessment has come a long way, there are a lot of practical experiences and analytical descriptions about what should be assessed and how. Thus, the second part of this article summarises the different dimensions of assessment and presents the different components that should be considered when comprehensively assessing interpretation.

Finally, assessment always means giving feedback. Even if this task needs a certain amount of sure instinct and empathy, there are still a number of con-

---

1   In line with Moser-Mercer (1996) the term 'assessment' refers to students' performances while 'evaluation' is used when professional interpreters' renderings are at stake.

siderations that are helpful in order to assure that the feedback will actually be of use to the students. Thus, the last part of the article contains some basic explanations about what good feedback is, why it is vital for the learning process, and how, therefore, it should be provided.

2. Quality in Interpreting

When it comes to quality in interpreting there are three main foci: the content, the presentation, and the reception. Henri Barik's (1971) analysis of omissions, additions, and errors in simultaneous interpreting laid the foundation for the so-called equivalence between the source and the target discourse which means nothing less than the correct rendering of the original speech in terms of content. Although this is the most important aspect for quality in interpreting, practitioners as well as researchers very soon became aware of the fact, that any severe assessment or evaluation must take into account a large number of diverse factors that vary with the respective situation – this is the main reason why a clear and unique definition of quality in interpreting has never been and can never be found.

In reference to evaluating interpreting performances Hildegund Bühler asked *"Who* should evaluate?" (BÜHLER 1986: 231, own emphasis) and set up 16 criteria which both peer interpreters (AIIC members) and users of the interpreting services considered important for quality in interpreting (although with different rankings). Since then, **eight** of these 16 criteria have been commonly used as a "reliable tool for evaluating quality" (SHLESINGER et al. 1997: 128):

*1) native accent, 2) **pleasant voice**, 3) **fluency of delivery**, 4) **logical cohesion of utterance**, 5) **sense consistence with original message**, 6) **completeness of interpretation**, 7) **correct grammatical usage**, 8) **use of correct terminology**, 9) **use of appropriate style**, 10) thorough preparation of conference documents, 11) endurance, 12) poise, 13) pleasant appearance, 14) reliability, 15) ability to work in a team, 16) positive feedback from delegates.* (BÜHLER 1986: 234)

Relying on these findings, other studies proved that the ranking of these criteria as well as the listeners' general expectations depend largely on the nature of the given conference and therefore on the respective type of users. European parliamentarians, participants in a technical or a medical conference, the interpreters themselves: for each group the ranking of the criteria differs – there is, however, consensus that sense consistency with the original message has to be one of the three most important aspects (cf. KURZ 1989: 144). That means that the evaluation of the different criteria for quality in interpreting always depends on the particular conference setting where the interpretation is performed. Accordingly, quality in interpreting can be defined as "quality as fitness for purpose" (GRIBĆ 2008: 247), and this is judged mainly by the listeners. Nevertheless this approach ignores an important fact that was put in a nutshell by Shlesinger: "Do our clients know what is good for them?" (SHLESINGER et al. 1997: 126). As the clients cannot assess the sense consistency with the original they are indeed not in the best position to judge the interpreters' performances. But as they are the clients and provide the fundamental reason that interpretation indeed exists in the first place, they cannot be ignored either – every interpreting setting has, first of all, an aim (i.e. the communication between the speaker and the listener) and therefore results in and consists of complex interaction between all the participants[2]. This means that, knowing the client's inability to evaluate sense consistency, it is the duty of the interpreter to assure the right rendering of the content – this is an essential part of the professional interpreter's "self-concept" (ANDRES 2011).

As the trainers' task is to shape future professional interpreters it is consequently their responsibility to guide the students so that they achieve such professional behaviour. Once the implementation of sense consistency is thereby guaranteed, attention has to be directed to the communicative event proper where "communication does not end in the booth" (SELESKOVITCH 1986: 236). 'After' the booth there are the listeners (i.e. the clients) with all their heterogeneity by reason of their respective backgrounds, their ways of information processing, their willingness (interest) and physical capacity (alertness or fatigue) to listen and to understand. And as a matter of course all these aspects come into play when the listeners are asked to evaluate the interpretation.

This approach, i.e. to consider the listeners' ways of understanding and judging (cf. BEHR 2013), refers, among other things, to the sociological factors

---

[2] This view, of course, was strongly influenced by Cecilia Wadensjø's work on community interpreting: *Interpreting as Interaction* (WADENSJÖ 1998).

that generally play an important role when evaluating the performance (or behaviour) of someone else. Hence, in line with the recent sociological turn in Interpreting Studies not only the 'hard facts', such as sense consistency, correct terminology etc. have to be considered, but also the 'soft facts', for example the cognitive effect of prosodic features on the user (cf. COLLADOS AÍS et al. 2011) or the impact these issues have on the listeners' judgment. The interpreting practitioners' approach to assessing quality in interpreting mostly focuses on the three aspects of content, style and technique/presentation (see table 1). While there is enough experience of, and knowledge about, the two first categories and their relevance, we know less about how and – even more importantly – to which degree the form of presentation has an impact on the users' judgment and therefore the observed quality. Studies showed that users tend to misevaluate the quality of an interpreting performance when it is presented less vividly or less fluently (COLLADOS AÍS et al. 2011). In doing so, most of these users totally ignore the fact that they are not suited to judge the quality in terms of sense consistency with the original speech. Thus, an appropriate evaluation of quality in interpreting, as well as sound training in interpreting, not only pays attention to content and correctness but also to the role and probable impacts of the cognitive effect on the users. The relevance of the respective setting and the particular audience has to be considered as an important factor in the training of interpreters: in line with the explanations above, quality in interpreting means an adaptive quality that not only embraces the conference type (cf. GILE 1989) and the topic, the register etc., but also respects the users and their heterogeneity.

There is still a lot of research to be done in this field but at the training level the trainers and the students have to bear in mind that users may evaluate on the basis of factors that are less 'objective' or content-based but far more 'subjective' and based on personal preference. With this in mind we will turn to the different types of assessment.

3. Assessing a Performance

The way an interpretation is assessed largely depends on the purpose of the evaluation[3]: is it for a university examination, for an entrance test to an institu-

---

3   As pointed out by Kalina, the quality of an interpretation basically also depends on the quality of

tion, or for training at different levels and therefore with different foci on the various skills and strategies that the students need to learn to master? And will the evaluation be made by a small jury with only two people or by a team of several jury members? According to these varying functions the evaluation will need to be adapted and different evaluation sheets should be used. Thus, three types of such evaluation sheets are presented below referring to a) interpreting practice, b) interpreting examinations and c) interpreting training.

3.1 Evaluation Sheets for Interpreting Practice

As mentioned above, evaluation in interpreting practice most prominently relies on three to four criteria as shown in table 1, which is the evaluation sheet of the GD Interpretation (SCIC), and which may serve as a sample for the interpreting practice in general. This form is used as a kind of peer evaluation inasmuch as the judges are themselves interpreters who also want to evaluate – beyond merely content and form – the interpreting techniques and the general and linguistic knowledge of the candidate.

1	Name of the speaker:		Subject of the speech:			Difficulty:			
	CONTENT			FORM		TECHNIQUE		KNOWLEDGE	
From: to:	Accuracy	Completeness	Internal coherence (links, contresens, etc.)	Target language (register, syntax, etc.)	Presentation	Technique: décalage, syntax, finishing sentences, etc.	Speed, stamina, etc.	Passive language	General knowledge
Good									
Sufficient									
Insufficient									

Table 1: Evaluation Sheet for Entrance Tests of the DG Interpretation (SCIC)

The advantage of this sheet lies in its simplicity: it is reasonably possible to evaluate all the aspects at the same time, even though it can be useful to agree beforehand that each jury member will evaluate only one criterion.

---

the source text, i.e. the original speech (cf. KALINA 2004; an updated English version of her article in German will be published in ZWISCHENBERGER & BEHR 2015).

3.2 Evaluation Sheets for Examinations

A good example of an evaluation form that can be used for such a split focus on criteria by different jury members, as mentioned above, is the evaluation sheet for both simultaneous and consecutive interpreting that is used for exams at the FTSK (see table 2).

Presentation	good	average	bad	comments
pronunciation				
prosody				
complete sentences				
communicative competence				
fluency				

Content	good	average	bad	comments
completness				
sense consistency				
cultural competence				
coherence				
monitoring				

Language	good	average	bad	comments
grammar				
syntax				
lexis				

Interpreting strategies	good	average	bad	comments
application of interpreting strategies				

Especially good/especially poor:

Total mark:

Table 2: Evaluation Sheet for Midterm and Final Exams at the FTSK

Although this matrix seems quite complex it can be employed in a simple way: either with several jury members (which should always be the case! (cf. BEHR 2013[4])) so that each member can concentrate on the different aspects of one of the principle domains (presentation, content, language or technique), or with only two examiners, who at least are able to focus on these main criteria without narrowing them down to the specific sub-criteria.

3.3 Evaluation Sheets for Training

It is obvious that good training does not consist of simply showing the students how a professional interpreter masters the task but entails explaining to the students what different skills are needed for the profession and – even more importantly – how they can be acquired. This can be done by showing them the respectively most efficient way (i.e. through helpful exercises) to improve in the different domains of the required skills. For that purpose, it will be necessary to break down the complex task of interpreting into several smaller – and thus manageable – subtasks. One way of doing this is to use an evaluation sheet with different macro- and micro-criteria, which was designed by Alessandra Riccardi (2002). Thanks to this comprehensive list of relevant aspects, the trainer can a) show the students all the criteria which are important and which will be marked when it comes to the final exams and b) select a particular item the students will need to concentrate on during a certain training phase. It is very useful to involve the students when choosing the criterion: on the one hand this allows setting clear learning goals and having a well-structured and efficient learning process, and on the other hand it enhances the students' motivation inasmuch as they take an active part in the teaching-learning process – this, in general, is beneficial to the atmosphere in the classroom and consequently favours the learning environment (which is one essential condition for effective learning). Or as Benjamin Franklin put it: "Tell me and I forget, teach me and I may remember, involve me and I learn" (FRANKLIN: online).

Table 3 (see below) shows Riccardi's evaluation matrix for simultaneous interpretation, which for the consecutive mode must be completed by the categories "eye contact" and "hand control and/or gesticulation and/or posture"

---

4   In her empirical study Behr showed that a single examiner tends to give different grades when evaluating the same interpretation twice whereas this effect can be compensated by evaluation by a group of examiners (BEHR 2013).

(RICCARDI 2002: 124). The list also contains certain 'soft' criteria – considering them is in line with what was said in the first part of this article, i.e. the psycho-sociological aspects influencing the users' judgment.

As set out, using this matrix allows trainers to identify and to set concrete learning goals by breaking down the complex interpreting process into several subtasks, i.e. into skills that can be learnt one by one. This not only permits each student to focus on individual problems, but also ensures that there is no cognitive overload of tasks – this, in turn, maintains the students' motivation and encourages them to aim higher towards the next tasks (every task has to be chosen corresponding to the particular student's learning stage: learning goals which cannot be attained may have a very counterproductive effect on the learner and their motivation to improve themselves). The success of such progressive learning depends on the one hand on the students' willingness, motivation and general skills, and on the other hand on the trainer's capacity to accompany this process well – which essentially is done by providing concrete and helpful feedback.

Evaluation sheet for CI examination

☐ consecutive from L1   into L2
☐ consecutive from L2   into L1

phonological deviations	☐ none	☐ some	☐ many
prosody deviations	☐ none	☐ some	☐ many
production deviations	☐ none	☐ some	☐ many
pauses (>3 sec.)	☐ none	☐ some	☐ many
eye contact	☐ none	☐ occasional	☐ frequent
hand control and/or gesticulation and/or posture	☐ none	☐ satisfactory	☐ good
lexical deviations (common)			
words	☐ none	☐ some	☐ many
collocations	☐ none	☐ some	☐ many
lexical deviations (technical)			
words	☐ none	☐ some	☐ many
collocations	☐ none	☐ some	☐ many
morphosyntactic deviations	☐ none	☐ some	☐ many
logical/semantic deviations	☐ none ☐ acceptable	☐ some ☐ serious	☐ many ☐ unacceptable
omissions	☐ none/some ☐ useful(coherence)	☐ few ☐ negligible	☐ many ☐ sense alteration
additions	☐ none/some ☐ useful(coherence)	☐ few ☐ negligible	☐ many ☐ intrusive
reformulation	☐ good	☐ satisfactory	☐ poor
calques	☐ none	☐ some	☐ many
register	☐ maintained	☐ modified	☐ altered
technique	☐ good	☐ satisfactory	☐ poor
successful solutions	☐ none/some	☐ few	☐ many
overall performance	☐ good	☐ satisfactory	☐ poor

Evaluation sheet for SI examination

☐ simultaneous from L1   into L2
☐ simultaneous from L2   into L1

phonological deviations	☐ none	☐ some	☐ many
prosody deviations	☐ none	☐ some	☐ many
production deviations	☐ none	☐ some	☐ many
pauses (>3 sec.)	☐ none	☐ some	☐ many
lexical deviations (common)			
words	☐ none	☐ some	☐ many
collocations	☐ none	☐ some	☐ many
lexical deviations (technical)			
words	☐ none	☐ some	☐ many
collocations	☐ none	☐ some	☐ many
morphosyntactic deviations	☐ none	☐ some	☐ many
logical/semantic deviations	☐ none ☐ acceptable	☐ some ☐ serious	☐ many ☐ unacceptable
omissions	☐ none/some ☐ useful(coherence)	☐ few ☐ negligible	☐ many ☐ sense alteration
incomplete sentences	☐ none/some	☐ few	☐ many
additions	☐ none/some ☐ useful(coherence)	☐ few ☐ negligible	☐ many ☐ intrusive
reformulation	☐ good	☐ satisfactory	☐ poor
calques	☐ none	☐ some	☐ many
register	☐ maintained	☐ modified	☐ altered
technique	☐ good	☐ satisfactory	☐ poor
successful solutions	☐ none/some	☐ few	☐ many
overall performance	☐ good	☐ satisfactory	☐ poor

Table 3: Evaluation Sheet for SI Examinations (RICCARDI 2002)

4. Feedback

The first conference interpreters, who excelled in their profession without any prior teaching, were certainly very talented but also highly exceptional. Since the need for professional – especially simultaneous – interpreters has increased over time, the role of training in interpreting has become more and more important. Generally, the key to becoming an expert in a special field lies – beyond having a basic aptitude (see CHABASSE in this volume) – in an approach that is called deliberate practice (see introduction by ANDRES and BEHR in this volume). Deliberate practice conceives learning as a two-step-method: first the individual skills that are required at an expert level need to be identified and broken down. Then, they should be rehearsed (as separately as possible) over and over again in order to reach a level where they can be applied automatically. Deliberate practice is considered the most efficient way to improve – and as an essential component it requires constant coaching feedback and therefore an active and competent trainer (cf. ERICSSON 1996, ANDRES 2013). This trainer should specify clear goals for improvement (i.e. learning tasks) and should guide the trainee in their learning process by giving feedback that allows the student a) to maintain or to increase their personal motivation, b) to clearly distinguish for themselves the faults and weaknesses of a performance and to receive concrete advice on how to overcome the problems identified and therefore c) to have all the necessary tools to train intensively and repetitively in order to develop the automatisms that are needed for a multi-operational task such as conference interpreting.

4.1 The Key to Good Feedback: Clear Tasks

A required condition sine qua non for good feedback is having a well-defined learning task in the first place. Only if the student knows exactly what they are asked to do, i.e. only if the challenge (just one at a time) is concrete enough and well explained to them, can the feedback that follows be sufficiently precise and thus productive. The (often only implicitly demanded) task to 'interpret the following text well' is too vague and therefore results in the fact that the students will interpret the text as well as they can, while they are neither aware of all the special challenges and problems that occurred, nor do they have any idea of how to solve these problems. This means that they will do acceptably well as long as the text does not pose any greater challenge, but that they will fail as soon as there is a problem they cannot deal with. Although the students will improve by applying such a method, progress will be so slow that the relatively short period of two years of a Master's curriculum at most universities will be insufficient.

Thus, presenting concrete tasks where problems can be detected will allow the students to have a clear goal to attain, and enable the trainer to refer concretely to this very task and to evaluate how well it was achieved – and this is the core of good feedback. With problem-related advice about how to overcome the difficulties they encountered while interpreting, such feedback afterwards enables students to practise deliberately (see DINGFELDER STONE (11) in this volume), i.e. to revise a text passage that caused problems repetitively (e.g. the syntactic structure, a particular expression, a level of high information density, an enumeration etc.) and to develop the necessary relative automatisms. The interpreting strategies thereby obtained (see KADER & SEUBERT in this volume) can be transferred afterwards to similar 'problems' in other contexts and texts.

But what does it really mean to set 'concrete' goals to enhance the learning process? They are effectively defined in the so called 'SMART' approach, where they have to be S-ignificant, M-eaningful, A-ppropriate, R-elevant and T-angible (MÜLLER 2013). Even if targets may be fixed in a more general way for the overall semester (e.g. 'Concentrate on strategies a and b.') they should be broken down into concrete step-by-step goals for a particular lesson or learning period (a week, a month) – for example: 'Wait longer before starting.' (lesson goal); 'Paraphrase whenever possible.' (weekly goal) or 'Try to establish more eye contact with the audience, meaning: be ahead with the reading of your consecutive notes while delivering the target speech.' (monthly goal). The fewer the goals are in number, the more the students can work towards them concretely and the more precise the feedback can be as well. But beyond the fact that good feedback must be tangible, it must also be carried out in a way that fosters the motivation of the student[5]. So, what are the particularities one has to know about giving feedback in order to guarantee this?

---

5 A student may sometimes fail to realise the potential shown in the entrance exams. If such a student ultimately proves to have no aptitude for interpreting after all, the feedback should help that student to become aware of this fact, for example by pointing out alternatives to the interpreting profession.

4.2 The Motivational Function of Feedback

When giving feedback one has to bear in mind that there are different types of learners (cf. KOLB 1984). The same feedback may therefore not have the same effect on every student. Knowledge of human nature as well as a certain amount of empathy and tact facilitate giving feedback in an individual and appropriate manner. Feedback in general should actively encourage the learners to aim higher (and to set their own learning goals, cf. ANDRES 2014). While normally, positive feedback has such an effect on students who themselves want to improve, it may cause a counterproductive reaction from those students who think that they are already good enough, provoking the feeling that there is no further need to get any better. In this case – as in all others – concrete feedback that is based on the content of the performance is presumably better suited to fostering the student's will to keep on practising. Negative feedback can help push a student to aim higher if it provokes a self-confident attitude: 'now more than ever'. If, on the contrary, students are less sure of themselves negative feedback may induce a defensive position – all the more if the feedback is not clearly tangible and thus taken as an overall assessment by the student who tends to simplify things and thinks 'generally, I'm not good at all'.

As we all know giving feedback in interpreting is very often a delicate issue: While in translation training, assessment refers to the written product on a sheet of paper or projected onto a screen, an evaluation in interpreting involves comments on personal characteristics of the student, such as posture, gesture, mimic, prosodic features, etc. – all these elements come into play in interpreting, especially when it is the user who evaluates a performance (see first part of this article). In terms of the importance of all these factors on their cognitive effect on the users, it may be helpful to remind the students of the psychological impact of the so-called primacy-recency-effect on the listener: in a series of information (as in an interpreted speech for example) it is the first and the last stimulus that are remembered the best (MURDOCK 1962). The first impression an interpreter imparts when they start the interpretation, as well as the last impression they give while leaving the rostrum, heavily influence the audience's information processing and judgment. These impressions serve as a basis upon which the listeners will evaluate the overall quality of the interpreter's performance. This applies especially to the consecutive mode where visual elements play a more important role, but it is also relevant to the simultaneous mode where – precisely due to the lack of visibility – the users refer just as much to non-content-based information (e.g. prosodic elements) when they listen to and judge the interpretation. Teachers therefore need to comment in some way on the personal behavioural traits students show while they interpret. But how can feedback that targets these delicate spheres be appropriate and constructive?

4.3 How to Provide Good Feedback

In order to avoid misunderstandings and to support the students with productive and helpful remarks, feedback has to be objective, i.e. based on the facts. The German psychologist and expert in communication Friedemann Schulz von Thun (1981) developed a model that shows the four facets of any utterance: the fact, the self-revealing, the relationship, and the appeal (SCHULZ VON THUN 1981). Teacher's comments like 'You were nervous' or 'Why do you fidget all the time?' are neither helpful nor based on the facts. They rather refer to both the appeal layer of communication (which for the student is very often taken as being condescending and provokes a defensive attitude), and to the relationship layer (which generates on the students' side the feeling that they are being judged purely at the mercy of the teacher who personally does not like them). On the contrary, to stick to the facts and to communicate the effect that the behaviour in question does or might have on the listener avoids these impressions. A better and far more objective way to make a remark on the use of gesture would be: 'I noticed that you gesture a lot, I was irritated/distracted by that/I was uncomfortable with the fact that…, it would help me if…/I would prefer a more discreet presentation'. This combines the matter-based aspect with the self-revealing facet: The first part of this criticism[6] is limited to the description of the observed facts while the second part describes first the perception and then expresses a desire or expectation (ideally worded in the first person) that already indicates some measures that could be taken to enhance the interpretation performance. Again, the perception should be based on concrete facts ('too many gestures hamper concentration on the content the user is interested in') and the expectation should be explained ('a less vivid presentation would allow better concentration on the content'). In order to give such feedback to students who are generally very reticent of feedback and who tend to take it personally, it can be helpful to explain beforehand how the feedback will be given; this puts the focus even more on the objectivity of the

---

6 Criticism means negative *and* positive comments on a person's behaviour or performance.

criticism. When it comes to perception, peer feedback can be of use, too: the trainer should not refer to personal preferences ('I don't like such vivid prosody') but should take the perspective of the audience ('a monotonous speech is generally considered less interesting') as it may be that the trainer's opinion represents an exception. Thus, asking the other students to express their impressions can justify the trainer's remark and allows the involvement of all the students at the same time. Sometimes peer feedback may entail criticism that is too general and therefore superficial ('I think he did well'/'I didn't miss anything'), especially when the students don't know each other very well, or if each and every student in a big class is asked to comment on one co-student's interpretation. However, in order to avail oneself of the advantages of peer feedback, the different criteria for assessment (see the second part of this article) can be divided so that every student only assesses and comments on one criterion[7]. This may furthermore contribute to a positive, constructive, and pleasant atmosphere in the class-room which, in turn, is beneficial to the learning process of the students in general.

The following overview summarises the most important aspects for good feedback.

Be prepared:
    Set clear learning goals for every learning unit on which basis feedback will be given afterwards.
Be simple:
    Feedback that refers to more than ca. three aspects will not or will only vaguely be remembered afterwards by the students and may have a negative effect on motivation.
Be concrete:
    Refer to the matter and do not judge subjectively, refer to the goal that was set beforehand and explain in which way it was not attained, give concrete examples of the aspects the evaluation is based on.
Be clear:
    Prioritise the feedback by emphasizing what can easily be improved and/or what clearly must be improved first.

---

[7] If the number of the students is very high, the peer feedback can be given by a few students for the first interpreting performance and by some others for the second etc.

Be sure:
> Recheck your feedback by asking the student to repeat the criticism you just offered to see if you made it clear and intelligible.

Be inclusive:
> Let the students themselves define the learning goals – this involves and therefore motivates them.
> Let them comment on their performance at first: what did they like, what was difficult for them, where did they manage well, what could have been improved and how?
> Ask for self-evaluation and self-reflection especially of those students who are less open to feedback.

Be comprehensive:
> With the students, analyse (or let them reflect at home on) their performances in order to know: Where did mistakes occur? What was probably the reason for it? Which exercises would be useful in order to overcome the particular difficulties?

Heeding this advice should facilitate good feedback. The reasons for this are explained in this article and can be recapitulated as follows:

At the outset of any training in interpreting there is a student who wants to become a professional interpreter. Along the challenging route to this profession, there is a trainer who accompanies the trainee in a competent and constructive manner. Such competence should be based on some theoretical knowledge (first part of this article) and on a degree of knowledge about the dimensions of assessment and the different perspectives of users evaluating an interpreting performance (second part of this article). Knowing how to provide good feedback (third part of this article) guarantees such a trainer's constructive supervision of the student's learning process in order to help them to improve and acquire all the necessary skills for the profession. The key to successful training is not only the willingness and motivation of the student, who wants to satisfy their hunger and thirst for knowledge or skills, but also a competent teacher who is able to provide constructive feedback, because "Feedback is the breakfast of champions" (BLANCHARD & JOHNSON 2011[4]).

References

ANDRES, Dörte (2011): "Ein integrativ konzipiertes Dolmetschprozessmodell", *Studia Universitatis Babes-Bolyai. Philologia* 2011(1), 81-103.

ANDRES, Dörte (2013): "Das Konzept Freitagskonferenz: Expertiseentwicklung durch berufsorientierte Lehre". In: HANSEN-SCHIRRA, Silvia & KIRALY, Donald (eds.): *Projekte und Projektionen in der translatorischen Kompetenzentwicklung.* Frankfurt a. M. : Peter Lang, 237-255.

ANDRES, Dörte (2014): "Lust verkürzt den Weg: Shakespeare und die Ausbildung im Dolmetschen". In: FORSTNER, Martin et al. (eds.): *CIUTI-Forum 2013. Facing the World's New Challenges. The Role of T & I in Providing Integrated and Efficient and Sustainable Solutions.* Frankfurt a. M.: Peter Lang, 181-192.

BARIK, Henri C. (1971): "A description of Various Types of Omissions, Additions and Errors of Translation Encountered in Simultaneous Interpretation", *Meta* 16(4), 199-210.

BEHR, Martina (2013): *Stimmung und Evaluation. Ein neuer Blick auf Qualität im (Simultan-)Dolmetschen.* Berlin: Frank & Timme.

BLANCHARD, Ken & JOHNSON, Spencer (2011[4]): *The One Minute Manager.* London: Harper Collins.

BÜHLER, Hildegund (1986): "Linguistic (semantic) and extra-linguistic (pragmatic) criteria for the evaluation of Conference Interpreters and Interpretation", *Multilingua* 5(4), 411-439.

COLLADOS AÍS, Ángela et al. (2011): *Qualitätsparameter beim Simultandolmetschen. Interdisziplinäre Perspektiven.* Tübingen: Gunter Narr.

ERICSSON, Anders K. (1996): *The Road to Excellence: The Acquisition of Expert Performance in the Arts and Sciences, Sports and Games.* Hillsdale: Lawrence Erlbaum Associates.

FRANKLIN, Benjamin: online: http://www.americanhistorycentral.com/entry.php?rec=469&view=quotes (19.06.2014).

GILE, Daniel (1989): "Les flux d'information dans les réunions inter-linguistiques et l'interprétation de conférence: premières observations", *Meta* 34(4), 649-660.

KALINA, Sylvia (2004): "Zum Qualitätsbegriff beim Dolmetschen", *Lebende Sprachen* 49(1), 2-7.

KOLB, David (1984): *Experiential Learning: Experiences as the Source of Learning and Development.* Englewood Cliffs: Prentice-Hall.

KURZ, Ingrid (1989): "Conference Interpreting – User Expectations". In: HAMMOND, Deanna L. (ed.): *Coming of Age. Proceedings of the 30th Annual Conference of the American Translator Association.* Medford: Learned Information, 143-148.

MOSER-MERCER, Barbara (1996): "Quality in Interpreting: Some methodological issues", *The Interpreters' Newsletter* 7, 43-55.

MÜLLER, Andreas (2013): Feedback in Lehrveranstaltungen. Workshop Johannes Gutenberg-Universität Mainz, 22.11.2013.

MURDOCK, Bennet (1962): "Serial Position Effect of Free Recall", *Journal of Experimental Psychology* 64(2), 482–488.

RICCARDI, Alessandra (2002): "Evaluation in Interpreting. Macrocriteria and Microcriteria". In: HUNG, Eva (ed.): *Teaching Translation and Interpreting. Building Bridges.* Amsterdam/Philadelphia: John Benjamins, 115-125.

SCHULZ VON THUN, Friedemann (1981): *Miteinander reden: Störungen und Klärungen. Psychologie der zwischenmenschlichen Kommunikation.* Reinbek: Rowohlt.

SELESKOVITCH, Danica (1986): "Comment: Who should assess an Interpreter's Performance?", *Multilingua* 5(4), 236.

SHLESINGER, Miriam et al. (1997): "Quality in Simultaneous Interpreting". In: GAMBIER, Yves; GILE, Daniel & TAYLOR, Christopher (eds.): *Conference Interpreting: Current Trends in Research.* Amsterdam/Philadelphia: John Benjamins, 123-131.

WADENSJÖ, Cecilia (1998): *Interpreting as Interaction.* London/New York: Longman.

ZWISCHENBERGER, Cornelia & BEHR, Martina (2015): *Quality in Interpreting: A Look Around and Ahead.* Berlin: Frank & Timme.

Professionalisation: A Systematic Didactic Approach

JACQUY NEFF
neff@uni-mainz.de
Johannes Gutenberg University Mainz/Germersheim, Germany

1. Introduction

With the implementation of the Bologna Declaration and its three-tier higher education system, universities within the European Higher Education Area were given the opportunity to redesign their curricula in order to make them more market-efficient. According to the Bologna Declaration, all degree levels "shall (also) be relevant to the European labour market as an appropriate level of qualification"[1] Skills to be taught should largely be practical skills. This requirement should be fulfilled through the "Adoption of a system of easily readable and comparable degrees, also through the implementation of the Diploma Supplement, in order to promote European citizens' employability and the international competitiveness of the European higher education system" (Bologna Declaration)[2].

The employability and international competitiveness of conference interpreters have always been at the heart of the conference interpreting training courses at the Faculty of Translation Studies, Linguistics and Cultural Studies at Johannes Gutenberg University in Germersheim, where the author of the present article is currently employed. However, switching from an eight-semester educational model to a postgraduate four term master's course was a compelling challenge. When our faculty faced this challenge, we redesigned the overall training concept in terms of its didactic approach and focused resolutely on skill-oriented teaching units. One of the major novelties concerned the introduction of a professionalisation course for all students regardless of their language combination. The following article pertains to this training unit

---

1   http://europa.eu/legislation_summaries/education_training_youth/lifelong_learning/c11088_en.htm
2   see above

as designed over the years by the author, starting with the first postgraduate Master of Arts degree in conference interpreting, which was introduced in the 2008/09 winter term.

1.1 Background

Professionalisation, as a technical concept in interpreting studies, is defined in a variety of ways covering various meanings, not all of which are relevant to the topics at hand.

Professionalisation may be a concern in an interpreting setting or domain as far as it has not yet acquired the necessary recognition by recipients of interpretation services as being a fully professionalized economic sector. When service providers (i.e. interpreters) are denied their status as professionals, interpreting fees decline and working conditions grow desperate. In order to secure its status, the profession has to first set up a sound foundation of academic training for future service providers. This in turn will 'professionalise' the sector that will be served. Furthermore, a professional organisation should ensure that recipients are served with loyalty, discretion, impartiality and neutrality (PÖCHHACKER 2003), by imposing statutes and codices of ethics and conduct (KÖGEL 2004: 91ff, GRBIĆ 1998: 613f) as well as setting up a quality assurance and litigation system. Other aspects of this kind of professionalisation would include the setup and regular updating of a membership directory made available to customers, a fee policy reflecting the true value of the service rendered without violating regulations governing competition, harmonized working conditions, quality standards and certification of interpreting service providers, for example those based on the EU accreditation scheme (HERWIG & MEYER 2013: 8). Professionalisation in the present sense has long been the norm for *conference interpreting* and their service providers (PÖCHHACKER 2003) and also for court interpreting (MAGNANI 2010). This definitely has not yet been the case everywhere for community interpreting, especially not in Europe, where efforts to secure this recognition only began in the late 1990s (PÖCHHACKER 2003, KALINA 2001).

Another way of obtaining professional recognition from recipients of interpreting services and thus 'professionalising' the interpretation setting is ensuring close cooperation between the recipients and the service providers or their association, in order to sensitize both parties to reciprocal needs and expectations. This, for example, is the case for conference interpreting since the creation of the annual meetings between the EU Commission and universities and university institutes that specialize in conference interpreting training (DG Interpretation Universities Conference) with the participation of 84 faculties currently from 37 countries. In addition, the International Association of Conference Interpreters (AIIC), as the sole truly international conference interpreter's organisation, periodically negotiates with various international and multilateral organisations such as the EU, the UN, the OECD, the Council of Europe, etc.

This kind of professionalisation can be found in other interpreting fields as well. In *court interpreting,* an example of such cooperation is the approach that is common in Zurich of setting up an expert contact group comprising judges, prosecutors, police authorities and the professional association of the Canton of Zurich (ALBL-MIKASA et al. 2011). Another example is *community interpreting* using the Vienna scheme (PÖCHHACKER 2001: 29 ff), where user expectation surveys in Viennese municipal hospitals and Youth Welfare Offices are mandated in order to infer an evidence-based quality profile and to set training criteria for conference interpreting training.

Based on the latter approach and together with feedback from practitioners of various interpreting fields, a third kind of professionalisation highlights users' expectations and evolving market realities as an integral part of an interpreter's training. Due to the above-mentioned close contacts with professional users of interpreting services, academic training is becoming more market- and customer-oriented.

In *community interpreting,* the already mentioned Vienna surveys have given a quality impetus to training approaches for community interpreters (development of so called competence models, PÖCHHACKER 2003) in both Austria and other European countries. Nevertheless, further consciousness-raising work still needs to be done. The same holds true for court interpreting with new curricula being developed. For example, in Germany at Stendhal University in Magdeburg or at the University of Hamburg, court interpreter education is continuously being updated by integrating quality and competence profiles emanating from empirical research, professional experiences and didactic requirements (THORMANN 2011:10 ff). A brief review of the presentation summary given at the Second International Conference organised by the German Federal Association of Interpreters and Translators (BDÜ) in Berlin in 2012 also bears witness to the variety and intensity of work going on in the field of community and court interpreting (BAUR et al. 2012: 15ff). In conference interpreting, training curricula have long been integrating market requirements in terms of text varieties, presentation speed and durations, themes and settings, new media etc. Thanks to the Internet, all types of speeches and presentations commonly encountered on the conference interpreting market are available in their original form and are widely used didactically. One might say that among all interpreting settings, it is conference interpreting that is the most professionalised (KALINA 2001: 53).

Another way to turn the trainees in interpreting schools into professionals pertains to the possibility of ensuring that they obtain hands-on practical experience during their training period. Some examples include: the weekly mock conferences organised in several German interpreting schools that are incorporated into the training curriculum (award-winning Germersheim 'Friday conferences'[3] for example), or the cross-institutional interpreting experience at Leipzig University's Institute for Applied Linguistics and Translation Studies (IALT) offered to MA students (HEROLD & ANDRÄ 2013: 40f). As from the 1990s, internships were offered by some of the EU-institutions, as it was the case of the European Parliament and European Court of Justice.

1.2 The Missing Link

In conference interpreting, training methods are nowadays evidence-based and integrate the latest developments found in markets and through research. Valuable input from customer groups, as in the case of the EU's pedagogical training assistance or train-the-trainers schemes by professional associations like AIIC is paramount for ensuring the preparation of market-relevant skills for future conference interpreters.

However, there still seems to be a missing link between professional education in regards to the conference interpreters and their market preparedness. More particularly, the questions to be asked are the following: are our graduates really aware of and up to date with the practical realities of the markets they are meant to serve? Furthermore, which markets should be looked at? What are the requirements of these markets and what possibilities are there to get a foothold in these markets once the training course is over? What fees need to be expected and what legal, regulatory and additional financial conditions must be met in order to be in line with common market practices? What are the rules of conduct towards colleagues and customers? There are so many

---

3 http://www.fb06.uni-mainz.de/stefl/117.php

unanswered questions to a newcomer in the conference interpreter's profession, making him/her unsure and prone to potentially fatal missteps.

This problem has been recognized by market practitioners for a long time but there still is no satisfactory answer on the level of interpreter training. In 2012 still, Ziegler noted that

Trotz der Bestrebungen der meisten deutschen Ausbildungsinstitute, die Studierenden der MA-Studiengänge zumindest mit einem grundlegenden Rüstzeug für eine erfolgreiche berufliche Betätigung als selbstständige Unternehmer auszustatten, ist in der Praxis sehr häufig zu beobachten, dass Absolventen unter unternehmerischen Gesichtspunkten nicht ausreichend auf die Praxis vorbereitet sind. Besonders auffällig manifestieren sich dabei die Defizite in den Bereichen Kostenkalkulation und Rentabilitätsberechnung sowie Marketing und Kundenkommunikation. (ZIEGLER 2012: 61)[4]

In the meantime, this missing link between education and market viability for conference interpreters has been partially filled by professional organisations. In Germany, the BDÜ-linked professional organisation *Verband der Konferenzdolmetscher im BDÜ* (VKD) has set up a mentoring scheme in 2007 whose target is to help newcomers getting started in the profession (PFLEGER 2008: 56). Mentors support up to two 'young' graduate colleagues with the same A- and B-languages and with less than one year of work experience, and accompany them over a two-year period. Mentees can always contact their mentors by phone or e-mail with regard to all questions related to practical topics, such as how to prepare a quote, calculate fees, VAT and the like. In addition, they are invited by mentors to sit in mute booths during conferences attended by mentors, and once a year to attend a 'professionalisation seminar' convening all mentors and mentees (PFLEGER 2008: 56f).

Another example is the beginners dedicated AIIC homepage[5] which helps to answer the questions asked most often by beginners in the profession. On a

---

4 "Although most of the German institutions of education and training are trying to provide their students with basic skills for their professional work as independent entrepreneurs, the graduates' practical work often reveals a lack of preparation for the market when it comes to applying these specific entrepreneurial skills. The most obvious deficiencies can be observed in the field of cost and profitability calculation as well as marketing and customer communication". (Translation by K. Ziegler)

5 http://aiic.net/page/1669/budding-interpreter-faq/lang/1

more regional level, AIIC organisations offer beginners a helping hand as they attempt to get started in the profession. AIIC Germany has designed a mentoring program similar to the VKD's for pre-candidates prior to full membership. This professional organisation goes a step further by also inviting non-candidates, who are still in master-level training courses, to a one-day training seminar, held on university premises. Finally, on a local level, all pre-candidates, and candidates with full membership, meet regularly with established colleagues. Themes that are discussed range from a variety of topics related to the practical aspects of market behaviour [6].

The problem with the unpreparedness of the alumnus is only partially solved; because of the constrained availability of so called 'buddies', these programs are rather limited in duration and therefore can only focus on the most urgent needs and questions newcomers might have. Unfortunately, they are unable to cover the whole scope that a professionalised market requires.

To compensate for this fact, the author of this article has designed a 30-hour compulsory training seminar covering all possible aspects of professionalisation prior to getting started. Professionalisation in the sense of the present article hence pertains to the preparation for market requirements, i.e. the imparting of practical skills needed to be a successful actor in the interpretation market.

1.3 The Professionalisation Course

The newly introduced, market-oriented preparation course is conceived as a one semester-long weekly seminar for students of all language combinations within the conference interpreting master course. The seminar is taught in German and split into three sections: Knowing Your Markets, Serving Your Markets and How to Behave in Markets. Each part of the course begins with a brief PowerPoint™ summary of market data and general information available, presented either by myself as the teacher in charge, a representative of a professional association or experts from different subject fields (lawyers and chartered accountants), followed by a discussion and a question & answer session. Some of the topics involve exercises (such as how to calculate a quote) or presentations to be completed by the students. At the end of the course, each student will receive a 60-page reader, comprising articles, general data and presentations made during the seminar.

---

[6] see: http://www.aiic.de/nachwuchs

The content that is provided is based on available empirical studies, like the annual world and regional surveys done by the AIIC on numerous aspects of the evolution of markets[7] or the BDÜ market fees survey "Honorarspiegel"[8] and publications by professional organisations like AIIC, BDÜ or EU information on interpreting activities[9]. In any case, it is not always desirable to only listen to individual colleagues, as there is always a risk of generalising an individual's experience, which might only provide a 'partial' perspective on the markets. Commonly available literature and dedicated publications by professional associations on different course topics are part of the seminar and are made available to students in the form of a bibliography that they can consult.

2. Section I: Knowing Your Markets

The course starts with an overview of general market features (private market sectors, agreement sector and special terms market) and market-related terminology as well as markets for German as a conference language. Available statistical data on these markets in comparison to other languages and language combinations are shown as annual surveys and time series (evolution of markets). The features include geographical information (work opportunities to be found in more than one country) and work volume data (interpreting days per country, clients etc.). In addition, research-based categorised information is also included, such as international and multinational organisations versus national entities, economic sectors most promising in terms of work volume, market niches, etc. (FELDWEG 1996; NEFF 2007). An important aspect related to this is the paradigm shift observed over the last ten years with regard to the interpreted languages used at conference events and, in particular, English as the ubiquitous conference language in all markets and countries. Therefore, consequences and the formal requirements of these different markets (languages, language combinations, specialisations, localisation etc.) and their various subsectors are also discussed.

---

7   The author is also AIIC's world statistical analyst.
8   http://www.bdue-fachverlag.de/fachverlag/schriftenreihe/detail_book/68
9   Statistics on working days, languages and interpreting days at EU SCIC are freely accessible, for instance (http://ec.europa.eu/dgs/scic/docs/about_dg_int/statistics-brochure.pdf) or are accessible only to SCIC-Universities conference participants (http://scic.ec.europa.eu/scicnet/jcms/prod61_539547/en/multilingualism).

The next unit then moves on to a detailed quantitative and qualitative picture of the status of the conference interpreters already working in these markets: number of freelancers, staff interpreters and mixed forms of conference interpreter's activities. This part also includes a general discussion of perceived or real advantages and disadvantages of becoming freelance or staff interpreters (in terms of freedom of choice, work and remuneration, diversification versus specialisation, job security/insecurity etc.) and more generally various objective and subjective criteria (personality check, life-planning, sociability etc.) to be taken into account when deciding which status of interpreting to pursue. Describing or presenting the life experiences of freelance and staff interpreters turns out to be a very effective way of confronting students' fears of being a freelance interpreter[10] or general apprehensions of working in a staff environment.

3. Section II: Serving Your Markets

Section II is dedicated to all aspects related to meeting market requirements and the matching of supply and demand (job matching) for both freelance and staff interpreters. It is divided into two parts, each part focused on one of the two interpreter types. However it is important to note that there are common aspects that need to be known by both types of interpreters because they serve the same market. The first part is dedicated to freelance interpreters since most interpreters fall into this category (88% versus 12% staff interpreters).[11]

The final objective is to make students aware that they will serve a market full of very diverse customers. While most of these customers have used interpreters for a long time and some are even long time signatories of detailed working agreements with the profession[12], other customers require the services of interpreters rarely but on a regular basis, and some are complete newcomers to the conference market. In any case, serving these customers' requirements requires high profile specialists who are aware of the added value they bring to potential clients and who will behave like entrepreneurs as actors on the supply side.

---

10 see for instance MDÜ 2/2007 dedicated to this subject
11   see: http://aiic.net/directories/interpreters
12 For a complete list of such agreements, see: http://aiic.net/directories/aiic/sectors/

3.1 Freelance Interpreters

3.1.1   Choosing one's Professional Domicile

The following session concerns the choice of a professional domicile versus, if applicable, legal residence. The choice should be based on market investigation (localisation, numbers of conference interpreters already in town and their language combinations, customer potential and requirements, congress and conference halls etc.), transport facilities, financial aspects and personal preferences. Regional or local experts of member directories edited by professional associations, such as AIIC or VKD, are of great help.

3.1.2   How to Become Established as a Conference Interpreter

Freelance interpreters as business-oriented entrepreneurs have to adopt a professional and legal profile that is used in most countries. Germany serves only as the most appropriate example for our students. According to German law, independent or self-employed interpreters are classified as independent entrepreneurs *(selbstständige Unternehmer)* and have a special status with respect to taxation and commercial law. Entrepreneurs of this kind may act as individuals (sole proprietor or *Einzelkaufmann*) or as a group. The most commonly found entrepreneurial associations on the supply-side of the interpreting market are civil law nonstock corporations (GbR), partnerships according to the German Partnership Law *(Partnerschaftsgesellschaftsgesetz)*, cooperatives *(Genossenschaften)* and office pools *(Bürogemeinschaften)*. Networks and other interpreter groups are not covered by a legal status, because each member of the group is considered an individual entrepreneur in terms of responsibility, fiscal status, etc. Despite this, their number has been growing since the late 1980s (BEER & JACOBS 2005: 6-15). Legal, fiscal, formal and strategic aspects related to each of these groups are discussed in class. The author usually invites a lawyer to explain all relevant aspects related to these various groups. In conclusion, interpreters in Germany are well advised to opt for one of the above-mentioned entrepreneurial statuses in order to work in the private sector.

3.1.3   USP – Unique Selling Proposition

After having decided on a location and a professional entrepreneurial profile, the next logical step for each individual interpreter consists in determining the kind of services to offer on the market. Although one might argue that conference interpreters are restricted to offering conference interpreting services, reality has taught otherwise. Conference interpreting markets have changed dramatically over the last 10 years, as the latest AIIC time series statistics (NEFF 2010: 12) suggest. Since the beginning of the new millennium, private markets in all European countries have, for instance, switched from multilingual to mostly bilingual events with both a national language and English as the most commonly represented conference language. In Europe, the number of interpreted conference days per interpreter has plummeted by almost 30% in the private sector, work for EU institutions has dropped by almost 40% since 2004 for conference interpreters working outside of Brussels, and by 2012 not even half of the conference interpreters based in Germany were able to make a living solely out of conference interpreting. Conference themes tend to grow more complex (ZIEGLER 2012: 57) whereby cultural bound domains still need interpretation services (NEFF 2007: 609).

From this evolution, the trend shows that future generations of conference interpreters will generally not be able to make a living solely from interpreting activities but will have to supplement their income with other activities. Furthermore, they will have to adapt in terms of what languages to offer (English is a must), specialisation (law, knowledge in various technical, scientific and financial fields), interpreting skills different from conference interpreting (media interpreting, interpreting for national civil and criminal courts, interpreting in industrial settings, banking sector etc.) and language related market services (translation work, language teaching, etc.). Most importantly, all these offerings must be based on solid skills and education in order to be competitive.

With an increasing number of Conference interpreting master's students coming from different academic backgrounds, prior educational and vocational specialisation can be effectively combined with conference interpreting skills: law graduates will be able to work for international and national courts of all kinds, such as patent organisations, attorneys in criminal and patent law, the EU Court of Justice, insurance companies, banking sector, etc. Students with first-hand knowledge of economics will serve companies in the financial, banking and insurance sectors, and so on. All of these possibilities will be discussed within each master's class as the backgrounds of the students may vary.

For master's students without a prior specialisation-oriented background (most of our students begin their studies with some sort of prior education in languages), specialised skills may be obtained in various ways, such as course offerings in the same faculty as their conference interpreting master's program. This is the case for translation skills, basic technical knowledge combined with commercial training for those wishing to work as industrial interpreters, basic training and further education courses in criminal law for those who wish to work for criminal and civil courts, the police, immigration authorities, etc. Training in other skills may also be offered on site, like voice-over techniques, subtitling, language teaching, etc. or more commonly available through continuing education courses offered by professional associations.

Students have to understand that without any kind of diversification and specialisation, their future as conference interpreters may be seriously compromised.

3.1.4 What to Charge for Your Services?

With these prerequisites in place, even before getting acquainted with the market, the most important question to be answered will relate to the price these services are to be offered for on the market. In this section, students are first asked, without any prior explanation, what they would charge for a day of simultaneous conference interpreting. From the answers collected, price formation – interpreting fees plus ancillary costs – will be discussed under different premises. Some of the questions raised, amongst others are: What does a fee represent? What kind of fees are commonly charged on national and international markets? What kind of restrictions or market-related price ceilings are there?

The most difficult part of this discussion is to convince students of their own value, since most of them have the perception that 'beginners' must charge lower fees than more experienced practitioners. In this situation, statistics on and publications by professional interpreters are of great help. In Germany, the BDÜ professional association has published an overview of rates ("Honorarspiegel", see above) bi-annually since 2005, and AIIC's annual surveys[13] regularly publish average daily fees for simultaneous and consecutive interpreting services by country. In the case of AIIC's statistics, one can see that there is no such a thing as age-related fees (NEFF 2010: 18). Fees negotiated by AIIC with major accounts (EU, UN, OECD, etc.), applicable to all interpreters whether they are members of this professional association or not, are pub-

---

13 see for instance the 2012 fee structure on http://aiic.net/page/6878/aiic-statistics-summary-of-the-2012-report/lang/1 (NEFF: 2012)

lished regularly (and included in the reader handed out to the students at the end of the course).

Taking a more commercial approach, fees that are being discussed are also a means of initial investment payback (ROI on education costs), effective time remuneration taking into account the preparation and travelling time necessary to cover an interpretation event, long-term professional investment plans, etc. (BÖHM 2012: 64ff), but also as a market-oriented tool (buyer's market versus seller's market). Fees finally need to be analysed as a (long-term) private life planning management instrument: fees as a basis for cost-of-living, health and pension insurance as well as standard of living (HOFFMANN 2012: 18ff). Finally, the difference between fees as remuneration of a service versus ancillary service-related costs (travel, accommodation, incidental expenses) will be made clear.

3.1.5 Market Presence

Before going to market, trainees have to be acquainted with a professional approach to basic marketing techniques. Beginner-related corporate identity will be presented with its subtopics of corporate design (logo, letterhead paper, business card, internet web page), corporate communication (marketing, advertising, public relation strategies, internet presence and hosting, social medias) and corporate behaviour (confidence-building and customer follow-up). Marketing and advertising as well as internet presence will ideally be addressed by marketing professionals or, if they are unavailable, the latest published papers (see for instance GOLMS 2013: 26ff; DIAMANTIDIS et al. 2013: 20ff; SCHIEMENZ 2013: 10ff; PIELOTH 2010: 28ff). Comparative studies of existing interpreter websites will illustrate the do's and don'ts of the art.

The second subsection relates to potential customer base and customer acquisition strategies. Differences will be made according to various customer types: customers with interpreting service departments (essentially international organisations), colleagues (consultant interpreters) and one's potential clients. Contact sources (departments and contact persons, websites and business directories experts with email addresses and phone numbers) as well as application forms will be presented and discussed. In addition, a detailed marketing strategy comprising of market segmentation, customer targeting and approach will be presented in order to acquire clients (NEIDHARDT 2010: 31ff, LEHMANN 2008: 36ff).

3.1.6 Insurance and Fiscal Regulations

This rather tedious section for interpreters-in-training covers legal, fiscal and regulatory business-related aspects of the work of freelance interpreters. The most important part relates to fiscal aspects which have to be presented in some detail: bookkeeping, VAT regulations according to turnover and place of delivery, tax and VAT identification number, place of taxation, basic income tax regulations, depreciation allowances, tax consultants. The author usually refers to a tax consultant of his acquaintance to cover this section. Concerning insurance matters, legally mandatory and optional insurances (sickness, accident, occupational invalidity insurance, professional indemnity insurance) also have to be addressed. For all of these aspects, the German regulations should always form the legal basis. For those students who will not remain in Germany after their master's degree, the system described may simply serve as an example and they should be aware of the necessity of getting legal advice in the country of their future residence. Other legal aspects pertain to the professional profile (see section "How to become established as a conference interpreter") and their tax incidences as well as to the adoption of standard terms and conditions of business.

3.1.7 Making One's Own Business Plan

All relevant elements of a simplified but cost-effective business plan have so far been put in place. An example of a simplified business plan (to be found on the Internet) will be presented, answering the basic questions of what, how and at what price to offer, as well as the return on investment of the chosen business model. From initial investments (initial rent, office equipment, office communication, membership fees in professional associations, insurances, business papers, branding and marketing campaign), financed alone or pooled, from one's own or borrowed money, to follow-up investments (advertising campaigns, active customer targeting on a regular, yearly or monthly base, order-related investments, fixed costs like rent and insurance premiums, variable business-related costs, leasing etc.), all costs are to be incorporated into a medium-term financing or budget plan. This business plan may be used for and required by funding agencies (denomination and contact data of German federal and regional agencies are being handed out) but its primary purpose is to serve as a roadmap for a long-term market presence.

3.1.8 Communicating With Your Clients

3.1.8.1 The Prerequisites

Before addressing a customer, one must be aware that time and resources at disposal are limited to convince clients of a service they cannot see, whose usefulness they are not entirely convinced of, whose price tag always seems to be exaggerated and who are not (yet) convinced that an unknown interpreter is able to solve their problem. Therefore, it is important to give students a detailed strategy to help them communicate more effectively and professionally with prospective clients. This detailed strategy should include a structured, compelling self-presentation and a detailed CV explaining who you are and what qualifications and references you possess (for example, 'tell me in 30 seconds why I should hire you'), preparation for recruitment meetings (such as gathering information on the prospective customer and possibly the meetings to be interpreted), and a check-list of questions to be asked in order to make an accurate quote.

Prior to the initial contact, detailed explanations regarding the standard practices of the profession are paramount for conveying a professional image of the services that will be offered (this includes team size, working conditions, the hiring conditions of team members, subsistence allowance, accommodation and travel conditions and costs, fee structure, non-working days, travel days, rest days, consultant interpreter, management and handling fees, terms of payment and more). The websites of many professional organisations and interpreters may serve as guides to the industry standards. Regarding the checklist of questions to be asked in order to make a quote, questions should be structured and direct (such as using the four w's: who, what, when, where). Some examples of usual information to write down include the position and contact information of the person in charge of organising the meeting, the type of meeting, the number of active and passive languages, the starting and ending dates of the event, the number of rooms in which interpreting will take place, what languages are to be provided for these rooms, location of the meeting, accommodation and so on.

The purpose of this preparation is to set a level of professionalism with clients who run million-dollar businesses or have huge interpretation and translation budgets, and to convince them of the quality of a service, which is currently unknown to them. This includes conversing with them and making a good impression on them and above all, appearing to the clients as a problem-solver, rather than a problem to be solved.

3.1.8.2 Initial Contact

Different strategies for conducting a recruiting or sales interview will be examined based on how the client will be contacted. In scenarios where the initial contact takes place by phone, strategies will of course differ slightly as compared to those during a physical meeting. Certain specific approaches can improve the impression interpreters give over the phone, such as having a confident tone of voice, being polite, showing interest and enthusiasm and asking structured questions. If some questions have to be asked that would not normally come up in a prepared meeting, they should be asked in a concise, direct manner. Some basic examples include 'who is the caller?' or 'what is his/her position?' This checklist of detailed questions concerning the meeting and the required interpretation service should always be accessible and filled in systematically as the conversation goes on. The purpose of this initial contact should always be to convince the caller of your professionalism and to persuade the potential client to request a quote from you.

In the event of actually meeting the prospective client, thorough preparation as discussed above is highly important. Beforehand, one should familiarise oneself with the person and the company one is meeting, prepare credentials (such as business cards and an updated CV), a short, well-prepared introduction speech and a checklist of questions to be asked. The rehearsal of questioning and answering techniques is also highly important. Always remember that we are our own brand and our own product; we should perform on a very consistent and professional level in order for the client to develop confidence in our abilities and services and subsequently, to be given a chance to submit a quote and to eventually be awarded the contract.

3.1.8.3 The Quote/Tender

Making a quote or bidding on a call for tenders requires a professional approach. In both cases, time limits must be observed. The bidding interpreter must be sure he or she can deliver the services promised at the stated rate and under the conditions offered by the customer. Binding quotes or estimates (the difference between these two will be explained later) should be made on the basis of an in-depth discussion with the client, paying special attention to precisely specifying the scope of the service that is to be provided. It should always be broken down into different components (such as honoraria, travel costs, accommodation, gastronomy allowance, handling fees and copyright) and categories (such as interpreting services, technical equipment, pre- and post-event translation work etc.).

Whereas quotes relate to one event, tenders usually cover a period of multiple events for one single customer with an offer involving a wider team of interpreters. In this case, besides normal working and remuneration conditions as stated above, other aspects that are relevant are technical merit (experience and references, client service and technical assistance), the quality of the proposed teams (interpreters' training, qualifications and experience, membership of professional associations and/or accreditation by international organisations, quality assurance system), effectiveness of team composition (direct interpreting versus indirectly through another interpreted language, native speakers working into each language) and price (itemise costs, management fees, cost-effectiveness). Professional associations such as AIIC may be of great help in this respect as they provide a set of standards and guidelines from which the above list is taken[14].

There will also be quotation exercises that will be undertaken by students in class and that will then be discussed.

3.1.8.4 Contracting

When entering into a final contract, whether it is based on a quotation or a tender, special attention is always required. As the final contract will be binding for both parties, it is necessary to verify and ensure consistency between the offer and the proposed contract terms on important issues such as the general terms and conditions of work, terms of payment, integration of ancillary costs and competent jurisdiction in case of disputes. Depending on national law, consultant interpreters (interpreters having signed the contract with the client and who organise the interpreter team) will be considered either as individual contractors, in which case each team member will sign a contract or order with the client, or as a primary contractor, in which case each team member (sub-contractor) will receive an individual order from the consultant interpreter. In the latter case, he or she is the sole contracting partner to each team member and will be liable, inter alia, for paying team members according to the payment terms agreed upon even if the customer defaults on his obligations.

....

14   see: http://aiic.net/page/6190/tenders-for-conference-interpreting-services/lang/1#attachment

3.1.9 The interpreting event
3.1.9.1 Preparation
Individual interpreters, members of an interpreter team and consultant interpreters must all undergo a thorough preparation phase prior to the event in order to guarantee the professional execution of the contract. This phase includes thematic preparation[15] (such as preparing a general topic, meeting documentation, agenda and list of participants and terminology work) and factual preparation (such as preparing hotel and travel arrangements, early vaccinations if necessary and planning/management of interpreting services as consultant interpreter (organising team(s) of interpreters and their work schedules, preparing individual contracts/orders, catering for conference documents, provision of equipment if such was included in the quotation/contract terms and mediating between clients and interpreters and between team members).

3.1.9.2 Performing the job
Be advised that this part of the interpreting service is the most nerve-racking for a customer who has either never worked with interpreters or is confronted with a new team of interpreters. It is wise to remind students that being professional means behaving without adding to the client's apprehensions! Aside from being thoroughly prepared and capable of doing the job, being punctual (at least 30 minutes early), chronologically organizing and arranging all relevant speeches and PowerPoint presentations, being polite and reserved with the client's representatives, team leader and team members, taking turns as scheduled[16] and being flexible in the likelihood of unforeseen events (such as a change in the speaker's order, accounting for additional speeches that have to be given, or running over schedule) will contribute to a smooth and reliable performance and help to reassure clients regarding their choice of team.

3.1.9.3 Debriefing and invoicing
A debriefing session between the consultant interpreter and the client one or two days after the end of event may be seen as an additional way of showing one's professionalism. During this time, asking about customer satisfaction, general feedback from listeners, as well as how possible incidents were man-

---
15 As a reminder but not part of the course as it is taught within individual interpreting classes.
16 For booth manners and social skills see section III.

aged, help to reassure clients about the value of the service they are receiving. Even if unforeseen negative incidents may have occurred, this is the perfect opportunity to discuss the cause, scope and people involved in the incident to ensure and propose a way for improvements to be made in the future.

While invoicing the client for the service rendered seems to be self-explanatory, it must still be addressed in detail, especially for students who are unaware of the existing legal stipulations. Since 2004, EU-directive 2001/115/EC[17] has been in force in most EU countries, making invoicing more transparent for customers and financial authorities. It is made up of nine different items, all of which have to be explained and supported with evidence. Billing exercises, which take into account contract terms, services rendered, different VAT rates, etc. will help students feel more comfortable with this part of the course.

Payment and dunning procedures (such as payment reminders and debt collection) will also be covered in this segment, preferably by experts (such as lawyers and accountants) in the field.

3.2 Staff interpreters

Although most of the aspects mentioned above relate to freelance interpreters, job application procedures for future staff interpreters will also be given special attention. Similarly, a systematic step-by-step approach is much better for helping students understand, than theoretical explanations. The focus is on helping students professionalise their formal presentation and convincing recruitment officers to invite applicants to pre-employment interviews and tests.

3.2.1 Identifying Potential Employers

When identifying potential employers for staff interpreters, whether they are searching for full- or part-time, permanent or temporary staff (like the EU Commission's newcomers scheme for young Auxiliary Conference Interpreters)[18], the first step is to use knowledge bases, such as AIIC's open-access dedi-

---

17 http://eur-lex.europa.eu/LexUriServ/LexUriServ.do?uri=OJ:L:2002:015:0024:0028:EN:PDF
18 ACI: Auxiliary Conference Interpreter is the official denomination of EU- accredited freelance interpreters. In the young ACI scheme, a one-year 80 conference days work contract is being offered by EU-Commission to freshly accredited newcomers in the profession

cated homepages[19] and search for organisations or employers both nationally and internationally[20].

There is also additional literature available (NEFF 2007: 181ff). Other sources related to the existing and future needs of staff interpreters may be found on the EU Interpretation Directorate's websites for the Commission, European Parliament and Court of Justice, or on the international network of international organisations employing conference interpreters (IAMLAPD)[21] homepage. German federal ministries, public authorities and multi- or bilateral organisations usually publish their vacancies on university boards and in national (weekly) newspapers. A periodical survey, which I conducted among German ministries on existing staff and expected vacancies, may also prove to be useful.

3.2.2 Applying for Employment

Although most major employers of conference interpreters currently conduct their recruitment process online, there are still application guidelines that need to be discussed, such as how to present oneself professionally in a CV, how to prepare for a recruitment interview and an employment test, how to behave during recruitment interviews, if applicable, how to negotiate working and remuneration terms, duration of the probationary period and final contract signing.

Special attention will be given to the EU's own recruitment procedure EPSO (European Personnel Selection Office)[22] with vacancy announcements in the Official Journal of the European Communities. The EPSO procedure is detailed in class and useful guidelines will be given to students who want to become permanent staff members of the EU institutions. As a brief overview, the admission test consists of computer-based verbal, numerical and abstract reasoning questions. Under the new competition procedures, EPSO uses a standard 'assessment centre' model for successful candidates. They are tested on general and specific competences. General competences are tested through

---

19   http://aiic.net/node/12/Staff-interpreters
20   http://aiic.net/directories/interpreters/organisations
21   IAMLADP: International Annual Meeting on Language Arrangements, Documentation and Publication is a forum and network of managers of international organisations employing conference and language services providers--mainly translators and interpreters (http://www.iamladp.org).
22   http://europa.eu/epso/index_en.htm

a structured interview, a group exercise and an oral presentation. Specific competences in the field of interpretation are tested through consecutive and simultaneous speeches for each language in the candidate's combination. Laureates who earn passing grades and the highest total score at the assessment centre are placed on a reserve list and may be invited by an institution for an interview.

4. Section III: Business Etiquette or How to Behave in the Market

Based on numerous complaints about the behaviour of young and inexperienced colleagues, the author took pains to elaborate on what is commonly known as business etiquette or professional behaviour. Although some important aspects have already been discussed in the previous section, the emphasis here is on common practices and the written and unwritten rules of behaviour towards colleagues and clients in our trade.

Taking stock of professional associations' rules of conduct (AIIC and VKD/BDÜ), students are handed out the texts related to the code of ethics[23]. Each item will be compared and explained. Real-life examples of infringements are given. In reference to non-written behavioural rules, these concern booth manners, social competence when interacting with clients, participants and staff and ethical behaviour in the profession. For booth manners, themes cover interacting with colleagues within a booth and team. For a comprehensive list, refer for instance to AIIC's 'Understanding booth manners,' which is available on their website[24]. Social skills also influence behaviour when interacting with clients and participants and therefore, the basic rules of behaviour with clients, participants and staff during breaks, lunches, official dinners are also highly important and will be discussed. When it comes to ethical profession-related behaviour, topics to be discussed and improved upon concern solidarity with the consultant interpreter (behave as if a client you work for was your own client), non-competitive actions (neither the client nor participants are your client if you are a member of a team), neutrality and ethical

---

23   http://aiic.net/code-of-ethics for AIIC and for VKD: http://konferenzdolmetscher-bdue.de/sites/default/files/2013.10.25.BEO_.pdf

24   http://aiic.net/page/1676

stance when confronted with unusual situations (misuse of insider knowledge).

5. Conclusion

This comprehensive, semester-long professionalisation unit turned out to be a real highlight within the conference interpretation master's course at our faculty. The unit is generally a lively, interactive and sometimes even controversial course. It provides much food for thought and ultimately helps students become aware of the imperative need to constantly display a professional attitude in order to succeed in the market. Satisfaction questionnaires at the end of the course have shown that the knowledge the students gain from the course have helped them becoming well-prepared for their future. The course contributes to conquering their fears of the unknown, especially of what the future may hold after graduation day.

References

ALBL-MIKASA, Michaela; GLASS, Anthony & HOFER, Gertrud (2011): "Professionalisierung des Gerichtsdolmetschens im Kanton Zürich: empirische Studie zur Umsetzung der Dolmetscherverordnung", *Working Papers in Applied Linguistics 2.* Zürich: Zürcher Hochschule für Angewandte Wissenschaften, Angewandte Linguistik.

BAUR, Wolfram; EICHNER, Brigitte; KALINA, Sylvia & MAYER, Bernd (2012): *Übersetzen in die Zukunft. Dolmetscher und Übersetzer: Experten für internationale Fachkommunikation. Tagungsband der 2. Internationalen Fachkonferenz des Bundesverbandes der Dolmetscher und Übersetzer e. V. (BDÜ), Berlin, 28. – 30. September 2012.* Berlin: BDÜ Fachverlag, 9-18.

BEER, Jochen & JACOBS, Wolfgang (2005): "Formen der Zusammenarbeit von freiberuflichen Dolmetschern und Übersetzern und ihre steuerliche Auswirkungen", *MDÜ* 2005(1), 6-15.

BÖHM, Julia (2012): "Rentables Arbeiten als Konferenzdolmetscher – Aufwand, Kosten, Honorare". In: BAUR, Wolfram; EICHNER, Brigitte; KALINA, Sylvia & MAYER, Bernd (eds.): *Übersetzen in die Zukunft. Dolmetscher und Übersetzer: Experten für internationale Fachkommunikation. Tagungsband der 2. Internationalen Fachkonferenz des Bundesverbandes der Dolmetscher und Übersetzer e. V. (BDÜ), Berlin, 28. – 30. September 2012.* Berlin: BDÜ Fachverlag, 64-72.

DIAMANTIDIS, Anne; TEMNENKOV Anastasia & KONZOK, Vanessa (2013): "Positionierung mit Social Media. Zwitschern Sie sich bekannt!", *MDÜ* 2013(2), 20-25.

FELDWEG, Erich (1996): *Der Konferenzdolmetscher im internationalen Kommunikationsprozess.* Heidelberg: Julius Groos.

GOLMS, Birgit (2013): "Stolperfalle vermeiden", *MDÜ* 2013(2), 26-28.

GRBIĆ, Nadja (1998): "Professionalisierung. Ein soziologisches Modell und ein Beispiel aus der Praxis des Gebärdensprachdolmetschens in Österreich", *Das Zeichen* 12/46, 612-623.

HEROLD, Susann & ANDRÄ, Vicky (2013): "Win-Win für alle", *MDÜ* 2013(1), 40-41.

HERWIG, Silke & MEYER, Bernd (2013): "Community Interpreting aus berufspolitischer und wissenschaftlicher Perspektive – ein Tätigkeitsfeld mit Zukunft für professionelle Dolmetscher?", *SpuK-Fachtagung,* Februar 2013, 1-16.

HOFFMANN, Roland (2012): "Ich kenne meinen Preis", *MDÜ* 2012(5), 18-21.

KALINA, Sylvia (2001): "Zur Professionalisierung beim Dolmetschen – Vorschläge für Forschung und Lehre". In: KELLETAT, Andreas (ed.): *Dolmetschen: Beiträge aus Forschung, Lehre und Praxis.* FASK Publikationen des Fachbereichs Sprach- und Kulturwissenschaft der Johannes Gutenberg-Universität Mainz in Germersheim. Reihe A – Abhandlungen und Sammelbände, Band 30. Frankfurt a. M.: Peter Lang, 51-64

KÖGEL, Steffi (2004): "Profession – Professionell – Professionalität: Eine terminologische Klärung aus wissenschaftlicher Perspektive", *Das Zeichen* 18/66, 89-93.

LEHMANN, Petra (2008): "Erfolgreich Kunden gewinnen", *MDÜ* 2008(2), 36-38.

MAGNANI, Michaela (2010): *Gebärdensprachdolmetschen: Professionalisierung und Rolle unter besonderer Berücksichtigung der Lage in Italien.* Unveröffentlichte Masterarbeit Universität Wien.

NEFF, Jacquy (2007): *Deutsch als Konferenzsprache in der Europäischen Union. Eine dolmetschwissenschaftliche Untersuchung.* Hamburg: Dr. Kovač.

NEFF, Jacquy (2010): *A Statistical Portrait 2005-2009*: http://aiic.net/page/3585/a-statistical-portrait-2005-2009/lang/1 (20.04.2014).

NEFF, Jacquy (2012): "AIIC Statistical Report 2012", *World Report.* http://aiic.net/page/6878/aiic-statistics-summary-of-the-2012-report/lang/1 (20.04.2014).

NEIDHARDT, Miriam (2010): "Gut gegoogelt ist halb gewonnen", *MDÜ* 2010(4), 31-33.

PFLEGER, Ralf (2008): "Professionalisierung durch Kollegen", *MDÜ* 2008(3), 56-57.

PIELOTH, Franziska (2010): "Sprachdienstleister 2.0", *MDÜ* 2010(1), 28-31.

PÖCHHACKER, Franz (2001): "Dolmetschen und translatorische Kompetenz". In: KELLETAT, Andreas (ed.): *Dolmetschen: Beiträge aus Forschung, Lehre und Praxis.* FASK Publikationen des Fachbereichs Sprach- und Kulturwissenschaft der Johannes Gutenberg-Universität Mainz in Germersheim. Reihe A – Abhandlungen und Sammelbände, Band 30. Frankfurt a. M.: Peter Lang, S. 19-36.

PÖCHHACKER, Franz (2003): "Dolmetschen im Asylverfahren: Perspektiven der Professionalisierung". In: *Tagung Sprachenrechte und Migration am 8.12.2003.* Wien: Institut für Übersetzen und Dolmetschen der Universität Wien.

SCHIEMENZ, Andreas (2013): "Machen Sie sich zur Marke", *MDÜ* 2013(2), 10-13.

THORMANN, Isabelle (2011): "Qualifikationen und Kompetenzen von Sprachmittlern im Justizbereich: Besondere Anforderungen", *MDÜ* 2011(1), 10-14 und 2011(2) (Fortsetzung), 43-46.

ZIEGLER, Klaus (2012): "Konferenzdolmetscher: Die letzten Generalisten oder hochmoderne Spezialisten? Veränderungen auf dem Markt und Konsequenzen für die Lehre". In: BAUR, Wolfram; EICHNER, Brigitte; KALINA, Sylvia & MAYER, Bernd (eds.): *Übersetzen in die Zukunft. Dolmetscher und Übersetzer: Experten für internationale Fachkommunikation. Tagungsband der 2. Internationalen Fachkonferenz des Bundesverbandes der Dolmetscher und Übersetzer e. V. (BDÜ), Berlin, 28. – 30. September 2012.* Berlin: BDÜ Fachverlag, 56-64.

(Self-)Study in Interpreting: Plea for a Third Pillar

MAREN DINGFELDER STONE
dingfel@uni-mainz.de
Johannes Gutenberg University Mainz/Germersheim, Germany

1. Introduction

Obtaining proficiency in interpreting has traditionally rested on two pillars: class sessions, where students receive teacher input on their performances, and private study sessions, where they rely on self-assessment and peer evaluation. As a rule, and certainly if there is no proper guidance, both centre heavily on the final product – the interpreted target text – and on repetition of the interpreting process as a whole. Drawing on the theories of capacity allocation, deliberate learning, and automation, this article proposes to complement these two pillars with a third: that of skill-oriented rather than comprehensive practice, and of subprocess-based rather than product-based self-study. Implemented in the form of a web-based platform, such an approach can provide targeted, purpose-built practice exercises to help students find more efficient ways of tackling weaknesses identified in class. One such platform is currently being developed at Germersheim. To illustrate its premises, the article first assesses the role of self-study in interpreting before introducing the concept and history of CAIT (Computer-Assisted Interpreter Training). It then introduces the findings of a survey among Germersheim students on their self-study routines, before explaining the basic design and features of the Germersheim self-study tool Moodle Online Platform for Self-Study in Interpreting (MOPSI).

2. Self-Study in Interpreting: Benefits and Pitfalls

Jean Herbert was the first of many to highlight the significance of self-study for interpreting proficiency. He considered such independent study a feasible option for supplementing the necessarily limited number of lecture hours and practice sessions provided by training institutes: "Da an den Fachschulen Vorträge und praktische Übungen nur während einer beschränkten Anzahl von Stunden gegeben werden können, erhebt sich die Frage, ob die Studenten ausserhalb der Kurse für sich allein üben können. Diese Frage kann man nur bejahen" (HERBERT 1952: 94). Sixty years later, Ursula Gross-Dinter echoes this sentiment almost literally: "Dass die verfügbaren Präsenzstunden allein nicht ausreichen, um Dolmetschstudierende zur Praxisreife zu führen, ist nicht erst in Zeiten knapper Ressourcen eine der Grunderkenntnisse der Dolmetschdidaktik" (GROSS-DINTER 2011: 273).[1] It is generally considered unlikely for a student of interpreting to acquire professional expertise merely by attending classes; additional individual and group work are seen as indispensable (SANDRELLI 2005: 15, see also HARTLEY et al. 2003: 2, and HEINE 2000: 213). Thus, learners traditionally complement their classroom training with weekly independent, self-organised and non-instructed study sessions. These sessions focus on repeating class practice material, or on interpreting speeches pulled from the internet (M.A.-KD SURVEY 2014), and require students to provide a meaningful assessment of their peers' efforts. In addition to improving interpreting skills and, potentially, linguistic and extra-linguistic expertise, such collaborative learning also helps to develop social skills and cooperative teamwork, both of which are essential for an interpreter's professional life (KALINA 2011: 423).

However, "[a]lthough students certainly need to develop good information searching skills for their future careers, they may not always be the best judges of what is suitable for their particular training stage" (SANDRELLI 2007: 4). Moreover, without proper guidance in their self-study, especially beginners may pick up bad habits, which then need to painstakingly be unlearned in later stages of the training (SANDRELLI 2007: 4). Optimal learning as defined by Ericsson et al. requires *deliberate practice* – in other words, performance improvement necessitates motivation, immediate informative feedback on the performance, repetition, and the inclusion of the learner's pre-existing knowledge (ERICSSON et al. 1993: 367).

Acknowledging its fundamental import, self-study in interpreting does not necessarily have to consist only of the monotonous practising of speech after

---

1 "That classroom sessions, by themselves, are insufficient to qualify interpreting students for the professional market is one of the basic insights of interpreting didactics not only in times of budgetary constraints".

speech. While this is a valuable part of a trainee's self-study if the material selected is appropriate and the learning objectives are realistic, publications throughout the years have also emphasised the need to hone the individual skills involved in the process in addition to practicing the process as a whole (SANDRELLI 2007: 3). If someone aspires to become a world-class sprinting champion, running a hundred meters again and again for years on end might make him die of boredom; it will not, however, win him an Olympic gold medal: "studies have shown that providing a motivated individual with repeated exposure to a task does not ensure that the highest levels of performance will be attained. Assessment of subjects' methods shows that inadequate strategies often account for the lack of improvement" (ERICSSON et al. 1993: 367, see also ANDERSON 2001: 305). In the world of professional athletics, the process of running will be separated into phases that are practised until automated: the fastest way to leave the blocks, the most efficient way to maintain velocity, the optimal stride, the perfect arm position. Such automation-geared practice will then be complemented by seemingly unrelated activities such as weight lifting (to build core muscles) or swimming (to gain upper-body strength), all of which combine to maximise the runner's potential.

Interpreter training, if taking seriously the theories of deliberate learning, should consider applying similar principles. Deliberate practice in interpreting first requires that learners be aware of a particular difficulty or failure trigger, and of the potential strategies for overcoming it (declarative knowledge). They then must gradually apply that knowledge in practice to an ever-increasing degree, until finally, appropriate strategies are selected and used intuitively and automatically, thus requiring fewer cognitive resources and decreasing reaction time (procedural knowledge) (ANDRES 2013: 240ff). Such (partial) automation is a key concept in contemporary interpreting training: "Within the limits and constraints given, interpreters have to find the best acceptable solution to hand, i.e. the constraint on the time and effort that can be invested determines the quality of the result. This means that operations that recur frequently have to be performed as routines that have become automated to a considerable degree. The teaching of interpreting has to develop ways for students' acquiring the necessary automatisms or routines" (KALINA 2000: 19).

For this purpose, it seems useful to enhance strategy selection and application skills by means of independent yet synchronised exercises. To be more precise, additional exercises that enhance automation – of figure processing, speed handling, input processing – might be added to the practice of speeches.

This is in line with the information-processing approach in interpreter training, which regards interpreting as a complex activity comprising a number of sub-skills, and "aims to develop the skills needed to perform each operation" by means of preparatory exercises and drills (SANDRELLI 2007: 3). In addition to general and specialised linguistic skills and the ability to speak and listen at the same time, interpreters must possess culture-specific knowledge, excellent memory skills, concentration, self-motivation, stress tolerance, professionalism with regard to preparation and ethics, and presentation skills (KALINA 2000: 4ff). A multitude of exercises have been suggested over the years to accomplish that goal (see CHABASSE & DINGFELDER STONE in this volume). A systematic, step-by-step approach, when combined with transparent instruction and controlled teaching results, builds up to the handling of real-life speeches by means of "sequences of specific exercises, with the relevant learning steps and teaching goals clearly defined"(KALINA 2000: 22).

Small, achievable goals with measurable progress might also help achieve another prerequisite for deliberate learning: that of learner motivation (see BEHR in this volume). Manfred Heine (2000) charges the interpreting teacher with motivating their students outside the classroom: "Ein kompetenter Dolmetschlehrer […] muss vor allem in der Lage sein, die Studenten, bei denen er Dolmetschfertigkeiten erkannt hat, so zu motivieren, dass sie ein effektives Selbststudium zur (Weiter-)Entwicklung ihrer Dolmetschfertigkeiten als Selbstverständlichkeit begreifen" (HEINE 2000: 214).[2] This sentiment is seconded by Peter Kornakov (2000) who specifies: "The instructor's role is to aid self-preparation, and to provide some useful guidelines and exercises that can be used outside the language laboratory" (KORNAKOV 2000: 241). Not all teachers feel comfortable with their role as motivational coaches, nor do they always have the skills, the resources, or the inclination to guide students toward an individually optimised, tailored practice approach. Research suggests that carefully chosen technology-assisted training tools may be one way to support those teachers and alleviate the problem of learner motivation. Inge Gorm Hansen and Miriam Shlesinger, for instance, found that the use of technology-assisted self-study tools, and video-based self-study material in particular, increased student motivation and effort. They explain this partly with "the

---

2 "A competent interpreting trainer […] must, above all, be able to motivate students that he feels show interpreting skills, so that these consider effective self-study a matter of course in (further) developing their interpreting skills".

options […] for self-paced and self-monitored practice" and the "adaptability to learning patterns of individual students" (GORM HANSEN & SHLESINGER 2007: 114). Sylvia Kalina, too, highlights the motivational potential of e-learning tools: "diese [Vorteile] liegen vor allem in der Motivation der Studierenden, die orts- und zeitgebunden üben können, ohne kritische Kommentare des Dozenten befürchten zu müssen, und dadurch weniger Stress empfinden. Diese Motivation kann zu höherer Übungsintensität und mehr repetitiver Übung führen, was gerade im Hinblick auf das Erlernen von Automatismen einen Lerneffekt bedeuten kann" (KALINA 2011: 425).[3]

3. CAIT: Technology-Assisted Self-Study Options

As shown above, interpreter instruction relies heavily on autonomous learning in the form of individual and collaborative self-study. In trying to ensure the efficiency and effectiveness of learners' self-studies, CAIT (Computer Assisted Interpreter Training) tools seem ideal to complement traditional teaching methods. The pedagogical rationale of CAIT is simple: it can "favour a shift from the *teacher-centred* (transmissionist) approach that prevails in most interpreter training programmes towards a *learner-centred* (constructivist) approach" (SANDRELLI & JEREZ 2007: 275, emphasis in original). Taking control of their own learning is an essential step for students, especially those from more passive learning traditions: "This is an integral part of the working interpreter's professional life and the earlier it starts the better" (CORSELLIS 2005: 157).

Over the years, projects have been instituted in a range of interpreting institutions that draw on electronic tools to create new forms of autonomous, oftentimes virtual interpreting learning. Many operate with a scenario akin to that of offline classrooms: context information, preparation material, and the speech itself are uploaded onto a platform; learners record their interpretation and receive online teacher feedback. Other tools are conceived as repositories, providing access to speech material often sorted by mode, degree of difficulty, language, word count, or other specifications. A small number target the de-

---

3 "The advantages are manifest mainly in students' motivation, as these can practice without the constraints of time and place, and thus experience less stress. This motivation can increase the intensity of practice and multiply repetitive practice, which can enhance learning in particular with regard to automation".

velopment of particular sub-skills, and a few select ones offer a combination of skill-based training, virtual classroom technology, and speech database.

Among the most noticeable developments are the European Union projects *Speech Repository,* a database of speeches that also allows for online recording and sharing of the interpretation (www.multilingualspeeches.tv), and *ORCIT,* a platform with English language resources "to introduce and allow for basic practice in interpreting skills and techniques" (www.orcit.eu). *Black Box,* developed by Annalisa Sandrelli and Jim Hawkins at the University of Hull, offers a custom-programmed, licence-based software solution for a *Virtual Interpreting Environment* (VIE) that allows for the recording and sharing of practice interpretations and offers additional authoring options for practice exercises (SANDRELLI & JEREZ 2007).[4] The community interpreting system implemented in Copenhagen, partly intended as a way to offset a reduction of contact hours and alleviate students' anxiety in the learning process, focuses largely on video-recorded practice scenarios that can be accessed online (GORM HANSEN & SHLESINGER 2007). IRIS, now discontinued, was set up at the University of Trieste as an interactive database of written, audio and video practice material, akin to what Marius now does at the University of Granada on a much larger scale (SANDRELLI & JEREZ 2007: 278). The *Virtual Institute* at ETI in Geneva comprises a database of teaching materials, useful links and resources, and video practice material (SANDRELLI & JEREZ 2007: 294); and the SDI in Munich has piloted an e-learning project that links contact classes and virtual self-study, and draws on internal and external speech resources to achieve guided and self-directed learning (GROSS-DINTER 2011).[5]

Each project has opted for a slightly different approach, taking advantage of whatever tool and set-up fit its needs most precisely. In choosing the appropriate scheme for Germersheim, several factors were taken into consideration: the tool was to be skill-based rather than product-based, and was to be suitable for all language combinations and levels of proficiency offered at Germersheim. Second, a web-based teaching tool was not to replace contact hours, but to complement them. Third, a license-free software solution was deemed the

---

4 *Black Box* derived from the prototype *Interpretation* developed at the University of Hull, which again evolved from *InterprIT*, developed in the 1990s for English-Italian community interpreting and consecutive at Trieste (SANDRELLI 2005, 2007, SANDRELLI & JEREZ 2007).

5 These are just a few of the more prominent examples; for more information on CAIT and e-learning for interpreting, see MAYOR & JIMÉNEZ IVARS 2007; BERBER-IRABIEN 2010; SANDRELLI & JEREZ 2007, FICTUMNOVÁ 2005; TYMCZYŃSKA 2009; GRAN, CARABELLI & MERLINI 2002; IBRAHIM-GONZÁLES 2011.

most prudent, both for budgetary reasons and because "'system-independent' teaching materials [...] can be developed, supplemented and easily replaced or uploaded without the constraints of dedicated software" (GORM HANSEN & SHLESINGER 2007: 101). And finally, the platform was intended to be largely teacher-independent – both to ensure its lasting acceptance and support among the teaching staff and administration at Germersheim, and to maximise the principle of autonomous, learner-centred training. As such, it was to supplement the abundant, excellent material available in speech databases both internally and externally, and the contact hours of classroom teaching.

In order to better understand the specific needs of students, and to assess more clearly the current situation regarding self-study at Germersheim, a brief survey was conducted among the Germersheim M.A. conference interpreting student body, the results of which have been integrated into the design of the platform and the selection of its contents.

4. Survey Results: Self-Study Habits and E-Learning Expectations

The survey was sent out to the students currently enrolled in the Germersheim M.A. Conference Interpreting programme.[6] The results of the survey show clearly that students are acutely aware of the significance of self-study as a prerequisite for passing the final exams; every single respondent emphasised its impact, ranking self-study as important (21%) or even very important (79%) for acquiring interpreting proficiency. At the same time, however, a full half of the respondents are satisfied with the structure of their self-study only occasionally or rarely, and almost as many report struggling with their self-organisation skills. In addition, the lack of evident, measureable progress appears to be a source of frustration: 64% of respondents list this as a major concern. It is reassuring that almost 54% of the respondents still feel their self-study is efficient and effective at least most of the time, and are confident that they manage to implement teacher feedback in their self-study sessions most of the time (42%) or at least occasionally (58%) (gratefully, however, no-one reported rarely or never being able to manage that feat). Nevertheless, re-

---

6   Of the 54 survey addressees, 39 responded. 33 responses were fully completed and thus were included in the survey analysis.

spondents also report that they find it hard to motivate themselves (54%), struggle to allocate enough time for self-study (48%), and doubt their self-assessment skills (45%). The overwhelming majority of students report working in offline tandems or working groups in their B- and/or C-languages, meeting once or even several times a week during the semester. In those sessions, they focus predominantly on re-visiting class material (67%) and/or working with independently researched study speeches (88%).[7]

Initial fears that students might view yet another study resource as burdensome or superfluous, or that the use of a new system might seem daunting for more technophobe learners, were quickly laid to rest – interest in an e-learning resource is significant, with 94% of respondents predicting that they will certainly (52%) or probably (42%) use such a resource. As to the content of the e-learning tool, interest in Interpreting Studies theory on the platform is practically non-existent; rather, every single respondent calls for practical exercises. They are also interested in useful tips (86%) and would appreciate options for further collaboration with other students outside their working groups (75%). One appeal stands out in particular: that there be a means of visualising progress to increase self-motivation and provide a sense of achievement. Curiously, there does seem to be an awareness for the link between learning objectives and motivation, as evidenced by comments in the wish section that ask for a clear outlining of such objectives as a way to enhance self-motivation. This awareness, however, apparently does not translate into the offline self-study where learning objectives play a very minor role: three quarters report setting learning objectives only occasionally (30%), rarely (36%), or never at all (9%).

5. MOPSI: Moodle Online Platform for Self-Study in Interpreting

The combination of student input and theoretical research, placed under the header of technological, administrative, and financial feasibility[8], finally result-

---

7   In the few cases without study groups, this is either to scheduling conflicts with suitable partners (1 answer), because the student feels that they work more efficiently and faster when studying alone (1 answer), or because the student consciously opted to avoid comparing their own performances to those of others, lest they begin to doubt themselves (1 answer).

8   The project only became possible through the generous funding of the University of Mainz's *Gutenberg Teaching Council* (GLK).

ed in MOPSI, a Moodle-based self-study platform offering practice exercises for Germersheim interpreting students. It follows Mariachiara Russo's recommendation to break down the complexity of the interpreting process into more manageable isolated features in order to enhance learner motivation, self-awareness, and focus (Russo 1995: 75). Rather than looking at the final product (the interpretation), the platform loosely follows Gile's Effort Model (GILE 2009) in defining separate but co-occurring skills that comprise the interpreting process (see CHABASSE & DINGFELDER STONE in this volume). However, the skills chosen as categories for the self-study resource deviate from Gile's Efforts for reasons of practicality. Language competence is essential in Gile's Listening Effort as well as his Production Effort; likewise, analytical competence influences Listening Effort, Note-Taking Effort, and Memory Effort at the same time. Rather than getting bogged down in tedious repetition, or lost in an increasingly intricate structure, the platform thus opts for seven more separable categories: Listening Comprehension, Production, Analysis, Memory, Note-Taking, Presentation, and Concentration. Each of these categories delineates a number of sub-skills required for handling particular failure triggers, and then sets out practice exercises purpose-designed to improve the handling of these failure triggers. As such, the platform is designed to provide students with an autonomous, web-based means of directly implementing teacher feedback in order to improve specific weaknesses at their respective levels.

Sections are interconnected where skills overlap to influence several processes – general knowledge is important, for instance, for both listening comprehension (to understand what is being said), analysis (to place it in its proper context), and production (to find the adequate target language phrase). Each section briefly explains the significance and role of its process within the interpreting task as a whole, and introduces the sub-skill; the sub-skill exercises themselves are each preceded by an explanation of their didactic purpose, a set-out of the strategies appropriate for handling the particular failure trigger, a detailed description of the exercise's implementation, and some means of evaluation and feedback. Since MOPSI is meant as a stepping stone for incorporating life-long learning into students' lives, each section furthermore provides tips for incorporating skill training into offline study groups and into learners' daily lives.

As an example, the category Listening Comprehension can illustrate MOPSI's underlying structure. Listening Comprehension comprises the sub-skill sections (1) Linguistic Competence, (2) Figures, (3) Accents/Dialects, (4) Active Listening, and (5) Speed. 'Linguistic Competence' offers students exercises for the use of synonyms, idioms, and collocations, as well as paraphrase exercises to train rapid input processing; 'Figures' includes exercises that take students from the auditory-mechanical processing of figures to the extraction, contextualisation, and ultimately automated notation of figures from speech material. 'Accents/Dialects' exposes learners to a range of dialects and accents, teaching them strategies to maximise their comprehension skills by means of shadowing, summarisation, and ultimately consecutive interpretation. 'Active Listening' provides a selection of informative video material of varying lengths and degrees of difficulty, so that students can slowly build up strategies to maximise memory recovery through mnemonic techniques such as visualisation and analysis. And finally, 'Speed' sets out strategies for handling different speeds of elocution, so that learners automate appropriate response strategies when confronted with a fast or slow speaker, or a speech with great internal speed differentials.

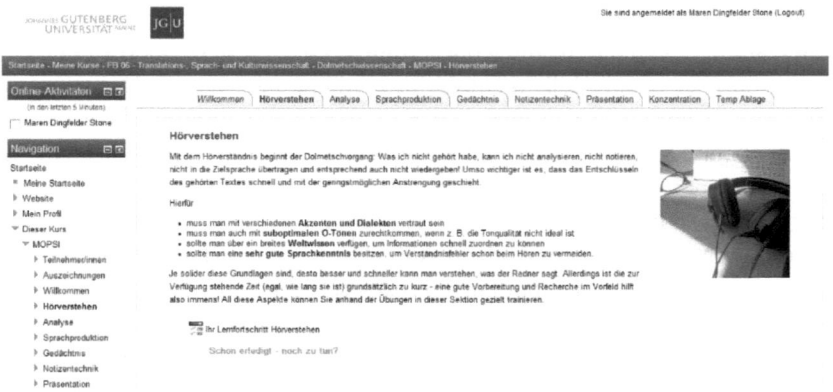

Each section will ultimately include materials from a variety of languages. The materials are classified according to their level of difficulty (beginners, intermediate, advanced); however, no restrictions have been put in place that would prohibit students to practice at a level that does not reflect their years of university enrolment. This pays tribute to the fact that even within one class, learners exhibit vastly different strengths and weaknesses, and that their skill levels concerning individual sub-skills do not necessarily reflect their competence in the interpreting process as a whole. Thus, a first-semester learner may well have analytical skills that match those of a second- or even third-semester student, but may be held back by weaker language skills. Forcing learners to limit themselves to exercises that are too undemanding bears the risk of dreariness and tedium, thus reducing motivation and learner satisfaction. Such learner's control of information input and processing, and the self-pacing that comes with it, maximises the principles of autonomous learning (KONRAD 2008: 16).

Once it is set up and the materials have been created/assembled, MOPSI is largely teacher-independent. Where it was possible to include answer sheets (i.e. in those instances where answers can be classified as right or wrong), those were incorporated into the Moodle structure. Where the evaluation requires a more nuanced, individual approach, students as a rule can choose one of two options – they can evaluate their own output based on guidelines provided on MOPSI, or they can ask another student to link up as an online or offline tandem and provide feedback on one another's performance. A third set of exercises are designed as group tasks, with students collaborating on a wiki, gathering data for a communal glossary, or comparing symbols for their note-taking systems in a dedicated forum. MOPSI also includes a Resources section that provides additional material, forms, website links, and glossaries. It has a chat function that allows students to interact with each other within the platform, and a who-is-online function that facilitates the formation of online tandems. There is a general discussion forum that is open to all, as well as separate forums for students to exchange thoughts on particular issues. Students have an individual blog that can serve as their MOPSI diary, and can mark tasks and exercises as 'done' to create a more tangible sense of accomplishment and thus enhance motivation.

The difficulties encountered in designing the platform were neither surprising nor unprecedented. Due to MOPSI's very autonomous learner approach, instructions had to be very explicit and comprehensible to ensure that even without immediate teacher guidance and input, exercises would be self-explanatory and manageable. Rather than simply abandoning students to their roles as assessors, the requirements for each task are outlined very specifically, as are the rules for self- and peer evaluation. In addition, students can resort to a form sheet for self- and peer assessment that is a more explicit, and more detailed, version of the assessment form used for Germersheim interpreting exams (see BEHR in this volume). These provisions should help boost students' faith in their own assessments, an important lesson to learn for professional life: "self-assessment skills and the ability to assess other interpreters' performances are essential for trainees, both to ensure progress and to maintain quality standards in their future careers as professional interpreters" (SANDRELLI 2007: 15). A second concern was the factor of motivation; as the platform is conceived as an independent study resource, and is not synched to an offline class, its use is entirely voluntary. Hence, it was even more crucial to create self-study materials which students would find motivating and appealing, a challenge already pointed out by Gorm Hansen and Shlesinger (2007: 99). For now, the platform mainly comprises learning material in German and English. However, it is devised to ultimately incorporate tasks and resources in all of the languages taught at Germersheim. Adding new materials will be an ongoing process; this might be made more manageable by including students and graduates more directly in the design of the teaching materials, potentially in the form of M.A. theses.

As a caveat, it must be pointed out that few of the exercises offered have been empirically validated for their usefulness in interpreter training yet. Where this was useful and possible, e.g. with regard to voice training and stress management, external experts were recruited to aid with designing or creating instructional material. For the rest, MOPSI follows Kalina's argumentation:

As there is no theory of interpreting or teaching and learning as yet which would allow us to justify or falsify such methods [specific exercises such as cloze, text completion or compression, shadowing etc.], the argument about some of these practical exercises has tended to become quite ideological. [...] Continuing the fierce argument about the pros and cons of individual teaching practices is therefore futile and will not result in any further insight into how interpreting competence is achieved. (KALINA 2000: 14)

In selecting the exercises, pointers were taken from sixty years of Interpreting Studies publications; rather than joining the (ultimately fruitless) discussion of which exercises are best suited to train which skill, however, it was deemed more prudent to supply students with a host of carefully chosen exercises and allow them to determine autonomously which ones they feel provide the most benefit. This input, which is to be collected in the form of another survey a few semesters down the line, will no doubt include some surprises, but will also help to make the platform a more tailored, useful tool.

6. Final thoughts

E-learning tools, whichever form they take, are no panacea, and one must remain humble in the expectations of their effects. However, if they follow a clear didactic design, provide student guidance and assessment options, and enhance learner motivation, they have the potential to complement traditional classroom instruction in a meaningful way. MOPSI was created as such a complement – a third pillar that helps students process and build on the input received in contact lessons, and provides new, motivating options for collaborative learning beyond the traditional study groups. Whether or not it succeeds remains to be seen.

References

ANDERSON, John R. (2001): *Kognitive Psychologie*. Heidelberg: Spektrum.
ANDRES, Dörte (2013): "Das Konzept Freitagskonferenz: Expertiseentwicklung durch berufsorientierte Lehre". In: HANSEN-SCHIRRA, Silvia & KIRALY, Donald (eds.): *Projekte und Projektionen in der translatorischen Kompetenzentwicklung*. Frankfurt a. M.: Lang. 237-255.
BERBER-IRABIEN, Diana-Cristina (2010): *Information and Communication Technologies in Conference Interpreting: A Survey of the Usage in Professional and Educational Settings*. Doctoral Thesis at the Universitat Rovira I Virgili, Tarragona. http://www.tdx.cat/bitstream/handle/10803/8775/tesi.pdf;jsessionid=F483F62C360 29589CBBD9B94BEDA127A. tdx2?sequence=1 (18.11.2014).
CORSELLIS, Ann (2005): "Training Interpreters to Work in the Public Services". In: TENNENT, Martha (ed.): *Training for the New Millennium: Pedagogies for Translation and Interpreting*. Amsterdam/Philadelphia: John Benjamins, 153-173.
ERICSSON, Anders K.; KRAMPE, Ralph Th. & TESCH-ROMER, Clemens (1993): "The Role of Deliberate Practice in the Acquisition of Expert Performance", *Psychological Review* 100(3), 363-406.
FICTUMNOVÁ, Jarmila (2005): "E-learning for Translators and Interpreters: The Case of CMS Moodle". In: CHOVANEC, Jan (ed.): *Theory and Practice in English Studies 3: Proceedings from the Eighth Conference of British, American and Canadian Studies*. Brno: Masarykova univerzita, 201-206.
http://www.phil.muni.cz/plonedata/wkaa/Offprints%20THEPES%203/TPES%203% 20%28201-206%29%20Fictumova.pdf (18.11.2014).
GILE, Daniel (1995, r. 2009): *Basic Concepts and Models for Translator and Interpreter Training*. Amsterdam/Philadelphia: John Benjamins.
GORM HANSEN, Inge & SHLESINGER, Miriam (2007): "The Silver Lining: Technology and Self-Study in the Interpreting Classroom", *Interpreting* 9(1), 95-118.
GRAN, Laura; CARABELLI, Angela & MERLINI, Raffaela (2002): "Computer-Assisted Interpreter Training". In: GARZONE, Giulia & VIEZZI, Maurizio (eds.): *Interpreting in the 21st Century. Challenges and Opportunities*. Amsterdam/Philadelphia: John Benjamins, 121-130.
GROSS-DINTER, Ursula (2011): "Zwischen Präsenzunterricht und Computerunterstützung, zwischen geführtem und selbstgesteuertem Lernen: Versuch eines integrierten didaktischen Konzepts für das Dolmetschstudium". In: SCHMITT, Peter A.; HEROLD, Susann & WEILANDT, Annette (eds.): *Translationsforschung. Tagungsberichte der LICTRA, IX*. Frankfurt a. M.: Peter Lang, 273-284.
HARTLEY, Anthony; MASON, Ian; PENG, Gracie & PEREZ, Isabelle (2003): *Peer- and Self-Assessment in Conference Interpreter Training*. York: Subject Centre for Languages. www.llas.ac.uk/resourcedownloads/1454/hartley.rtf (18.11.2014).

HEINE, Manfred (2000): "Effektives Selbststudium – Schlüssel zum Erfolg in der Dolmetschausbildung". In: KALINA, Sylvia et al. (eds.): *Dolmetschen: Theorie – Praxis – Didaktik.* St. Ingbert: Röhrig, 213-230.

KALINA, Sylvia (2000): "Interpreting Competences as a Basis and a Goal for Teaching", *The Interpreters' Newsletter* 10, 3-32.

KALINA, Sylvia (2011): "Die Dolmetschlehre im elektronischen Zeitalter". In: SCHMITT, Peter A.; HEROLD, Susann & WEILANDT, Annette (eds.): *Translationsforschung. Tagungsberichte der LICTRA, IX.* Frankfurt a. M.: Peter Lang, 419-431.

KONRAD, Klaus (2008): *Erfolgreich selbstgesteuert lernen. Theoretische Grundlagen, Forschungsergebnisse, Impulse für die Praxis.* Bad Heilbrunn: Klinkhardt.

KORNAKOV, Peter (2000): "Five Principles and Five Skills for Training Interpreters", *Meta* 45(2), 241-248.

M.A.-KD SURVEY by DINGFELDER STONE, Maren (2014): Umfrage zum Selbststudium im M.A. Konferenzdolmetschen am FTSK Germersheim September/Oktober 2014.

MAYOR, María J. Blasco & JIMÉNEZ IVARS, Amparo (2007): "E-Learning for interpreting", *Babel* 53:4, 292–302.

IBRAHIM-GONZÁLES, Noraini (2011): "E-Learning in Interpreting Didactics: Students' Attitudes and Learning Patterns, and Instructor's Challenges", *Journal of Specialised Translation* 16, 224-241. http://www.jostrans.org/issue16/art_gonzalez.php (18.11.2014).

RUSSO, Mariachiara (1995): "Self-Evaluation: The Awareness of One's Own Difficulties as a Training Tool for Simultaneous Interpretation", *The Interpreters' Newsletter* 6, 75-85.

SANDRELLI, Annalisa (2005): "Designing CAIT (Computer-Assisted Interpreter Training) Tools: Black Box". In: GERZYMISCH-ARBOGAST, Heidrun & NAUERT, Sandra (eds.): *MuTra 2005 – Challenges of Multidimensional Translation.* Saarbrücken: St. Jerome, 1-15. http://www.euroconferences.info/proceedings/2005_Proceedings/2005_proceedings.html (18.11.2014).

SANDRELLI, Analisa (2007): "Designing CAIT (Computer-Assisted Interpreter Training) Tools: Black Box". In: NAUERT, Sandra (ed.): *MuTra 2005 – Challenges of Multidimensional Translation: Conference Proceedings.* Saarbrücken: St. Jerome. http://www.euroconferences.info/proceedings/2005_Proceedings/2005_Sandrelli_Annalisa.pdf

SANDRELLI, Annalisa & JEREZ, Jesús de Manuel (2007): "The Impact of Information and Communication Technology on Interpreter Training", *The Interpreter and Translator Trainer* 1(2), 269-303.

TYMCZYŃSKA, Maria (2009): "Integrating In-Class and Online Learning Activities in a Healthcare Interpreting Course Using Moodle", *Journal of Specialised Translation* 12, 148-164. http://www.jostrans.org/issue12/art_tymczynska.php (18.11.2014).

TRANSKULTURALITÄT – TRANSLATION – TRANSFER

Bd. 1   Cornelia Zwischenberger: Qualität und Rollenbilder beim simultanen Konferenzdolmetschen. 434 Seiten. ISBN 978-3-86596-527-1

Bd. 2   Sarah Fünfer: Mensch oder Maschine? Dolmetscher und maschinelles Dolmetschsystem im Vergleich. 150 Seiten. ISBN 978-386596-548-6

Bd. 3   Dörte Andres/Martina Behr (Hg.): Die Wahrheit, die reine Wahrheit und nichts als die Wahrheit. Erinnerungen der russischen Dolmetscherin Tatjana Stupnikova an den Nürnberger Prozess. 242 Seiten. ISBN 978-3-7329-0005-3

Bd. 4   Larisa Schippel (Hg.): Magda Jeanrenaud: Universalien des Übersetzens. 332 Seiten. ISBN 978-3-86596-444-1

Bd. 5   Sylvia Reinart: Lost in Translation (Criticism)? Auf dem Weg zu einer konstruktiven Übersetzungskritik. 438 Seiten. ISBN 978-3-7329-0014-5

Bd. 6   Sophia Scherl: Die deutsche Übersetzungskultur in der zweiten Hälfte des 18. Jahrhunderts. Meta Forkel-Liebeskind und ihre Übersetzung der *Rights of Man*. 152 Seiten. ISBN 978-3-7329-0020-6

Bd. 7   Thomas Kammer: Basiswissen für Dolmetscher – Deutschland und Spanien. 204 Seiten. ISBN 978-3-7329-0035-0

Bd. 8   Dorothee Jacobs: Basiswissen für Dolmetscher – Deutschland und das Vereinigte Königreich Großbritannien und Nordirland. 192 Seiten. ISBN 978-3-7329-0036-7

Bd. 9   Sophia Roessler: Basiswissen für Dolmetscher – Deutschland und Italien. 212 Seiten. ISBN 978-3-7329-0039-8

Bd. 10 Annika Selnow: Basiswissen für Dolmetscher – Deutschland und Frankreich. 192 Seiten. ISBN 978-3-7329-0040-4

Bd. 12 Alice Leal: Is the Glass Half Empty or Half Full? Reflections on Translation Theory and Practice in Brazil. 334 Seiten. ISBN 978-3-7329-0068-8

Bd. 13 Kristina Werner: Zwischen Neutralität und Propaganda – Französisch-Dolmetscher im Nationalsozialismus. 130 Seiten. ISBN 978-3-7329-0085-5

Bd. 14 Larisa Schippel/Magda Jeanrenaud/Julia Richter (Hg.): „Traducerile au de cuget să îmblînzească obiceiurile …". Rumänische Übersetzungsgeschichte – Prozesse, Produkte, Akteure. 368 Seiten. ISBN 978-3-7329-0087-9

Bd. 15 Elena Kalašnikova (Hg.): „Übersetzer sind die Wechselpferde der Aufklärung". Im Gespräch: Russische Übersetzerinnen und Übersetzer deutscher Literatur. 254 Seiten. ISBN 978-3-7329-0097-8

Frank & Timme

TRANSKULTURALITÄT – TRANSLATION – TRANSFER

Bd. 16   Dörte Andres/Martina Behr (eds.): To Know How to Suggest … Approaches to Teaching Conference Interpreting. 260 Seiten. ISBN 978-3-7329-0114-2

Bd. 17   Tatiana Bedson/Maxim Schulz: Sowjetische Übersetzungskultur in den 1920er und 1930er Jahren. Die Verlage *Vsemirnaja literatura* und *Academia*. 182 Seiten. ISBN 978-3-7329-0142-5

Bd. 18   Cécile Balbous: Das Sprachknaben-Institut der Habsburgermonarchie in Konstantinopel. 90 Seiten. ISBN 978-3-7329-0149-4

Bd. 19   Cornelia Zwischenberger/Martina Behr (eds.): Interpreting Quality: A Look Around and Ahead. 334 Seiten. ISBN 978-3-7329-0191-3

Bd. 20   Mehmet Tahir Öncü: Basiswissen für Dolmetscher – Deutschland und die Türkei. 232 Seiten. ISBN 978-3-7329-0154-8

Bd. 21   Marc Orlando: Training 21st century translators and interpreters: At the crossroads of practice, research and pedagogy. 158 Seiten. ISBN 978-3-7329-0245-3

Bd. 22   Christian Trollmann: Nationalsozialismus auf Japanisch? Deutsch-japanische Beziehungen 1933–1945 aus translationssoziologischer Sicht. 154 Seiten. ISBN 978-3-7329-0281-1

Bd. 23   Ursula Gross-Dinter (Hg.): Dolmetschen 3.0 – Einblicke in einen Beruf im Wandel. 226 Seiten. ISBN 978-3-7329-0188-3

Bd. 24   Lieven D'hulst/Carol O'Sullivan/Michael Schreiber (eds.): Politics, Policy and Power in Translation History. 256 Seiten. ISBN 978-3-7329-0173-9

Bd. 25   Dörte Andres/Julia Richter/Larisa Schippel (Hg.): Translation und „Drittes Reich". Menschen – Entscheidungen – Folgen. 352 Seiten. ISBN 978-3-7329-0302-3

Bd. 26   Julia Richter/Cornelia Zwischenberger/Stefanie Kremmel/Karlheinz Spitzl (Hg.): (Neu-)Kompositionen. Aspekte transkultureller Translationswissenschaft. 404 Seiten. ISBN 978-3-7329-0306-1

Bd. 27   Barbara den Ouden: Translation und Emotion: Untersuchung einer besonderen Komponente des Dolmetschens. 438 Seiten. ISBN 978-3-7329-0304-7

Bd. 28   Larisa Schippel/Cornelia Zwischenberger (eds.): Going East: Discovering New and Alternative Traditions in Translation Studies. 540 Seiten. ISBN 978-3-7329-0335-1

Bd. 29   Dörte Andres/Klaus Kaindl/Ingrid Kurz (Hg.): Dolmetscherinnen und Dolmetscher im Netz der Macht. Autobiographisch konstruierte Lebenswege in autoritären Regimen. 280 Seiten. ISBN 978-3-7329-0336-8

Frank & Timme

TRANSKULTURALITÄT – TRANSLATION – TRANSFER

Bd. 30 Martina Behr/Sabine Seubert (Hg.): Education is a Whole-Person Process. Von ganzheitlicher Lehre, Dolmetschforschung und anderen Dingen. 516 Seiten. ISBN 978-3-7329-0324-5

Bd. 31 Simone Kellner: Basiswissen für Dolmetscher und Übersetzer – Österreich. 108 Seiten. ISBN 978-3-7329-0370-2

Bd. 32 Simon Zupan/Aleksandra Nuč (eds.): Interpreting Studies at the Crossroads of Disciplines. 204 Seiten. ISBN 978-3-7329-0045-9

Bd. 33 Hilke Effinghausen: Zwischen Neutralität und Propaganda – Spanisch-Dolmetscher im Nationalsozialismus. 178 Seiten. ISBN 978-3-7329-0394-8

Bd. 34 Lars Felgner: Nonverbale Kommunikation beim medizinischen Dolmetschen. 428 Seiten. ISBN 978-3-7329-0386-3

Bd. 35 Annika Schlesiger: Berufsschutz für Übersetzer und Dolmetscher in Deutschland. Vergangenheit – Gegenwart – und Zukunft? 200 Seiten. ISBN 978-3-7329-0408-2

Bd. 36 Lena Skalweit: Dolmetscher und ihre Ausbildung im Zeitalter der europäischen Expansion. Osmanisches Reich und Afrika. 312 Seiten. ISBN 978-3-7329-0371-9

Bd. 37 Samantha Blai: Basiswissen für Dolmetscher und Übersetzer – Deutschland und Polen. 306 Seiten. ISBN 978-3-7329-0446-4

Bd. 38 Jette Knapp: Basiswissen für Dolmetscher und Übersetzer – Deutschland und USA. 248 Seiten. ISBN 978-3-7329-0447-1

Bd. 39 Thomas Baumgart/Mona Gerlach: Basiswissen für Dolmetscher und Übersetzer – Deutschland und Spanien. 254 Seiten. ISBN 978-3-7329-0465-5

Bd. 40 Amrei Bahr/Katja Hagedorn: Basiswissen für Dolmetscher und Übersetzer – Deutschland und das Vereinigte Königreich Großbritannien und Nordirland. 236 Seiten. ISBN 978-3-7329-0467-9

Bd. 41 Saskia Isabelle Riemke/Eleonora Pepe: Basiswissen für Dolmetscher und Übersetzer – Deutschland und Italien. 276 Seiten. ISBN 978-3-7329-0468-6

Bd. 42 Miriam Heike Schroers: Basiswissen für Dolmetscher und Übersetzer – Deutschland und Frankreich. 280 Seiten. ISBN 978-3-7329-0485-3

Bd. 43 Charlotte P. Kieslich: Dolmetschen im Nationalsozialismus. Die Reichsfachschaft für das Dolmetscherwesen (RfD). 428 Seiten. ISBN 978-3-7329-0515-7

Bd. 44 Viktoria Fedorovskaja/Tatiana Yudina: Basiswissen für Dolmetscher und Übersetzer – Deutschland und Russland. 264 Seiten. ISBN 978-3-7329-0487-7

Frank & Timme